The Theatrical Notebooks of Samuel Beckett

VOLUME IV

The Shorter Plays

The series of
The Theatrical Notebooks of Samuel Beckett
has been prepared under the
General Editorship of James Knowlson,
Emeritus Professor of French at the University of Reading.
It consists of:

VOLUME I
Waiting for Godot
edited by James Knowlson and Dougald McMillan

VOLUME II
Endgame
edited by S. E. Gontarski

VOLUME III
Krapp's Last Tape
edited by James Knowlson

VOLUME IV
The Shorter Plays
edited by S. E. Gontarski

THE THEATRICAL NOTEBOOKS OF

SAMUEL BECKETT

GENERAL EDITOR: JAMES KNOWLSON

VOLUME IV

The Shorter Plays

with revised texts for
Footfalls, *Come and Go* and *What Where*

EDITED WITH AN INTRODUCTION
AND NOTES
BY S. E. GONTARSKI

Grove Press
New York

First published in the UK in 1999
by Faber & Faber Limited
Bloomsbury House, 74–77 Great Russell Street
London WC1B 3DA

First published in the USA by Grove Atlantic
154 West 14th Street
New York, NY 10011

This paperback edition first published in 2021

Photoset by Wilmaset Ltd, Birkenhead, Wirral
Printed in England by CPI Group (UK) Ltd, Croydon, CR0 4YY

All rights reserved

No part of this book may be reproduced in any form or by any electronic or mechanical means, including information storage and retrieval systems, without permission in writing from the publisher, except by a reviewer, who may quote brief passages in a review. Scanning, uploading, and electronic distribution of this book or the facilitation of such without the permission of the publisher is prohibited. Please purchase only authorized electronic editions, and do not participate in or encourage electronic piracy of copyrighted materials. Your support of the author's rights is appreciated. Any members of educational institutions wishing to photocopy part or all of the work for classroom use, or anthology, should send inquiries to Grove Atlantic, 154 West 14th Street, New York, NY 10011 or permissions@groveatlantic.com

Footfalls, Come and Go and *What Where* revised texts © Estate of Samuel Beckett, 1999, 2021
Introduction, notes and editorial matter © S. E. Gontarski, 1999, 2021

The right of S. E. Gontarski to be identified as editor of this work has been asserted in accordance with Section 77 of the Copyright, Designs and Patents Act 1988

A CIP record for this book
is available from the British Library

ISBN 978-0-8021-5952-6

The colour scans of the original notebooks are reproduced with the assistance of the Beckett Digital Manuscript Project, with permission from the Beckett Estate and the Beckett International Foundation / Special Collections, University of Reading.

MIX
Paper from responsible sources
FSC® C013604

2 4 6 8 10 9 7 5 3 1

For Jane,
ma mignonne, toujours

GENERAL EDITOR'S NOTE

Nothing can ever truly be said to be definitive in the theatre. A play or a role is constantly open to reinterpretation. A different directorial approach, different actors and actresses, a different stage space and the end result must inevitably differ. And Samuel Beckett's own productions illustrated this just as clearly as do anyone else's. It is a misconception to think that he believed he or anyone else could 'fix' his plays. He stressed that other productions would have a different 'music' from his own and he accepted different configurations of the stage set. On the very few occasions when he objected to certain directorial proposals it was because he felt that fundamental changes were being made that radically altered his plays.

When Beckett came to direct his own plays for the stage, he introduced numerous changes to the printed texts that consisted of cuts and additions as well as revisions. This was usually because he regarded these changes as improvements that he had discovered either as he was preparing to stage the plays or in the course of rehearsals themselves. Again it is worth stressing that his directorial decisions were inevitably determined by variable circumstances – the kind of actor that he was working with, the limitations of the stage set and so on. As with anyone else, they may even have derived from changes of mind on his part.

There is, none the less, a remarkable consistency in Beckett's changes. For the revisions appear to represent a further dynamic stage in the writer's own encounter with his texts and are of considerable interest for that very reason. In fact, some of the stage directions or, in the case of *Waiting for Godot*, with Beckett as director or aide to the director, whole sections of the text have *never* been played as printed in the original editions. It may surprise readers to learn that some of the cuts in Beckett's 1975 Schiller-Theater production in German of *Waiting for Godot* had already been made, as an annotated script shows, over twenty years earlier for the French world première. It is simply that, in the past, Beckett's texts have not been revised to take account of these changes – partly because of a somewhat ambiguous attitude on the part of the author towards his originals. Our aim in printing (at last with Beckett's full agreement) revised texts that are based on his productions has been to set down the changes that were made there. The texts are now as close as possible to how Beckett wanted them to be. And in presenting his theatrical notebooks our aim has also been to record, put into context and try to explain some of his directorial decisions.

Beyond that it would only be too easy to misunderstand or misrepresent what this series is intended to do. We too are decidedly not attempting to 'fix' the plays by limiting directorial freedom. How each director uses the production notes of the author will be up to him or her. And, in establishing a revised text, again it will be a matter of individual judgement as to whether readers, directors or actors prefer the revision to the original. On all occasions we have printed in the textual notes exactly what Beckett deleted and indicated what was added or revised. My own judgement is that practical experience confirms the rightness of most of the author's decisions concerning his texts. It is indeed a rather curious experience now, after one has seen Beckett's own revised versions, to watch a production that includes all of the text and follows the stage directions of the originals.

It is often said that authors are not the best directors of their own work. All I can say is that, to take *Waiting for Godot* as my example, the Schiller Theater and San Quentin productions by Beckett were two of the most beautiful productions of that play that I have ever seen. Once again misunderstandings or myths have arisen concerning Beckett's productions, as memory fades. Some critics have written as if they were uniformly serious, even heavy, when – as any glance at a video recording of the Schiller production shows – they blended comic and serious elements very successfully. What Beckett also did was to see the work in terms of clear visual patterns with movements so carefully charted that the word 'choreography' can quite properly be applied to a meticulously planned direction.

Detailed moves varied, of course, from production to production. And one would not want it otherwise. There is after all nothing worse in the theatre than a dull imitation. We have then incorporated such moves into the text itself only when they override the original stage directions or when they have importance as part of a complex piece of revised stage business. Otherwise, when such information is of interest, it has been placed in the textual notes. And although these volumes are specifically intended as editions of *production* texts, we have not hesitated to include other explanatory material in our notes whenever it seemed worthwhile.

We have also chosen to include a large amount of our information in the notes to the text rather than in the notes to the theatrical notebooks because it allowed more naturally for variants, because the notebook entries themselves often appeared to be self-explanatory and because such a system of reference seemed more convenient to a reader. And if, as well as providing approved revised texts, we are also (as John Lahr suggested in the *Guardian* in anticipation of the publication of these editions) preserving 'Beckett's blocking in the aspic of scholarship', the specimens that are offered here are, I contend, not dead museum pieces at all but living creatures that may be seen evolving during a final phase of the author's creative process.

James Knowlson, October 1991

CONTENTS

APPENDIX: *Not I*

ACKNOWLEDGEMENTS

Scholarship, like theatre itself, is a collaborative effort even when a single name is credited on the title page, and so I am pleased to have this opportunity to acknowledge the many collaborators on this volume. For direct economic support I am grateful to the American Philosophical Society for a timely grant to travel to the Beckett Archive at the University of Reading and to the National Endowment for the Humanities whose Fellowship for University Teachers allowed for full-time, uninterrupted research on this volume. I am pleased as well to acknowledge logistical support from the Department of English at Florida State University, John Fenstermaker, Chair, and from the Florida State University London Program, Eugene Crook, Director. Teaching on the London campus in the autumn of 1991 allowed for frequent access to the Beckett Archive at the University of Reading, where, as usual, Archivist Michael Bott and Beckett International Foundation Fellow Mary Bryden were cheerful and helpful despite their own overburdened schedules.

Walter Asmus, Samuel Beckett's principal assistant for most German productions, has provided not only indispensable copies of Beckett's annotated texts for *Spiel* (*Play*), *Kommen und Gehen* (*Come and Go*), *He Joe* (*Eh Joe*), and *Damals* (*That Time*) but welcome hospitality in Hanover, Germany. The generosity and hospitality of my General Editor, James Knowlson, has once again far exceeded the bounds of collegiality and professional friendship as I became a fixture in the first-floor back bedroom of 'Rivendell'. This book owes as much to the 'Rivendell' breakfasts, long Sunday dinners and late-night conversations as it does to the Beckett Archive at the University of Reading. I am delighted to acknowledge as well the diligent assistance of Fita Ferguson, a friend who became a colleague on this project, and Maria Lehmann, a colleague who became a friend; both helped immeasurably with the German texts and notebooks. Remaining errors are, of course, wholly my responsibility.

As we approach completion of this complicated publication project with the final volume of Samuel Beckett's theatrical notebooks, it should be abundantly clear to most readers what an exceptional job the design and editorial teams at Faber and Faber have done; they deserve special mention, particularly Charles Boyle, Jill Burrows, Ron Costley, Frank Pike and Tracey Scoffield.

By the time work on this volume was underway in earnest, Samuel Beckett had died, and so the careful attention he lavished on the *Endgame* and *Krapp's Last Tape* volumes in this series was sorely missed. Much of the impetus for this project, however, grew from working directly with him on staging the English-language première of the revised text of *What Where* at the Magic Theater in San Francisco in the autumn of 1986. Rethinking and reconstructing the details of that production for this volume, particularly our meetings over production details, was bitter-sweet, evoking simultaneously the warmth of those encounters and the extent of the loss. Those of us working on his theatre must now learn to get along without his direct help. These *Theatrical Notebooks* may, however, at least in some small way, maintain his presence in the theatres of the world – that indeed would be a tribute to his impact on the literature of the post-World War II era. The notebooks are, of course, no substitute for the man, but they suggest that what survives is what he always wanted to survive, the work, and here in the exacting detail of his conception.

Adieu, Sam.

INTRODUCTION
De-theatricalizing Theatre: The Post-*Play* Plays

To the objection that visual component too small, out of all proportion with aural, answer: make it smaller, on the principle that less is more.
That Time notes

The call of the theatre is strong.
Letter to Barney Rosset, 20 March 1959

In the early 1960s the nature of Samuel Beckett's writing for the theatre changed profoundly as he increased his direct advisory role in productions of his work and as he took the next step and finally began taking full charge of directing his own plays. The experiences of staging himself had a double effect, altering his writing of new plays and, as important, offering him the opportunity to rethink, rewrite, and so complete previously published work.

As Beckett began *officially* to take charge of staging his own plays (first in 1967 with the Schiller-Theater production of *Endspiel* (*Endgame*) and continuing strongly – despite constant pledges to the contrary – until the 1986 rewrite of his stage play *Was Wo* (*What Where*) for German television), he took those opportunities to complete the creative process, to *realize* his plays fully. If what we tend to call Beckett's late style began with *Play*, then all of Beckett's theatre works are finally 'late plays', written in the 'late style', that is, all of Beckett's stage plays are 'written' (i.e. completed) after the publication of *Play* – even *Play* itself. That Beckett was re-creating his dramatic corpus, reinventing himself as a dramatist, rewriting history in effect during this mid-1960s period, is a perspective of singular critical significance, and yet one largely ignored in current theatre history.

In many respects the new theatre grew more overtly formalist and patterned as it became more visual. Beckett balanced a theatre of concrete visual images with a theatre of poetic images. With *Play* the Beckettian bricks were no longer tossed directly at naturalism – that particular victim already on life-support by 1960 – but against modernism, if not against literature itself. With *Play* Beckett's theatre finally grew more static than active, more lyric than dramatic. It was for Beckett, in a very practical sense, the end of literature – and the beginning of theatre. The change is evident to anyone who has tried to read *Play*, *Breath*, *Come and Go*, *Ghost Trio*, *. . . but the clouds . . .* or especially *Quad* without access to productions. On the page, without the full visual counterpart, the works are denuded, skeletal, finally unreadable – in any traditional literary sense, that is, if by unreadable we mean to suggest that their primary effect is extra-linguistic.

These aesthetic changes were signalled in a pair of radio plays with titles and themes more suggestive of the concert hall than of the theatre, *Words and Music* written in English at the end of 1961, and its counterpart or counterpoint, *Cascando*, written in French the following year. The first stage play of this new period was begun in the spring of 1962 as Beckett was completing *How it is*.[1] As he wrote to a colleague of Lawrence Harvey, Herbert Myron, on 31 May, '*How it is* still awaiting revision. Haven't done a [tap?] of work for months, but idea for a new act, one hour, three faces (mouths) and lights.'[2] Finished that summer, the piece was entitled simply *Play*, and with it Beckett began to turn theatre back on itself with renewed vigour, deliberately exploring, stretching, re-evaluating, playing with the forms of drama – as he had with *Eleuthéria*, written, as the manuscript note indicates, 'Prior to *Godot*'. By the following April (1963) Beckett approached film in the same spirit, in a work called *Film*, his first and only *pure* excursion into that medium (although he went on to write at least five works for television). But it was *Play* that was to have the most profound resonances on Beckett's dramatic art for the next two and a half decades.

In these works Beckett was moving theatre to a new aesthetic plane. The nature of theatrical 'character' itself, for example, was being redefined, dispersed. Words and music were personified, becoming protagonists – or antagonists – in the radio plays. Beckett began to dramatize his creative, aesthetic conflicts directly within the works, as he had in narrative as early as *Dream of Fair to Middling Women* written in 1932. In the radio plays music struggles with words, the lyric with the dramatic, for attention, even for supremacy. That conflict is central to the creation of poetry, and *Words and Music* ends with one of Beckett's most poignant poems.[3] In *Film* part of the self is represented by a camera and so the machine is drawn into the perceptual frame, although like Godot it never physically appears. (There are limits or impediments, after all, to self-perception. The image of the camera photographing itself photographing itself becomes a trope for the paradox of self-perception.) In *Film* the machine is as much a character as O and so, while the camera is person-ified, O is object-ified – as indeed his name, O, denotes. Like the human eye with which *Film* begins, the camera is never, we realize, simply a neutral, objective observer. It records and participates, intruding on, affecting what it records.

Play seems in many respects to be an assault on itself, on theatre – as *Eleuthéria* and *Godot* had been a decade earlier – drama playing against itself, theatre against the very idea of theatre. If *Godot* eliminated 'action' from the stage, *Play* all but eliminated motion. If *Godot* eliminated intelligible causality, *Play* all but eliminated intelligibility itself. Beckett modified his stage directions on tempo from the 'whole movement as rapid as possible' in Typescript 5 to the final 'Rapid tempo throughout' (p. 307), but he evidently urged the former tempo to director George Devine, much to the chagrin of the National Theatre's Literary Manager Kenneth Tynan. Productions of *Play* seem to have generated a whole new set of conflicts between producers and directors, or between those who understood and accepted Beckett's aesthetic shift and those who could not. As Billie Whitelaw recalls it, 'Rows between Sir Laurence Olivier and Ken Tynan turning up at rehearsals and saying "you cannot possibly go as quickly as this" and everyone keeping very quiet, as George Devine had no intention of going any slower – and neither had Beckett . . .'.[4] Tynan, in fact, attacked Beckett's presence at rehearsals, finding his influence finally intrusive and detrimental, as he noted in an acrimonious exchange of letters with the play's director:

> Before Sam B. arrived at rehearsals, *Play* was recognisably the work we all liked and were eager to do. The delivery of the lines was (rightly) puppet-like and mechanical, but not wholly dehumanized and stripped of all emphasis and inflections . . . it seems that Beckett's advice on the production has changed all that – the lines are chanted in a breakneck monotone with no inflections, and I'm not alone in fearing that many of them will be simply inaudible . . . The point is that we are not putting on *Play* to satisfy Samuel Beckett alone . . . I trust the play completely, and trust your production of it – up to the advent of the author. What I don't especially trust is Beckett as co-director.

Devine (ever the soldier) retorted:

> The presence of Beckett was a great help to me, and to the actors. . . . To play the play as you indicate would be to demolish its dramatic purpose and turn it into *literature* [emphasis added] . . . I certainly would never have leased the play to the National Theatre if I had thought the intention was to turn it into something it isn't, to please the majority.[5]

Critic Bamber Gascoigne, however, shared Tynan's reservations and complained of the English première (*Observer*, 12 April 1964), 'The words are to be gabbled so fast that we can't understand them (we may seem to catch them the second time round but not in such a way as to appreciate them).'[6] Undeterred by such charges, Beckett went on to write yet another 'unintelligible' play, *Not I*. When actress Jessica Tandy complained that the play's suggested running time of 23 minutes rendered the work unintelligible to audiences, Beckett telegraphed back his now famous (but oft misinterpreted) injunction, 'I am not unduly concerned with intelligibility. I hope the piece may work on the nerves of the audience, not its intellect.'[7] The play certainly worked on the nerves of at least one actress, Billie Whitelaw: '*Not I* came through the letter-box. I opened it, read it, and burst into tears, floods of tears. It had a tremendous emotional impact on me. I knew then that it had to go at great speed.'[8] For Whitelaw, the work on *Play* nearly a decade earlier had thoroughly prepared her for the extraordinary ordeal of *Not I.* The experience was finally nerve-racking for her. Blindfolded, with yet another hood secured over her face, she suffered sensory deprivation in performance. 'The very first time I did it, I went to pieces. I felt I had no body; I could not relate to where I was; and, going at that speed, I was becoming very dizzy and felt like an astronaut tumbling into space . . . I swore to God I was falling.'[9]

Earlier, the American première of *Play* fared even less well with its producers than the National Theatre production. Beckett's instructions to Alan Schneider were that '*Play* was to be played through twice without interruption and at a very fast pace, each time taking no longer than nine minutes,'[10] that is, 18 minutes overall. The producers, Richard Barr, Clinton Wilder, and, of all people, Edward Albee, threatened to drop the play from the programme if Schneider followed Beckett's instructions. Schneider, unlike Devine, capitulated, and wrote to Beckett for permission to slow the pace and eliminate the *da capo*: 'For the first and last time in my long relationship with Sam, I did something I despised myself for doing. I wrote to him, asking if we could try having his text spoken only once, more slowly. Instead of telling me to blast off, Sam offered us his reluctant permission.'[11]

Admittedly, *Play* was unusual theatre for audiences in 1963. Overall, it was perhaps no more shocking than *Godot* had been a decade earlier, yet it shattered another set of theatrical conventions and audience expectations. It featured three apparently post-mortem characters. But even 'characters' is not the right word. They are rather voices, instruments, or things, part of the funeral urns which appear to have swallowed – like some leviathan – all but their protruding heads. As the girth of the urns and the diameter of their openings decreased, rendering movement all but impossible, and as the faces took on the texture and complexion of the earth-encrusted urns, as they did in the English première which Beckett oversaw (or, as Tynan claims, co-directed), the stage image became less a grouping of characters than a set of sculpted icons, a bas-relief triptych. Dialogue, in essence, disappeared. Side by side, the figures never speak to one another but respond only to the mechanical stimulus, an inquisitorial light which functions as a fourth character. In George Devine's rehearsal notes he reminds himself, 'Rehearse separately to start with to get the idea of cues from the light and *not from each other*'[12] (emphasis added). And Billie Whitelaw recalls that, 'We used to rehearse it with the stage manager playing the light, pointing a finger at us, giving us a cue. And before each performance, we sat down, the three of us and he, pointing his finger.'[13]

In *Play* Beckett redoubled his attack on literature with a plot remarkable for its banality, as language or meaning was devalued from the opening 'largely unintelligible' chorus, and with an assault against the very idea of resolution – ending, and so completion – with, at least as originally written, overt repetition. The play's *da capo* structure, even as revised in rehearsals, suggests that these figures are trapped not only in urns but in a play, in a Möbius strip of narrative. Beckett would recast that image visually nearly a decade later in the pacing figure of *Footfalls*. Circularity and repetition were, of course, already implicit in the structure of *Waiting for Godot*, *Endgame*, and *Happy Days*, but in *Play* the repetition grew even more sinister, more punishing (especially for the performers); the characters are less corporeal, more dehumanized than in anything Beckett had heretofore written for the stage. Devine would refer to the light in rehearsals as a dental drill. Billie Whitelaw took it a step further, 'It was an instrument of torture.'[14]

The visual image of *Play* suggests that Beckett had returned to his fiction for tropes, as the stage iconography echoed less that of Beckett's earlier drama than that of his more disembodied prose narratives. One of the narratological voices of *The Unnamable*, for example, notes, '. . . a collar, fixed to the mouth of the jar, now encircled my neck. And my lips which used to be hidden . . . can now be seen by all and sundry.' *Not I* may emerge from the same jar.

Structurally, the dramatic movement of *Play* is staccato, incessantly interrupted, a series of short bursts, which in rehearsals for his own 1978 production Beckett compared to the action of a manual lawn-mower – a burst of energy followed by a pause; a renewed burst followed by yet another pause. It is an image Beckett incorporated into the play itself. 'He went on and on,' notes the play's 'other' woman, called simply W2, 'I could hear a mower. An old hand mower.' Her lover, M, repeats the image shortly thereafter, 'Some fool was cutting grass. A little rush, then another' (pp. 310–11). In the Brown Notebook, the second of the two he prepared for his Schiller-Theater production of *Spiel*, Beckett describes the voices as, 'Broken, breathless – exhorted' and quotes M's line about hearing the hand mower, 'Ein rascher Ruck, dann wieder einer.'

From *Play* onwards, Beckett's stage images would grow increasingly dehumanized, reified, and metonymic, featuring dismembered or incorporeal creatures as Beckett's became a theatre of body parts and spectres, a theatre striving for transparency rather than solidity, a theatre, finally, trying to undo itself. And as plot and character dissipated, the playing space grew more delimited, circumscribed, controlled. The proscenium arch is indispensable to these works, framing a playing space. The works from *Play* onwards make little sense performed on modern, thrust stages or in the round. In his programme notes to the English première, director George Devine, clearly echoing Beckett on the subject, sounds prophetic:

> . . . very often in Beckett words are not used for their intellectual content or their emotional impact. This is especially so in *Play*, where 'story and dialogue' are of a deliberately banal order. Here the words are used more as sounds, as 'dramatic ammunition', to quote Beckett's own phrase, and they take equal place with the visual action but do not dominate it.

Despite Devine's implication that the anti-literary nature of the dialogue – or rather the three monologues – in *Play* is characteristic of Beckett's work, his comments ill fit the original texts and productions of *Waiting for Godot*, *Endgame*, *Krapp's Last Tape*, or *Happy Days*. But it is precisely the aesthetic perspective Beckett was to bring to revising these works. Devine's observation presages not only the theatre Beckett would write from *Play* onwards but also anticipates Beckett's revisionist need to reconstitute all his theatre works through an aesthetic that percolates through *Play*.

Play, moreover, drew Beckett further into the theatrical process, since it demanded a level of technical sophistication and precision unknown in his earlier work, and it was the writing of *Play* that may have, finally, forced Beckett – reluctant as he was – to assume full directorial responsibility for his own works. Beckett had introduced technology to his theatre with *Krapp's Last Tape* in 1958, shortly after working on his first radio play, *All That Fall*, at the BBC and then hearing a tape recording of the production. And the exploding umbrella of *Happy Days* still gives producers and fire wardens headaches. But the single inquisitorial spotlight – part torturer, part orchestra conductor, even part theatre director – situated amid the footlights, which instantaneously flashes from face to face, was not part of any technical director's repertoire of contraptions in 1963. And Beckett kept a hand in all major European performances to ensure that technological compromise – three separate spotlights, for instance – did not compromise performances. In the second of the *Spiel* notebooks, the Brown Notebook, Beckett clearly indicates his desire for a single spot even when all three urns are simultaneously illuminated: 'as if a single gaze widening for 3', he notes.

Written in English in 1962, *Play* would have its première in German, and Beckett reviewed the German translation by Elmar Tophoven (although as the first of the two *Spiel* notebooks, the Red Notebook, makes abundantly clear, when he came to direct the play himself in German in 1978, he revised the published translation extensively), and he attended final rehearsals for Deryk Mendel's *Spiel*, at the Ulmer-Theater, Ulm-Donau, Germany, which premièred 14 June 1963, with his American director, Alan Schneider. Beckett was, however, according to Michaël Lonsdale, less than pleased with the German production: 'En Allemagne, les jarres étaient trop rondes et trop éloignées les unes des autres.' [In Germany the urns were too round and too separated from one another.][15] Shortly thereafter Beckett began an extensive correspondence with the American director, Schneider, in preparation for the

English-language première at the Cherry Lane Theater, New York, on 4 January 1964. In that correspondence Beckett re-emphasized the importance of his working directly in the theatre. To Schneider's queries of 21 November 1963, Beckett responded on 26 November: 'I realize that no final script is possible until I work on rehearsals.'[16] This apparently simple observation on the nature of the theatrical process was to have a profound impact on Beckett's work since it affected not only subsequent creations, but drew him further into the theatrical process to reread, rethink, and finally rewrite his earlier work.

For Beckett the early productions of a work were especially important because they set a standard of production. Writing to his American publisher, Barney Rosset, on 1 April 1958, he said of the première of *Krapp's Last Tape*, 'I'd hate it to be made a balls of at the outset and that's why I question its being let out to small groups beyond our controp [*sic*] before we get it done more or less right and set a standard of fidelity at least.'[17] On 10 April 1958 Beckett wrote to Rosset that he was off to London to oversee McWhinnie's *Krapp's Last Tape*, 'where I hope to get the mechanics of it right'. The first two productions of *Play*, the Mendel production in Ulm and the Schneider production in New York, set unacceptable standards, and so Beckett increased his participation with Serreau in Paris and Devine in London. Neither production went smoothly and so the inevitable next step for Beckett was to set his own standard. In the mid-1960s he decided to do just that. The result was not only Beckett's staging his work as originally conceived and written but his reconceiving it for and directly on the stage.

That Beckett's involvement in practical theatre – and its attendant frustrations – began to dominate his creative life is evident from the letters of this period. But it is precisely this saturation that finally made Samuel Beckett a man of the theatre. On 23 September 1963, for example, Beckett wrote to Jack MacGowran, who played Clov to George Devine's Hamm in the 1958 *Endgame* at the Royal Court Theatre:

> Start rehearsals with Madeleine [Renaud] next week [for *Oh les beaux jours*]. Afraid no chance of getting to London this 'summer'. Shall be over end of year or early next to assist George [Devine] in his production of *Play* for the National Theatre. [Jean-Marie] Serreau will do it here [in Paris] about the same time.[18]

The National Theatre production finally opened at the Old Vic on 7 April 1964 and, less than a week later, on his birthday, Beckett was again lamenting his heavy rehearsal schedule, this time to friend and sometime literary agent, George Reavey:

> I seem to have been rehearsing practically without pause since January. Just back from 3 weeks in London on rehearsals of *Play*. Very pleased with results – rather different from N.Y. from what I have heard. Start tomorrow – or rather resume – French version [*Comédie*] with Serreau, opening

next month. Then back to London in June for *Endgame* at the Aldwych. Then I hope a long retreat at Ussy to try to collect what wits remain.[19]

That London production of *Play* – coming as it did in the midst of the rehearsals for *Comédie* – was an event of far-reaching consequences since it offered the English theatre-going public a play transformed from that available in local bookshops. Working uneasily in Paris with Jean-Marie Serreau on staging the French text before the London rehearsals, Beckett decided on some fundamental changes to the play, and he wrote to British director George Devine on 9 March 1964 – less than a month before the scheduled opening – to warn him of necessary script adjustments:

The last rehearsals with Serreau have led us to a view of the *da capo* which I think you should know about. According to the text it is rigorously identical with the first statement. We now think it would be dramatically more effective to have it express a slight weakening, both of question and of response, by means of less and perhaps slower light and correspondingly less volume and speed of voice.[20]

These revisions were unprecedented since they called not for temporary textual concessions made to appease the likes of the Lord Chamberlain, for example, or those necessitated by production: to adjust the play to a particular playing space or to the strengths or weaknesses of particular actors. They were, instead, the result of the author's dissatisfaction with his own text as *published*, his recognition that his original script, even if published, was unfinished, in need of revision. In addition to altering the *da capo* ending, for instance, Beckett revised the fundamental relationship between the inquisitorial light and its urn-imprisoned victims: 'The inquirer (light) begins to emerge', continued Beckett, 'as no less a victim of his inquiry than they and as needing to be free, within narrow limits, literally to act the part, i.e., to vary if only slightly his speeds and intensities.' While the French production was still in rehearsals, Beckett left for London with his revisions to ensure their incorporation into the English première. Subsequently, he produced a document that he called 'Notes made *after* the National Theatre Production' (italics added) which varies only slightly from the original letter he sent to Devine before the London rehearsals. The complex changes to the text of *Play* were publicly announced by the English publisher of Beckett's fiction, John Calder, in a letter to the *Times Literary Supplement* on 23 April 1964:

Since although the present editions of Beckett's play *Play* state 'repeat play exactly' your readers might be interested to hear that during the London rehearsals Beckett made a number of changes in the order of the cues so that although each actor has his lines in the same order as the light interrogates him, the light interrogates in a different order. This makes it impossible for the actors

> to take cues from each other but only from the light and lets us assume that on a third round many things might be different.

The multiple productions of *Play* signalled then not only Beckett's increasingly frenetic involvement with the productions of his work in three languages, French, German and English, but also that he was prepared to change and even at times substantially rewrite the published versions of his texts based on the practicalities, realities, and insights that working in stage space literally brought to light, and this at a time when he was rethinking the staging of all his work. Roger Blin, for example, was directing *Oh les beaux jours* with Beckett in Paris in October of 1963. Beckett was heavily involved with Anthony Page's staging of *Waiting for Godot* at the Royal Court in December of 1964. And he was also preparing two new productions of *Endgame* with Jack MacGowran, one that opened in Paris at the Studio des Champs-Elysées (in English) in February 1964 and one with the Royal Shakespeare Company opening at the Aldwych in London in July of that same year. Such close and frequent theatrical work began to suggest various insufficiencies or clumsiness in his texts so that the changes that Calder announced would soon become a pattern with every play Beckett subsequently directed. The principle that Beckett emphasized to Alan Schneider, 'that no final script is possible until I work on rehearsals', would now apply to all of his work.

Two years after the French première of *Comédie*, the production was reprised, and Beckett now found that there was 'no escape' from assuming total direction of the work himself. He wrote to MacGowran on 8 September 1966:

> Up to my eyes in theatre again for my sins and despite rows rehearsing *Play* with new cast for new season at Théâtre de France. Hope to try it a different way. Serreau *nominally in charge* is off to Dallas and N.Y. for 10 days on theatre prospection, so no escape. [Emphasis added.]

What Beckett could no longer 'escape' was full directorial responsibility or self-collaboration. Serreau appeared as the director of record, but it was Beckett's productions of *Comédie*, *Va-et-vient*, and Robert Pinget's *L'Hypothèse* that opened at the Petite Salle, Odéon Théâtre de France on 28 February 1966. That production of *Comédie* began a long period of Beckett's working through Beckett, this time as an *auteur/metteur-en-scène* in collaboration with himself. Directing became a crucial part of his creative process, and turning a directorial eye on his earlier plays gave him the opportunity to 'correct' (Beckett's word) the theatrical insufficiencies he found there and to reshape the works with an aesthetic that coalesced with the writing and staging of *Play*. The shift in aesthetics was towards a radical simplification, a disencumberment, a further de-theatricalization of theatre. It tended to substitute extended monologues, often delivered in monotone, for dialogue, and feature renewed emphasis on the static stage image, still-points, *tableaux vivants*, or *Wartestelle*, literally waiting points, which bear more resemblance to painting or sculpture than to traditional theatre.

What John Calder's letter to the *Times Literary Supplement* announced was that the printed texts available for Beckett's plays were for various reasons neither always reliable nor even fully acceptable to the author; that is, they did not represent the author's final (if such were ever possible with Beckett) and certainly not his most recent and so most complete thinking about his work. The particular textual problems with *Play* seem to have been easily solved. Beckett's 'Notes', with a few variants, were incorporated into subsequent printings, beginning with the 1969 Faber and Faber reprint. That would seem to have solved the problem. But the post-publication revisions of *Play* were not an anomaly. Beckett began to direct in earnest from September the following year, 1967, at the Schiller-Theater Werkstatt with *Endspiel* (*Endgame*). In all, between the Odéon *Va-et-vient* in 1966 and the valedictory television version of *Was Wo* which was aired by Süddeutscher Rundfunk on Beckett's eightieth birthday, 13 April 1986, Beckett directed some sixteen stage productions of his work and some seven works for German television, each time making at least adjustments to his texts, each time creating the final text in rehearsals.

Not all aesthetic and theatrical issues, however, were resolved during productions. Having worked closely with Anthony Page on the 1973 Royal Court Theatre production of *Not I* (see Appendix for Beckett's notes) and having directed it himself in 1975 at the Théâtre d'Orsay, Beckett still remained ambivalent about the visual image of the play. The best advice that he could finally offer directors of *Not I* was to omit the Auditor. As he wrote to a pair of directors on 16 November 1986, 'I should have . . . advised you simply to omit the auditor. He is very difficult to stage (light – position) and may well be of more harm than good. For me the play needs him but I can do without him. I have never seen him function effectively.'[21] Beckett's comment presumably includes the English production he supervised closely, the 1973 Royal Court production with Billie Whitelaw, directed by Anthony Page. For the 1978 French productions with Madeleine Renaud which he directed himself, Beckett omitted the Auditor all together, as did the BBC film production of the Billie Whitelaw performance. To date no script for the play suggests that the elimination of the Auditor is an option.

By 1986 the textual variations of Beckett's productions suggested a repudiation of his originally published texts. Not only did Beckett's *oeuvre* now exist in multiple versions because he revised as he translated; that is, each self-translation became a textual transformation, the translation not a literary equivalent but essentially a new text, and one that did not supersede the original. Now even within each language multiple versions or texts existed. Critics and directors were forced into a position of building interpretations and mounting productions of Beckett's work not so much on corrupt texts such as almost all English versions of *Waiting for Godot*, but on those the author himself found unsatisfactory, unfinished. With *Footfalls*, for example, Faber and Faber, eager to make the play available for opening night, set its first edition from a typescript that Beckett had not fully tested on the stage. Beckett subsequently changed the pattern of May's pacing from seven to nine steps in both of the productions that he directed, and detailed the significance of that change in both theatrical notebooks. Faber and Faber went on to correct its text in the collected edition *Ends and Odds*, but the revised text (never identified as such) remains incorrect and internally inconsistent. Faber indeed changed the number of May's footsteps from seven to nine in the stage directions, for instance, but left her counting her steps from one to seven in the dialogue.[22] Stagings of *Footfalls* based on any of the published versions of the play, either the first edition (1976), the incompletely revised version in *Ends and Odds* (1977), or that in *The Complete Plays of Samuel Beckett* (1986), will inevitably introduce unnecessary confusion into the production.

Much of this major aesthetic shift, this second phase of Beckett's theatre, begins then with productions of *Play* and the increased amount of authorial oversight it necessitated, and fortunately much of it is documented in Beckett's own theatrical notebooks. As Beckett began to direct his work himself, his preparations became methodical and committed to paper. He outlined his plays again and again and again and again in an obsessive search for patterns, linguistic and visual echoes, parallels of any sort. He developed detailed notes on staging, and meticulously revised his texts whether in German, French or English to accommodate a more formalist post-*Play* aesthetic.

The two notebooks that Beckett prepared for his 1978 Schiller-Theater production of *Spiel* (*Play*) are a case in point. They demonstrate his near-obsession with language (German in this case), structure, and formal detail – all three of which are, of course, inextricably entwined. Beckett's notebooks not only comprise a motif index to his plays, they constitute as well a remarkably detailed external record of the artist's internal process and struggles. They document Beckett's continued aesthetic and stylistic development. At the head of a series of notes he prepared for Donald McWhinnie's 1976 Royal Court production of *That Time* Beckett wrote what amounts to a one-sentence theatrical manifesto, the most succinct and explicit statement of his late aesthetics that we have, 'To the objection that visual component too small, out of all proportion with aural, answer: make it smaller, on the principle that less is more.' As Beckett adapted the aesthetics of architect Mies van der Rohe that 'less is more', as he developed his own 'mania for minimalism', or what he punningly called a 'Process of elimination' in the *What Where* notebook, he also seized directorial opportunities to re-create his work according to principles more in keeping with sculpture, painting or even architecture than drama, and to test the results directly on the stage.

The *Eh Joe* notebook that Beckett prepared for the second of his German productions outlines succinctly the central thematic and theatrical conflicts of this, his first teleplay. While Joe may be 'Out of sight, [and so apparently out of] reach', for example, he would not feel safe even without the assailing voice because of his 'Fear of Dark'. Beckett outlined the ten scenes of the play as follows:

1. Out of sight, reach. Fear of dark.
2. Rupture formula – 'Best to come' (1)
3. Voices in head – behind the eyes. Mental thugee.
4. Present voice last, then his own to still, then silence till God's, unstillable
5. Clues for voice and hearer. Worse when nearly home. What if final whisper unstillable?
6. God to him 1
7. Deficient in kindness, strength, intelligence, looks, cleanliness, normality.
8. Green one. 'Best to come' 2. Duly laid
9. Same as 4.
10. Voice falling to whisper.

In the notebook for *Tritte* (*Footfalls*) Beckett made explicit the relationship among the imbedded characters of that play in his discussion of voices. In the dialogue within the monologues (Parts II and III), for example, the Mother's, 'What do you mean, May, not enough' of Part II should be echoed by the voice of Mrs W in Part III, 'What do you mean, Amy, to put it mildly', according to Beckett. 'Same style for both relationships,' he noted. The *Kommen und Gehen* (*Come and Go*) notebook details Beckett's preoccupation with pattern in theatre space. *Kommen und Gehen* (finally directed by Walter Asmus not Beckett) was on the programme with *Spiel* (*Play*) at the Schiller-Theater Werkstatt in October of 1978. While Beckett rethought the *da capo* ending of *Spiel*, he considered adding a similar repetition to *Kommen und Gehen*. Although he outlined the pattern of what would amount to a second act to the play in his directorial notebook, he finally dismissed the possibility as 'mathematically desirable [but] logically impossible'.

As we credit Beckett with redefining modern theatre in January of 1953 with *En attendant Godot*, which made the theatrical tradition at the time seem bloated, we need to understand that Beckett's aesthetic and theatrical development did not stop then. With the composition of *Play*, which drew the performative fully into his creative process for the first time, Beckett redefined his theatre yet again, increasing the significance of the performative and ruthlessly rejecting anything dispensable. The result was a minimalism and formal simplicity that made even *Godot* and *Endgame* seem operatic. Simultaneously, Beckett tried to rectify what he perceived as defects in that chronologically and aesthetically earlier work through his own direction, drawing that work as well closer to the iconic, sculptural qualities of the post-*Play* theatre. These rewritten texts are not aberrations or curiosities but the main line of Beckett's artistic development. Beckett's 1967 Schiller *Endspiel* produced not only a faithful stage production of an existing text but created a major new text in the canon. His productions of *Footfalls* and *What Where* did likewise (those texts printed in this volume in completely revised form for the first time). As another Vladimir observed, this one with the family name of Nabokov, 'The best part of a writer's biography is not the record of his adventures, but the story of his style.' *The Theatrical Notebooks of Samuel Beckett* record nothing less than the biography of Samuel Beckett's developing theatrical style.

Notes to the Introduction

1 – The letter to Myron is actually dated 31 May 1961, but that seems to be an error since it refers to Lawrence Harvey's sabbatical in Paris. Harvey did not go to Paris on his Guggenheim Fellowship, however, until the summer of 1962. See also, for example, Beckett's letter to Thomas McGreevy, 22 July 1962: 'I have been here for the past week struggling with a new short play I can't get right . . . Back to the battle, lights and voices' (Beckett cited by Bair, p. 462).
2 – The earliest version of the play was written for a woman and two men, Syke and Conk. These figures were contained not in the urns of the published version but in white boxes. For additional details see Gontarski, 1985, pp. 90–100.
3 – All references to Beckett's drama are from *The Complete Dramatic Works* (*CDW*). The *Words and Music* poem appears on pp. 293–4. Subsequent page numbers are in parentheses.
4 – James Knowlson, 'Practical Aspects of Theatre, Radio, and Television: Extracts from an Unscripted Interview with Billie Whitelaw', *Journal of Beckett Studies*, no. 3 (summer 1978), p. 85.
5 – The accuracy of Devine's analysis of Tynan seems to have been borne out some five years later when Beckett sent Tynan a playlet, *Breath*, for a theatrical review Tynan proposed, whose title is derived from the surrealist pun, 'Oh quel cul t'as.' Tynan seized the opportunity to demonstrate his sensitivity to Beckett's texts by overtly revising Beckett's typescript. To Beckett's 'Miscellaneous rubbish' Tynan added, 'including naked people'. ('Mene, mene,' Hamm might have said.) And Beckett's two cries, one of birth and one of death, were performed as erotic groans. To add to the folly, the amended text of *Oh! Calcutta!* was published by Beckett's American publisher, Grove Press, with Beckett's contribution, identified as such and now called 'Prologue', facing a production photo of rubbish and naked bodies. Beckett found that his American contract forbade his intervention in this production, but he did succeed in forbidding use of the 'Prologue' in all other countries where the 'Entertainment' was produced, including the United Kingdom.
6 – Michaël Lonsdale, who played M in Serreau's French première, notes of Beckett's instructions, 'Il voulait qu'on parle à une vitesse de mitrailleuse.' [He would like it spoken with the speed of a machine-gun.] Elisabeth Auclair-Tamaroff et Barthélémy, *Jean-Marie Serreau Découvreur de Théâtres* (L'Arbre Verdoyant Editeur, Paris, 1986), p. 75.
7 – Enoch Brater, *Beyond Minimalism: Beckett's Late Style in the Theater* (Oxford University Press, New York, 1987), p. 23.
8 – Knowlson, op. cit., p. 86.
9 – Ibid.
10 – Alan Schneider, *Entrances: An American Director's Journey* (Viking Press, New York, 1986), p. 341.
11 – Ibid.
12 – Notes on deposit at the University of Reading Samuel Beckett Archive, MS 1581/15.
13 – Knowlson, op. cit., p. 86.

14 – Ibid.
15 – *Jean-Marie Serreau*, p. 75.
16 – Alec Reid made something of the same point in the posthumously published 'Impact and Parable in Beckett: A First Encounter with *Not I*', published in a tribute issue of *Hermathena*, no. 141 (1986), edited by Terence Brown and Nicholas Grene: Beckett 'will speak of the first run-through with actors as the "realization" of the play and when it has been performed publicly, he will say that it has been "created"'. Delivering the first Annenberg Lecture at the University of Reading's Beckett Archive in May of 1993, Billie Whitelaw made the following observation of *Not I*: 'I very much had the feeling that it was a work in progress.'
17 – It would be Alan Schneider who set the 'standard of fidelity' for the American *Krapp's Last Tape* but not, of course, for *Play*.
18 – *No Symbols Where None Intended: A Catalogue of Books, Manuscripts and Other Material Relating to Samuel Beckett in the Collections of the Humanities Research Center*, selected and described by Carlton Lake (Austin, Texas: Humanities Research Center), p. 129.
19 – Ibid.
20 – This letter to Devine has been published in its entirety in *New Theatre Magazine* (Samuel Beckett issue), vol. 2, no. 3 (1972), pp. 16–17.
21 – Letter to David Hunsberger and Linda Kendall, dated 16 November 1986.
22 – See my 'Texts and Pre-texts of Samuel Beckett's *Footfalls*'.

ABBREVIATIONS

In the notes to this edition, the following abbreviations are used throughout:

CDW Samuel Beckett, *The Complete Dramatic Works*, Faber and Faber, London, 1986.

Play

Spiel(SB) Annotated copy Beckett prepared for the Schiller-Theater Werkstatt production, 6 October 1978.

Spiel(WA) Copy of annotated text with additional production notes by Walter Asmus.

Red Nb See page 5.

Brown Nb See page 145.

Come and Go

KuG(WA) Director's copy of *Kommen und Gehen*, from *Theater Heute* by Walter Asmus. Annotations and revisions in his hand, but the textual revisions were initiated by Beckett and conform with the notes in the *Kommen und Gehen* notebook.

Brown Nb See page 217.

Eh Joe

He Joe(RC) Beckett's annotated copy of the Suhrkamp Verlag edition of *Samuel Beckett/Film/He Joe.* The autograph presentation reads, 'for Rick (Cluchey)/ affectionately/from Sam/Stuttgart/January 1979'.

Brown Nb See page 245.

Footfalls

Footfalls(SB) Revised text Beckett prepared for the Royal Court Theatre production in 1976. Reading University Library MS 2828.

Footfalls(CI) A second revised text Beckett prepared for the Royal Court Theatre production inscribed 'for Calvin & Joann/Sam. Beckett'. On deposit, Boston University.

RC Nb See page 289.

German Nb See page 313.

That Time

TT(SB) Revised text of *Samuel Beckett: That Time/Damals* Beckett prepared for his 1976 Schiller-Theater Werkstatt production.

RC ms See page 357.

German Nb See page 367.

What Where

WW(SB) Annotated copy of *Theater Heute* edition of *Was Wo* Beckett prepared before and revised during the filming of *What Where* in Stuttgart, 18–28 June 1985. Reading University Library MS 3097.

QO(PC) Revised French text Samuel Beckett prepared for Pierre Chabert's French stage première of the revised text, Théâtre du Rond-Point, April 1986.

WW(SEG) Revised English text Samuel Beckett prepared for S. E. Gontarski's English-language stage première of the revised text, Magic Theater, San Francisco, December 1986.

Stuttgart Nb See page 423.

Play

Spiel, Ulmer Theater, Ulm-Donau, 14 June 1963

Director Deryk Mendel
Nancy Illig
Sigrid Pfeiffer
Gerhard Winter

Revived 16 November 1963
Ruth Hausmeister
Gisela Stein
Holger Kepick

Play, Cherry Lane Theater, New York, 4 January 1964

Director Alan Schneider
Frances Sternhagen
Marian Reardon
Michael Lipton

Play, National Theatre Company, Old Vic Theatre, London, 7 April 1964

Director George Devine
Rosemary Harris
Billie Whitelaw
Robert Stephens

Comédie, Pavillon de Marsan, Paris, 14 June 1964

Director Jean-Marie Serreau
Eléonore Hirt
Delphine Seyrig
Michaël Lonsdale

Comédie, Petite Salle, Odéon-Théâtre De France, Paris, 28 February 1966

Director Jean-Marie Serreau
Eléonore Hirt
Danielle van Bercheyke
Michaël Lonsdale
(Beckett to Jack MacGowran, 8 September 1966: 'Serreau nominally in charge.')

Play, Abbey Theatre, Dublin, 7 October 1967

Director Edward Golden
Joan O'Hara
Angela Newman
Patrick Laffan

Play, Royal Court Theatre, London, 20 May 1976

Director Donald McWhinnie
Anna Massey
Ronald Pickup
Penelope Wilton

Spiel, Schiller-Theater Werkstatt, Berlin, 6 October 1978

Director Samuel Beckett
F1 Hildegard Schmahl
F2 Sybille Gilles
M Klaus Herm

Come and Go

Kommen und Gehen, Schiller-Theater Werkstatt, Berlin, 14 January 1966

Director Deryk Mendel
LO (FLO) Lieselotte Rau
MEI (VI) Charlotte Joeres
SU (RU) Sibylle Gilles

Va-et-vient (with *Comédie*), Petite Salle, Odéon–Théâtre de France, Paris, 28 February 1966

Director Samuel Beckett
FLO Annie Bertin
VI Madeleine Renaud
RU Simone Valère

Come and Go, Abbey Theatre Company at the Peacock Theatre, Dublin, 28 February 1968

Director Edward Golden
FLO Deirdre Purcell
VI Aideen O'Kelly
RU Kathleen Barrington

Come and Go, Royal Festival Hall, London, 9 December 1968

Director William Gaskill
FLO Joan Plowright
VI Billie Whitelaw
RU Peggy Ashcroft

Come and Go, Arts Laboratory, Drury Lane, London, 1 July 1969

Director Hovhannes I. Pilikian
FLO Cleo Sylvestre
VI Gilli Fraser
RU Aletta Lohmeyer

Kommen und Gehen, Schiller-Theater Werkstatt, Berlin, 6 October 1978

Director Walter Asmus
LO (FLO) Christine Prober
MEI (VI) Charlotte Joeres
SU (RU) Karin Remsing

Eh Joe

He Joe, Süddeutscher Rundfunk, Stuttgart, 13 April 1966

Director Samuel Beckett
Deryk Mendel
Nancy Illig

Eh Joe, BBC2, London, 4 July 1966

Director Alan Gibson
Jack McGowran
Sian Phillips

He Joe, Süddeutscher Rundfunk, Stuttgart, January 1979

Director Samuel Beckett
Heinz Bennet
Irmgard Först

Not I

Not I, Repertory Theater of Lincoln Center, New York, 22 November 1972

Director Alan Schneider
MOUTH Jessica Tandy
AUDITOR Henderson Forsythe

Not I, Royal Court Theatre, London, 16 January 1973

Director Anthony Page
MOUTH Billie Whitelaw
AUDITOR Brian Miller

Pas Moi, Petite Salle, Théâtre d'Orsay, Paris, 8 April 1975

Director Samuel Beckett
Madeleine Renaud

Pas Moi, Grande Salle, Théâtre d'Orsay, Paris, 11 April 1978

Director Samuel Beckett
Madeleine Renaud

Footfalls

Footfalls, Royal Court Theatre, London, 20 May 1976

Director Samuel Beckett
MAY Billie Whitelaw
VOICE OF MOTHER Rose Hill

Tritte, Schiller-Theater Werkstatt, Berlin, 1 October 1976

Director Samuel Beckett
MAY Hildegard Schmahl
STIMME DER MUTTER Charlotte Joeres

Pas, Théâtre d'Orsay, Grande Salle, Paris, 11 April 1978

Director Samuel Beckett
MAY Delphine Seyrig
VOICE OF MOTHER Madeleine Renaud

That Time

That Time, Royal Court Theatre, London, 20 May 1976

Director Donald McWhinnie
LISTENER AND VOICE Patrick Magee

Damals, Schiller-Theater Werkstatt, Berlin, 1 October 1976

Director Samuel Beckett
GESICHT UND STIMME Klaus Herm

What Where

What Where (original text), Harold Clurman Theater, New York, 15 June 1983

Director Alan Schneider
BAM David Warrilow
BIM Donald Davies
BEM Rand Mitchell
BOM Daniel Wirth

Was Wo (revised text), Süddeutscher Rundfunk, Stuttgart, 13 April 1986

Director Samuel Beckett
BAM Friedhelm Becker
BIM Alfred Querbach
BEM Edwin Dorner
BOM Walter Lagnitz

Quoi Où (revised text), Théâtre du Rond-Point, Paris, April 1986

Director Pierre Chabert
BAM David Warrilow
BIM Guy Cambreleng
BEM Phillipe Krijbich
BOM Dominique Ehlinger

What Where (revised text), Magic Theater, San Francisco, November 1986

Director S. E. Gontarski
BAM Tom Luce
BIM Dave Peichert
BEM Richard Wagner
BOM Morgan Upton

PART I

Play

Samuel Beckett's Production Notebooks for *Spiel* (*Play*) at the Schiller-Theater Werkstatt, Berlin, October 1978

DAMALS
SPIEL

FACSIMILE OF BECKETT'S PRODUCTION NOTEBOOK
WITH TRANSCRIPTION AND TRANSLATION

Note on Manuscript I: The Red Notebook

Samuel Beckett's production notes for his 1978 Schiller-Theater production of *Spiel* (*Play*) are divided between two notebooks. The first is a red, hard-covered, 90-folio, Square-ruled notebook measuring 20.5 × 14.5 cm., on deposit at the University of Reading Samuel Beckett Archive, MS 1976. Across the front cover Beckett wrote 'DAMALS' (*That Time*) and beneath it 'SPIEL'; on the back cover, overturned, Beckett wrote 'TRITTE' (*Footfalls*). The unpaginated notebook contains blank endpapers (blue) and notes for Beckett's 1976 Schiller-Theater *Damals*, which begin on the recto of folio 1 and continue to the recto of folio 6. On the verso of folio 6 Beckett began to outline *Spiel* for his 1978 Schiller-Theater production and, from the recto of folio 8, to write out and revise the German text, grouping and numbering consecutively each character's speeches to the recto of folio 30 (folio 25 having been crudely cut away and removed). Folios 31–81 are blank, but the verso of folio 82 contains the final notes, upside-down, of the 1976 Schiller *Tritte*, since Beckett prepared notes for *Damals* and *Tritte* in the same notebook, beginning *Tritte* from the back of the notebook, on the recto of folio 1 (if the text were being foliated from this direction) or the verso of folio 90. The *Tritte* notes, counting from the back of the notebook, the way they were written, begin on the recto of folio 1 and continue to the recto of folio 9. Interpolations, usually English translations, are bracketed. The bracketed English throughout the notebook, however, is not necessarily a literal translation of the German but the equivalent phrase in the English text. Variations from the trilingual German edition, *Samuel Beckett: Dramatische Dichtungen in drei Sprachen* (Suhrkamp Verlag, Frankfurt am Main, 1981), are also indicated within brackets.

SPIEL

F1	1-14	Present 1	14
	15-19	Others	5
	20-25	Present 2	6
F2	1-10	Present 1	10
	11-14	Others	4
	15-25	Present 2	11
M	1-8	Present 1	8
	9-16	Others	8
	17-31	Present 2	15

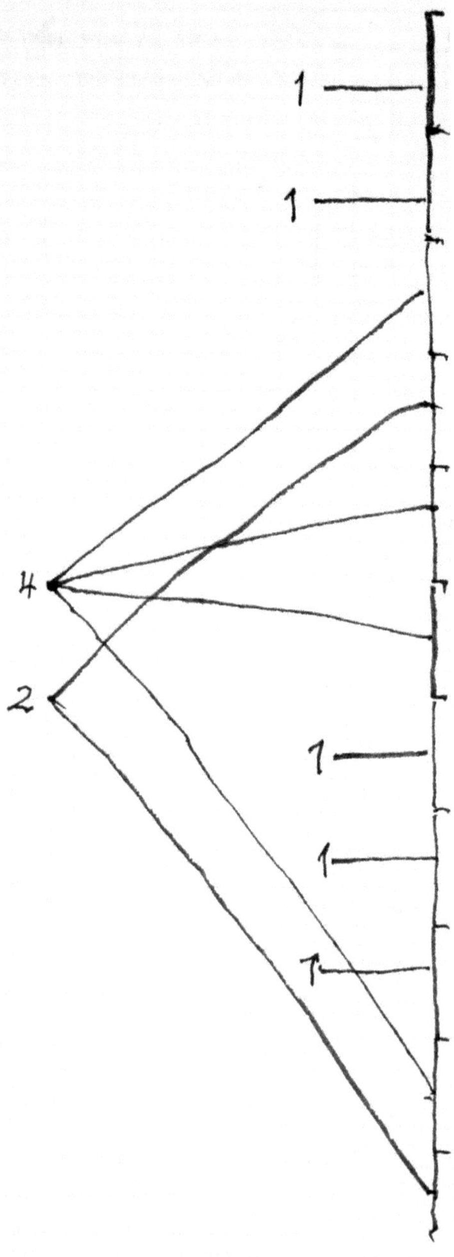

order

I

F1
F2
M
F2
F1
M
F2
M
F1
M
F2
F1
F2
M
F1
F2
M
F1
F2
F1
F2
F1
M
F2
F1
M
F1
F2
M
F1
M
F2

32

II

M
F1
1 F2.
F1
M
2 F2.
M
F2
3 F1.
M
F2
4 F1.
M
F2
5 M.
F1
F2
6 M.
F1
F2
7 M.
F1
F2
8 M.
F1
M
1 F2.
M
F2
2 M.
F1
F2
3 F1.
M
F1
4 F2.

36

M
F1
5 F2
F1
F2
6 M
F1
M
7 F2
M
F1
8 F2
F2
M
1 F2
F1
M
2 F2
F1
M
3 F2
M
F1
4 M
F2
F1
5 M
F1
F2
6 M
F1
M
7 F1
F2
M
8 F1

36

M
F2
1 F1
M
F1
2 M.
F2
M.
3 M

9
36
36

81

[*fol. 6v*]

SPIEL[1]

F1	1–14	Present 1	–	14
	15–19	Others	–	5
	20–25	Present 2	–	6
F2	1–10	Present 1	–	10
	11–14	Others	–	4
	15–25	Present 2	–	11
M	1–8	Present 1		8
	9–16	Others		8
	17–31	Present 2		15

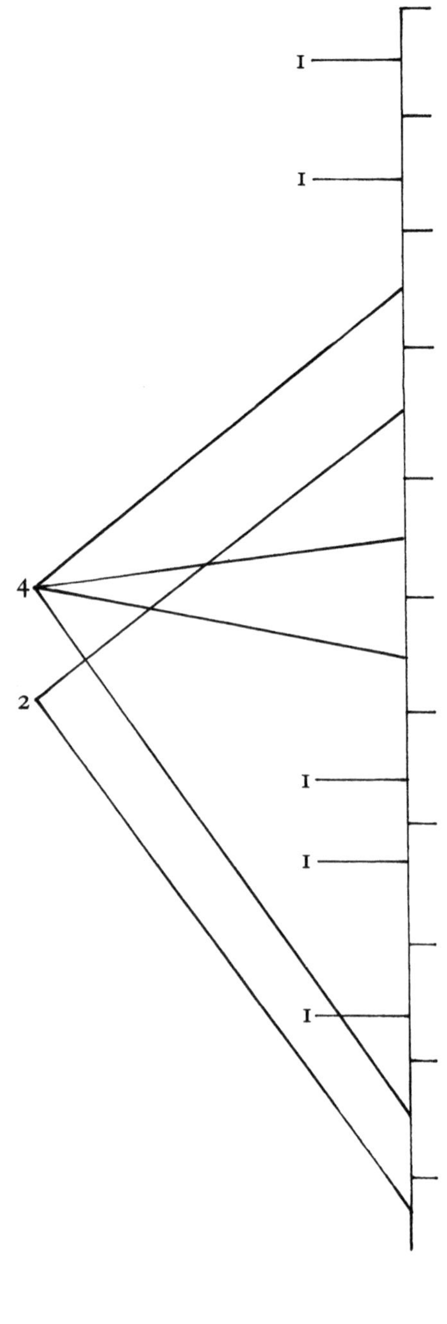

F2 15–20

Order

I	
1	F1
1	F2
1	M
2	F2
2	F1
2	M
3	F2
3	M
3	F1
4	M
4	F2
4	F1
5	F2
5	M
5	F1
6	F2
6	M
6	F1
7	F2
7	F1
8	F2
8	F1
7	M
9	F2
9	F1
8	M
10	F1
10	F2
9	M
11	F1
10	M
11	F2
32	

	II		Group
	1	M	
	1	F1	
1	1	F2	
	2	F1	
	2	M	
2	2	F2	
	3	M	
	3	F2	
3	3	F1	
	4	M	
	4	F2	
4	4	F1	
	5	M	
	5	F2	
5	6	M	
	5	F1	
	6	F2	
6	7	M	
	6	F1	
	7	F2	
7	8	M	
	7	F1	
	8	F2	
8	9	M	
	8	F	
[X]	10	M	
1	9	F2	1
	11	M	
	10	F2	
2	12	M	1
	9	F1	
	11	F2	
3	10	F1	1
	13	M	
	11	F1	
4	12	F2	1
	36		

			Group
	14	M	
	12	F1	
5	13	F2	2
	13	F1	
	14	F2	
6	15	M	1
	14	F1	
	16	M	
7	15	F2	2
	17	M	
	15	F1	
8	16	F2	3
	17	F2	
	18	M	
1	18	F2	
	16	F1	
	19	M	
2	19	F2	
	17	F1	
	20	M	
3	20	F2	
	21	M	
	18	F1	
4	22	M	
	21	F2	
	19	F1	
5	23	M	
	20	F1	
	22	F2	
6	24	M	
	21	F1	
	25	M1	
7	22	F1	
	23	F2	
	26	M	
8	23	F1	
	36		

	27	M
	24	F2
1	24	F1
	28	M
	25	F1
2	29	M
	25	F2
	30	M
3	31	M
	9	
	36	
	36	
	81	

Bewunderung

~~??~~ F1 (chor)

Ja seltsam – lieber dunkel – und je dunkler – je schlimmer – bis alles dunkel – dann alles gut – eine Zeitlang – doch es wird kommen – die Zeit wird kommen – das Ding ist da – du wirst es sehen – mich lassen – verlassen – alles dunkel – alles still – ~~[illegible]~~ alles vorbei – ausgelöscht

—

Ich sagte zu ihm, Gib sie auf – (chor)

1

Ich sagte zu ihm, Gib sie auf. Ich schwor bei allem, was mir lieb u. teuer –

— 2

obgleich ich monatelag einen erstklassigen Mann auf seine Fährte setzte, kam keine Spur von einem Beweis heraus. Und es liess sich nicht leugnen, dass er noch genauso ... galant ~~[illegible]~~ wie immer war. Dies u. sein Abscheu vor der rein platonischen Masche liessen mich manchmal fragen, ob ich ihn nicht zu unrecht beschuldigte. Ja.

— 3

Man stelle sich also mein Erstaunen vor, als er eines schönen Morgens, ~~[illegible]~~ da ich wie erschlagen im Frühstückszimmer sass, hereinschlich, vor mir auf die Knie sank, sein Gesicht in meinem Schoss bettete und ... beichtete.

— 4

Ich gehe zu, meine erste Regung war Erstaunen. Was für ein Kerl!

—

[*fol. 7v*]

[*erasure*] F1 (Chor)

Ja, seltsam – lieber dunkel – und je dunkler – je
schlimmer – bis alles dunkel – dann alles gut –
eine Zeitlang – doch es wird kommen – die Zeit
wird kommen – das Ding [der Sinn] ist da – du wirst es [ihn]
sehen – mich lassen – verlassen – alles dunkel –
alles still – [*erasure*] alles vorbei – ausgelöscht

[Yes, strange, darkness best, and the darker the worse, till all dark, then all well, for the time, but it will come, the time will come, the thing is there, you'll see it, get off me, keep off me, all dark, all still, all over, wiped out –]

Ich sagte zu ihm, Gib sie auf – (chor)

[I said to him, Give her up –]

1

Ich sagte zu ihm, Gib sie auf. Ich schwor bei
allem, was mir lieb und teuer –

[I said to him, Give her up. I swore by all I held most sacred –]

— 2

Obgleich ich monatelag [*recte* monatelang] einen erstklassigen Mann
auf seine Fährte setzte, kam keine Spur von einem
Beweis heraus. Und es liess sich nicht leugnen,
dass er noch genauso . . . galant [*erasure*] wie immer
war. Dies u. [und] sein Abscheu vor der rein platonischen
Masche [Tour] liessen mich manchmal fragen, ob ich ihn
nicht zu unrecht [Unrecht] beschuldigte. Ja.

[Though I had him dogged for months by a first-rate man, no shadow of proof was forthcoming. And there was no denying that he continued as . . . assiduous as ever. This, and his horror of the merely Platonic thing, made me sometimes wonder if I were not accusing him unjustly. Yes.]

Transcription continues on pp. 14–15.

Bewunderung

— 3

Man stelle sich also mein Erstaunen vor, als er
eines schönen Morgens, [*erasure*] da ich wie erschlagen
im Frühstückszimmer sass, hereinschlich, vor
mir auf die Knie sank, sein Gesicht in meinen
Schoss bettete und . . . beichtete.

[Judge then of my astonishment when one fine morning, as I was sitting stricken in the morning room, he slunk in, fell on his knees before me, buried his face in my lap and . . . confessed.]

— 4

Ich gebe zu, meine erste Regung war Erstaunen {Bewunderung}!
Was für ein Kerl!

[I confess my first feeling was one of wonderment. What a male!]

Dann verzieh ich ihm. Wozu Liebe sich nicht hergibt! Ich schlug einen kleinen Ausflug vor, um es zu feiern, zur Riviera oder zu unserer geliebten grossen kanarischen Insel. Er sah blass aus. Shitz. Aber es war da gerade nicht möglich. Berufliche Verpflichtungen.

– 6

Als ich keinen Zweifel mehr hatte, dass alles aus war, ging ich zu ihr, um es auszukosten. Eine ganz gewöhnliche Nutte. Was er nur an ihr gefunden haben konnte, wo er mich doch hatte –

– 7

Puddinggesicht, pummelig, Pickel, wabbeliger Mund, Hängebacken, keinen Hals, Titten, dass man –

– 8

Waden wie Sektpullen.

– 9

Er war also wieder mein. Ganz mein. Ich war wieder glücklich. Ich ging herum u. sang. Die Welt –

– 10

Dann roch ich sie ihm doch wieder an. Ja.

– 11

Ehe ich was unternehmen konnte, verschwand er. Dass hiess, die hatte gesiegt. Die Schlampe! Ich konnte es nicht glauben. Ich war wochenlang wie erschlagen. Dann fuhr ich zu ihr. Es war alles verriegelt u. verrammelt. Alles grau von eisigem Tau. Auf dem Rückweg über Esch u. Rodtland –

[*fol. 8v*]

vergab

5

?

Dann (verzieh) {vergab} ich ihm. Wozu |Liebe|sich| nicht
hergibt! Ich schlug einen kleinen Ausflug [eine kleine
Vergnügungsreise] vor,
um es zu feiern, zur Riviera oder zu unserer
geliebten grossen Kanarischen Insel. Er sah blass
aus. [,] spitz. Aber es war da gerade nicht möglich.
Berufliche Verpflichtungen.

[Then I forgave him. To what will love not stoop! I suggested a little jaunt to celebrate, to the Riviera or our darling Grand Canary. He was looking pale. Peaked. But this was not possible just then. Professional commitments.]

— 6

Als ich keinen Zweifel mehr hatte, dass alles aus war,
ging ich zu ihr, um es auszukosten. Eine ganz
gewöhnliche Nutte. Was er nur an ihr gefunden
haben konnte, wo er mich doch hatte –

[When I was satisfied it was all over I went to have a gloat. Just a common tart. What he could have found in her when he had me –]

— 7

Puddinggesicht, pummelig, Pickel, wabbeliger
Mund, Hängebacken, keinen Hals, Titten, dass
man –

[Pudding face, puffy, spots, blubber mouth, jowls, no neck, dugs you could –]

— 8

Waden wie Sektpullen.

[Calves like a flunkey –]

— 9

Er war also wieder mein. Ganz mein. Ich war
wieder glücklich. Ich ging herum u. [und] sang. Die Welt –

[So he was mine again. All mine. I was happy again. I went about singing. The world –]

Transcription continues on pp. 20–21.

lag

— 10

Dann roch ich sie ihm doch wieder an. Ja.

[Then I began to smell her off him again. Yes.]

— 11

Ehe ich was unternehmen konnte, verschwand er.
Das hiess, sie hatte gesiegt. Die Schlampe! Ich
konnte es nicht glauben. Ich (war) {lag} wochenlang wie
erschlagen. Dann fuhr ich zu ihr. Es war alles
verriegelt u. [und] verrammelt. Alles grau [Grau] von eisigem
Tau. Auf dem Rückweg über Esch u. [und] Rottland –

[Before I could do anything he disappeared. That meant she had won. That slut! I couldn't credit it. I lay stricken for weeks. Then I drove over to her place. It was all bolted and barred. All grey with frozen dew. On the way back by Ash and Snodland –]

II

Gnade, Gnade (chor)

– 1

Gnade, Gnade, die Zunge lechzt noch nach Gnade. Sie wird kommen. Du hast mich nicht gesehen. aber du wirst mich sehen. Dann wird sie kommen

– 2

Oder du wirst meiner müde. Mich lassen.

– 3

Höllisches Halblicht.

– 4

Lass mich! Lass mich!

– 5

~~Kann~~ sollte es sein, dass ich nicht die Wahrheit sage, sollte es dann sein, dass ich irgendwann irgendwie vielleicht endlich die Wahrheit sage, u. dann endlich kein Licht mehr, für die Wahrheit?

– 6

Sollte es das sein?

– 7

Ich kann nichts tun … für niemanden mehr … Gott sei dank. Es kann also nur etwas sein, was ich sagen muss. Wie der Kopf immer noch funktioniert.

–8

Aber ich habe alles gesagt, was ich sagen kann. Alles, was du mich sagen läßt. Alles, was ich –

– 9

Sollte es etwas sein, daß ich mit dem Gesicht tun muss, etwas anderes als sprechen? Weinen?

[*fol. 9v*]

II
Gnade, Gnade (chor)
[Mercy, mercy –]

— 1

Gnade, Gnade, die Zunge lechzt noch nach Gnade.
Sie wird kommen. Du hast mich nicht gesehen. Aber
du wirst mich sehen. Dann wird sie kommen.

[Mercy, mercy, tongue still hanging out for mercy. It will come. You haven't seen me. But you will. Then it will come.]

— 2

Oder du wirst meiner müde. Mich lassen.

[Or you will weary of me. Get off me.]

— 3

Höllisches Halblicht [Halb-Licht].

[Hellish half-light.]

— 4

Lass mich! Lass mich!

[Get off me! Get off me!]

— 5

[*erasure*] Sollte es sein, dass ich nicht die Wahrheit sage,
sollte es das sein, dass ich irgendwann irgendwie
vielleicht endlich die Wahrheit sage, u. [und] dann
endlich kein Licht mehr, für die Wahrheit?

[Is it that I do not tell the truth, is that it, that some day somehow I may tell the truth at last and then no more light at last, for the truth?]

— 6

Sollte es das sein?

[Is that it?]

Transcription continues on p. 27.

— 7

Ich kann nichts tun . . . für niemanden mehr . . .
Gott sei Dank. Es kann also nur etwas sein, was
ich sagen muss. Wie der Kopf immer noch
funzioniert [*recte* funktioniert] [arbeitet!].

[I can do nothing . . . for anybody . . . any more . . . thank God. So it must be something I have to say. How the mind works still!]

— 8

Aber ich habe [hab'] alles gesagt, was ich sagen kann. Alles,
was du mich sagen lässt. Alles, was ich –

[But I have said all I can. All you let me. All I –]

— 9

Sollte es etwas sein, das<s> ich mit dem Gesicht tun muss,
etwas anderes als sprechen? Weinen?

[Is it something I should do with my face, other than utter? Weep?]

nicht den geringsten. /

~~irgendanderswo~~

- 10

Meine Zunge abbeissen u. sie verschlucken? Sie ausspucken? Würde das dich versöhnen? Wie der Kopf immer noch funktioniert, erstaunlich!

- 11

Wenn ich nur denken könnte, dies hat keinen Sinn ... auch dies nicht. Ich kann es nicht.

- 12

und dass alles fällt, alles gefallen ist, von Anfang an, ins Leere. Dass gar nichts verlangt wird. Dass niemand auch nur das geringste von mir verlangt.

- 13

Ich kann es nicht.

- 14

Ich kann es nicht. Der Verstand weigert sich. Er würde weichen müssen. Ja.

- 15

Sie war nicht mittellos, sag' ich mir, u. lebte doch wie eine Sau.

- 16

Vielleicht hat sie ihre mitgenommen, um anderswo zu leben -- irgendwo in der Sonne.

- 17

Vielleicht sitzt sie irgendwo, am offenen Fenster, die Hände im Schoss gefaltet, u. blickt weit hinab über die Oliven -

- 18

Weit hinab über die Oliven, dann die See, u. fragt sich, warum er wohl so spät kommt, fröstelnd. Schatten schleichen über alles. Kriechen. Ja.

[*fol. 10v*]

10
9
5

nicht den geringsten

wohl /

— 10

Meine Zunge abbeissen u. [und] sie verschlucken? Sie
ausspucken? Würde das dich versöhnen? Wie
der Kopf immer noch funzioniert [*recte* funktioniert] [arbeitet],
erstaunlich!

[Bite off my tongue and swallow it? Spit it out? Would that placate you? How the mind works still to be sure!]

— 11

Wenn ich nur denken könnte, dies hat keinen
Sinn . . . auch dies nicht/{nicht den geringsten}, Ich kann es nicht.

[If only I could think, There is no sense in this . . . either, none whatsoever. I can't.]

— 12

Und das alles fällt, alles gefallen ist, von Anfang an,
ins Leere. Dass gar nichts verlangt wird. Dass
niemand auch nur das geringste von mir verlangt.

[And that all is falling, all fallen, from the beginning, on empty air. Nothing being asked at all. No one asking me for anything at all.]

— 13

Ich kann es nicht.

[I can't.]

— 14

Ich kann es nicht. Der Verstand weigert sich.
Er würde weichen müssen. Ja.

[I can't. The mind won't have it. It would have to go. Yes.]

— 15

Sie war {wohl} nicht mittellos, (sag' ich mir,) u. [und] lebte doch
wie eine Sau.

[She had means, I fancy, though she lived like a pig.]

Transcription continues on pp. 32–33.

<irgendanderswo> [somewhere else]

— 16

Vielleicht hat sie ihn mitgenommen, um anderswo
zu leben . . . irgendwo in der Sonne.

[Perhaps she has taken him away to live . . . somewhere in the sun.]

— 17

Vielleicht sitzt sie irgendwo, am offenen Fenster,
die Hände im Schoss gefaltet, u. [und] blickt weit hinab
über die Oliven –

[Perhaps she is sitting somewhere, by the open window, her hands folded in her lap, gazing down out over the olives –]

— 18

Weit hinab über die Oliven, dann die See, u. [und] fragt
sich, warum er wohl so spät kommt, fröstelnd.
Schatten schleichen über alles. Kriechen. Ja.

[Gazing down out over the olives, then the sea, wondering what can be keeping him, growing cold. Shadow stealing over everything. Creeping. Yes.]

~~21~~

~~Höllisches Halblicht~~

Waren?

22

Höllisches Halblicht

19

Die Ärgste. Die Ärgsten.

-20

Büssen, ja, zur Not, sühnen, man war darauf gefasst, aber nein, das scheint es nicht zu sein: – auch das nicht.

- 21

Stille u. Dunkel war alles, wonach ich sehnte. Nun ja, ich bekomme etwas von beiden. Denn sie sind eins. Vielleicht ist es noch Sünde, um mehr zu flehen.

- 23

Dürstend nach Dunkel – u. je dunkler je schlimmer. Seltsam.

- 24

Ja, u. alles ist da, gellt da, starrt dir ins Gesicht. Du wirst es sehen. Mich lassen. Oder müde werden.

- 25

Müde des Spiels mit mir. Mich lassen. Ja.

[*fol. 11v*]

<21>
<Höllisches Halblicht>

Waren?

22
Höllisches Halblicht ←

19

Die Ärmste. Die Ärmsten.

[Poor creature. Poor creatures.]

— 20

Büssen, ja, zur Not, sühnen, man war darauf
gefasst, aber nein, das scheint es nicht zu sein . . .
auch das nicht.

[Penitence, yes, at a pinch, atonement, one was resigned, but no, that does not seem to be the point either.]

— [*erasure*] 21

Stille u. [und] Dunkel war alles, wonach ich sehnte [was ich verlangte].
Nun ja, ich bekomme etwas von beiden. Denn
sie sind eins. Vielleicht ist es noch Sünde [frevelhafter]
um mehr zu flehen [bitten].

[Silence and darkness were all I craved. Well, I get a certain amount of both. They being one. Perhaps it is more wickedness to pray for more.]

{22}

{Höllisches Halblicht.}

[Hellish half-light.]

— 23

Dürstend nach Dunkel – u. [und] je dunkler je
schlimmer. Seltsam.

[Dying for dark – and the darker the worse. Strange.]

— 24

Ja, u. [und] alles ist da, ganz da, starrt dir ins
Gesicht. Du wirst es sehen. Mich lassen. Oder
müde werden.

[Yes, and the whole thing there, all there, staring you in the face. You'll see it. Get off me. Or weary.]

— 25

Müde des Spiels mit mir. Mich lassen. Ja.

[Weary of playing with me. Get off me. Yes.]

ernst

ist mein

in Lebensgrösse

Ihr

9

könnte

F2 (Chor)

Ja vielleicht - leicht verwirrt - nehme ich an - könnte man sagen - armes Ding - leicht verwirrt - nur ganz leicht - im Verstand - Lachen - nur ganz leicht - aber ich glaube nicht - ich glaube nicht - nicht ernstlich - mir fehlt nichts - noch gar nichts - tu' mein Bestes - was ich kann

-

Eines Morgens, als ich im Zimmer - (Chor)

1

Eines Morgens, als ich im Zimmer am offenen Fenster nähte, platzte sie herein u. fuhr mich an. Geben Sie ihn auf, schrie sie, er gehört mir. Die Fotos von ihr waren schmeichlerisch. Als ich sie [50] zum ersten Mal in Fleisch u. Blut / sah, begriff ich, warum er mich vorzog.

2

Wovon reden Sie nur? sagte ich, weiternähend. Jemand, der Ihnen gehört? Wen aufgeben? Ich riech' Sie ihm an, schrie sie, er stinkt nach Luder.

3

Da ich fürchtete, dass sie mir Gewalt antun könnte, klingelte ich nach Gustav, damit er sie hinausbringe. Beim Weggehen sagte sie, wie er bezeugen kann, wenn er noch lebt u. es nicht vergessen hat, bei seinem Kommen u. Gehen auf Erden, beim Leute-Hereinlassen u. Leute-Hinausbringen, gab sie zu verstehen, dass sie mich kaltmachen würde. Ich geb zu, dass es mich ein wenig beunruhigte, seiner Zeit.

ernst

ist mein

in Lebensgrösse

Ihr

F2 (chor)

Ja, vielleicht – leicht verwirrt – nehme [nehm'] ich an –
könnte man sagen – armes Ding – leicht verwirrt –
nur ganz leicht – im Verstand – Lachen –
nur ganz leicht – aber ich glaube nicht – ich glaube
nicht – nicht ernstlich – mir fehlt nichts – noch
gar nichts – tu' mein Bestes – was ich kann –

[Yes, perhaps, a shade gone, I suppose, some might say, poor thing, a shade gone, just a shade, in the head – [*faint wild laugh*] – just a shade, but I doubt it, *I* doubt it, not really, I'm all right, still all right, do my best, all I can –]

Eines Morgens,[2] als ich im Zimmer – (chor)

[One morning as I was sitting –]

— 1

Eines Morgens, als ich im Zimmer am offenen
Fenster [*erasure*] nähte, platzte sie herein u. [und] fuhr mich
an. Geben Sie ihn auf, schrie sie, er
gehört mir {ist mein}. Die [*erasure*] Fotos von ihr waren
schmeichlerish [*recte* schmeichlerisch] [schmeichelhaft]. Als ich sie {so} zum
ersten Mal in
Fleisch u. [und] Blut[3] {in Lebensgrösse} sah, begriff ich, warum er
mich vorzog.

[One morning as I was sitting stitching by the open window she burst in and flew at me. Give him up, she screamed, he's mine. Her photographs were kind to her. Seeing her now for the first time full length in the flesh I understood why he preferred me.]

— 2

Wovon reden Sie nur? sagte ich, weiternähend.
Jemand, (der Ihnen gehört) {Ihr}? Wen aufgeben?
Ich riech' Sie ihm an, schrie sie, er stinkt
nach Luder.

[What are you talking about? I said, stitching away. Someone yours? Give up whom? I smell you off him, she screamed, he stinks of bitch.]

Transcription continues on pp. 42–43.

könnte

— 3

Da ich fürchtete, dass sie mir Gewalt antun könnte,
klingelte ich nach Gustav, damit er sie hinaus –
bringe. Beim Weggehen sagte sie, wie er bezeugen
kann {könnte}, wenn er noch lebt u. [und] es nicht vergessen
hat, bei seinem Kommen u. [und] Gehen auf Erden,
beim Leute-Hereinlassen u. [und] Leute-Hinausbringen,
gab sie zu bestehen [*recte* verstehen] [ungefähr], dass sie mich kaltmachen würde.
Ich gebe zu, dass es mich ein wenig beunruhigte,
seinerzeit.

[Fearing she was about to offer me violence I rang for Erskine and had her shown out. Her parting words, as he could testify, if he is still living, and has not forgotten, coming and going on the earth, letting people in, showing people out, were to the effect that she would settle my hash. I confess this did alarm me a little, at the time.]

Sich die Lippen leckend.

sagte sie,

Das hiess, er war zu ihr zurückgekehrt.

9

4

Warum haust du mich ab, sagte ich, als er anfing über sein Leben zuhause zu jammern, es ist offensichtlich nichts mehr zwischen euch. oder doch?

5

Was zwischen uns, sagte er, wofür hältst du mich, für eine --- Dingsda - Maschine? Und natürlich bestand bei ihm nicht die Gefahr der ... rein seelischen Masche. Warum haust du denn mich ab? sagte ich. Ich fragte mich manchmal, ob er nicht ihres Geldes wegen mit ihr zusammenlebte.

6

Sie kam wieder. Einfach hereinspaziert. Katzenfreundlich. Leckte sich die Lippen. Armes Ding. Ich machte gerade meine Nägel, am offenen Fenster. Er hat mir alles darüber erzählt, sagte sie. Wer er, sagte ich weiterfeilend, u. worüber. Ich weiss, welche Qualen Sie ausstehen müssen, u. ich bin gekommen, um ~~[illegible]~~ Ihnen zu sagen, dass ich keinen Groll gegen Sie hege. Ich klingelte nach Gustav.

7

Als er wiederkam, sprachen wir uns aus. Mir war sterbenselend. Er redete noch darüber, warum er ~~es~~ ihr hatte sagen müssen. Zu riskant u. so weiter. Was bedeutete, dass er zu ihr zurückgekehrt war. Zurück zu ~~[illegible]~~ so was!

8

Er redete immer weiter. Ich hörte einen Rasenmäher. Einen alten Handmäher. Ich ~~[illegible]~~ schnitt ihm das Wort ab u. sagte, dass ich, wie auch immer mir zumute sei, keine dämliche Drohungen parat habe - (dass ich) aber auch nicht viel Lust auf ihre Abfälle (~~[illegible]~~ hätte) Das gab ihm ein Weilchen zu denken.

Sich die Lippen leckend.

sagte sie,

4

Warum haust du nich [*recte* nicht] ab, sagte ich, als er anfing,
über sein Leben zuhaus zu jammern, es ist [doch]
offensichlich [*recte* offensichtlich] nichts mehr zwischen euch. Oder
doch?

[Why don't you get out, I said, when he started moaning about his home life, there is obviously nothing between you any more. Or is there?]

5

Was zwischen uns, sagte er, wofür hältst du mich,
für eine . . . Dingsda-Maschine? Und natürlich
bestand bei ihm nicht die [keine] Gefahr der [für die] . . . rein
seelischen Masche [seelische Tour]. Warum haust du denn nich [*recte* nicht] ab?
sagte ich. Ich fragte mich manchmal, ob er nicht
ihres Geldes wegen mit ihr zusammenlebte.

[Anything between us, he said, what do you take me for, a something machine? And of course with him no danger of the . . . spiritual thing. Then why don't you get out? I said. I sometimes wondered if he was not living with her for her money.]

6

Sie kam wieder. Einfach hereinspazierte [hereinspaziert]. Katzen-
freundlich. Leckte sich die Lippen. {Sich die Lippen leckend.} Armes Ding.
Ich machte gerade meine Nägel, am offenen
Fenster. Er hat mir alles darüber erzählt,
sagte sie. Wer er, sagte ich weiterfeilend, u. [und]
worüber? Ich weiss, welche Qualen Sie ausstehen
müssen, {sagte sie,}/u. [und] ich bin gekommen, um [*erasure*]
Ihnen zu sagen, dass ich keinen Groll gegen
Sie hege. Ich klingelte nach Gustav.

[She came again. Just strolled in. All honey. Licking her lips. Poor thing. I was doing my nails, by the open window. He has told me all about it, she said. Who he, I said filing away, and what it? I know what torture you must be going through, she said, and I have dropped in to say I bear you no ill-feeling. I rang for Erskine.]

Transcription continues on pp. 48–49.

Das hiess, er war zu ihr zurückgekehrt.

7

Als er wiederkam, sprachen wir uns aus. Mir
war sterbenselend. Er redete noch darüber,
warum er es {ihr} hatte sagen müssen. Zu riskant u. [und] so
weiter. Was bedeutete, dass er zu ihr zurückgekehrt {Das hiess, er war zu ihr zurückgekehrt.}
war. Zurück zu [*erasure*] so was!

[When he came again we had it out. I felt like death. He went on about why he had to tell her. Too risky and so on. That meant he had gone back to her. Back to that!]

8

Er redete immer weiter. Ich hörte einen Rasenmäher [Grasmäher].
Einen alten Handmäher. Ich [*erasure*] schnitt ihm das Wort ab [Ich fiel ihm ins Wort] u. [und]
sagte, dass ich, wie auch immer mir zumute sei,
keine dämlichen Drohungen parat habe – (dass ich)
aber auch nicht viel Lust auf ihre Abfälle ([*erasure*] hätte).
Das gab ihm ein Weilchen zu denken.

[He went on and on. I could hear a mower. An old hand mower. I stopped him and said that whatever I might feel I had no silly threats to offer – but not much stomach for her leavings either. He thought that over for a bit.]

meiner müde

9

Es gab nur eine Lösung. Zusammen zu verreisen. Er schwor, dass wir es tun würden, sobald er seine Geschäfte geregelt hätte. Derweil sollten wir so weitermachen wie zuvor. Er meinte, so gut wir könnten.

10

Als er nicht mehr kam, war ich darauf gefasst. Mehr oder weniger.

11

Ich packte seine Sachen zusammen u. verbrannte sie. Es war November u. das Müllfeuer schwelte. Die ganze Nacht roch ich, wie sie qualmten.

Ich sage ~~...~~ nicht, das (Chor)

1

Ich sage nicht, dass ich nicht enttäuscht sei, nein, ich bin es. Ich hatte es mir etwas besser vorgestellt. Etwas ruhiger.

2

Weniger verwirrt. Weniger verwirrend. Und trotzdem ist dies mir lieber als ... das andere. Ganz entschieden. Es gibt erträgliche Momente.

3

Wenn du erlischst – u. ich erlösche. Eines Tages wirst du mich satt haben u. erlöschen ... endgültig.

4.

Wirst du ~~mich~~ mich aufgeben wie eine hoffnungslose Sache. Wirst du weggehen, um jemand anderes zu packen u. darauf herumzuhacken. Andererseits –

[*fol. 14v*]

9

Es gab nur eine Lösung, zusammen zu verreisen.
Er schwor, dass wir es tun würden, sobald er
seine Geschäfte geregelt hätte. Derweil sollten
wir so weitermachen wie zuvor. Er meinte[,] so gut
wir könnten.

[The only solution was to go away together. He swore we should as soon as he had put his affairs in order. In the meantime we were to carry on as before. By that he meant as best we could.]

10

Als er nicht mehr kam, war ich darauf gefasst.
Mehr oder weniger.

[When he stopped coming I was prepared. More or less.]

11

Ich packte seine Sachen zusammen u. [und] verbrannte sie.
Es war November[,] u. [und] das Müllfeuer [Freudenfeuer] schwelte. Die
ganze Nacht roch ich, wie sie qualmten.

[I made a bundle of his things and burnt them. It was November
and the bonfire was going. All night I smelt them smouldering.]

Ich sage [sag'] [*erasure*] nicht, das [dass] (chor)

[To say I am –]

1

Ich sage [sag'] nicht, dass ich nicht enttäuscht sei, nein,
ich bin es. Ich hatte es mir etwas besser vorgestellt.
Etwas ruhiger.

[To say I am not disappointed, no, I am. I had anticipated something better. More restful.]

2

Weniger verwirrt. Weniger verwirrend. Und trotzdem
ist dies mir lieber als . . . das andere. Ganz
entschieden. Es gibt erträgliche Momente.

Transcription continues on pp. 54–55.

meiner müde

[Less confused. Less confusing. At the same time I prefer this to . . . the other thing. Definitely. There are endurable moments.]

3

Wenn du erlischst – u. [und] ich erlösche. Eines Tages
wirst du mich satt haben {meiner müde} u. [und] erlöschen . . . endgültig.

[When you go out – and I go out. Some day you will tire of me and go out . . . for good.]

4

Wirst du <mich> mich aufgeben wie eine hoffnungslose
Sache. Wirst du weggehen, um [dir] jemand anderes
zu packen u. [und] darauf herumzuhacken. Andererseits –

[Give me up, as a bad job. Go away and start poking and pecking at someone else. On the other hand –]

5

andererseits könnten sich die Dinge verschlimmern, das ist die Gefahr.

6

Du könntest böse werden u. mich um meinen Verstand bringen. Nicht wahr?

7

Nicht wahr?

8

aber ich glaube nicht. Es wäre eigentlich nicht deine Art. Und du weisst doch, dass ich mein Bestes tu'. Oder nicht?

9

Ich nehme an, dass ich den gleichen Fehler mache wie einst, als es die Sonne war, die schien, nämlich nach Sinn zu suchen, wo möglicherweise keiner ist.

10

Hörst du mir zu? Hört irgend jemand mir zu? Kümmert sich überhaupt irgend jemand um mich?

11

Ist mein Name tabu? Nicht unbedingt, nun da alle Gefahr ... abgewandt. Die Ärmste – ich kann sie hören – die Ärmste.

12

Die Ärmste, die dich verführen wollte, was mag wohl aus ihr geworden sein, denkst du dir – ich kann die hören. Armes Ding.

13

Sie würden womöglich Mitleid mit mir haben, wenn sie mich sehen könnten. aber nie soviel Mitleid wie ich mit ihnen.

[*fol. 15v*]

blaze
brennen?

5

Andererseits könnten sich die Dinge verschlimmern,
das ist die Gefahr.

[On the other hand things may disimprove, there is that danger.]

6

Du könntest böse werden u. [und] mich um meinen
Verstand (bringen) {'brennen', Beckett queries, may be closer to the English
'blaze'} Nicht wahr?

[You might get angry and blaze me clean out of my wits. Mightn't you?]

7

Nicht wahr?

[Mightn't you?]

8

Aber ich glaube nicht. Es wäre eigentlich nicht deine
Art. Und du weisst doch, dass ich mein Bestes tu'.
Oder nicht?

[But I doubt it. It would not be like you somehow. And you must know I am doing my best. Or don't you?]

9

Ich nehme an, dass ich den gleichen [denselben] Fehler mache
wie einst, als es die Sonne war, die schien,
nämlich nach Sinn zu suchen, wo möglicher-
weise keiner ist.

[No doubt I make the same mistake as when it was the sun that shone, of looking for sense where possibly there is none.]

10

Hörst du mir zu? Hört irgend jemand mir zu? [Sieht irgend jemand mich an?]
Kümmert sich überhaupt irgend jemand um mich?

[Are you listening to me? Is anyone listening to me? Is anyone looking at me? Is anyone bothering about me at all?]

Transcription continues on p. 61.

11

Ist mein Name tabu? Nicht unbedingt, nun da
alle Gefahr (. . .){?} abgewandt. Die Ärmste – ich kann
sie hören – die Ärmste.

[Am I taboo, I wonder. Not necessarily, now that all danger is averted. That poor creature – I can hear her – that poor creature –]

12

Die Ärmste, die dich verführen wollte, was mag wohl
aus ihr geworden sein, denkst du dir – ich kann sie
hören. Armes Ding.

[That poor creature who tried to seduce you, what ever became of her, do you suppose? – I can hear her. Poor thing.]

13

Sie würden womöglich Mitleid mit mir haben, wenn
sie mich sehen könnten. Aber nie soviel Mitleid wie
ich mit ihnen.

[They might even feel sorry for me, if they could see me. But never so sorry as I for them.]

thri dauren Küsse kliessend

erlischet
it 3

One word

Stofe –

14

Die ihre sauren Küsse küssen.

15

Was machst du, wenn du ausgehst? alles sondern?

16

Wie das Rollen einer dicken Walze an einem glühend heissen Tag. Die Mühle … sie in Bewegung zu setzen, sie kommt in Schwung –

17

Halt – und wieder die Mühle.

18

Und dabei hast du vielleicht Mitleid mit mir u. denkst, Armes Ding, sie braucht etwas Ruhe.

19.

Ich weiss es nicht.

20

Nein.

21

Bin ich nicht vielleicht schon ein wenig aus dem Lot.

22

Ich sagte, bin ich nicht vielleicht schon ein wenig aus dem Lot. Ein wenig nur. Ich glaube nicht.

23

Leicht verwirrt. Im Verstand. Ganz leicht. Ich glaube nicht.

24

Ich glaube nicht. (Lachen)

[*fol. 16v*]

Ihre sauren Küsse küssend.

erlischst
cf 3

one word

Stop –

14

Die ihre sauren Küsse küssen. {Ihre sauren Küsse küssend.}

[Kissing their sour kisses.]

15

Was machst du, wenn du ausgehst {erlischst}? Alles
sondern [sieben]?

[What do you do when you go out? Sift?]

16

Wie das Rollen einer dicken Walze an einem glühend
heissen Tag. Die Mühe . . . sie in Bewegung zu
setzen, sie kommt in Schwung –

[Like dragging a great roller, on a scorching day. The strain . . . to get it moving, momentum coming –]

17

Halt {Stop} – und wieder die Mühe.

[Kill it and strain again.]

18

Und dabei hast du vielleicht Midleid [*recte* Mitleid] mit mir u. [und]
denkst, Armes Ding, sie braucht etwas Ruhe.

[And you perhaps pitying me, thinking, Poor thing, she needs a rest.]

19

Ich weiss es nicht.

[I don't know.]

20

Nein.

[No.]

21

Bin ich nicht vielleicht schon ein wenig aus dem Lot. [?]

[Am I not perhaps a little unhinged already?]

Transcription continues on p. 67.

22

Ich sagte, bin [Bin] ich nicht vielleicht schon ein
wenig aus dem Lot. [?] Ein wenig nur. Ich glaube nicht.

[I say, Am I not perhaps a little unhinged already? (*Hopefully*) Just a little? (*Pause.*) I doubt it.]

23

Leicht verwirrt. Im Verstand. Ganz leicht. Ich glaube
nicht.

[A shade gone. In the head. Just a shade. I doubt it.]

24

Ich glaube nicht. (*Lachen*)

[*I* doubt it. (*Pause. Peal of wild low laughter . . .*)]

(Lachen) 25

[*fol. 17v*]

25

(Lachen)

[*Laugh.*]

ich könne ohne sie

M (chor)

Ja Friede – dachte man – alles aus – alle Qual – alles wie – nie ~~gegeben~~ gewesen – es wird kommen – <u>Schluckauf</u> Verzeihung – dies hat keinen Sinn – oh ich weiss – immerhin – dachte man – Friede ich meine – nicht nur – alles vorbei – sondern wie – nie gewesen

—

Wir waren nicht lang zusammen – (chor)

1

Wir waren nicht lang zusammen, als sie Wind davon bekam. Gib die Hure auf, sagte sie, oder ich schneide mir die Kehle durch – <u>Schluckauf</u> – Verzeihung – so wahr mir Gott helfe. Ich wusste, dass sie nichts beweisen konnte. Also sagte ich zu ihr, ich wüsste nicht, wovon sie redete.

2

Worüber kannst du dich eigentlich beklagen? sagte ich. Hab' ich dich etwa vernachlässigt? Wie könnte man so wie wir miteinander leben, wenn da noch eine andere wäre? Da ich sie so liebte, nämlich von ganzem Herzen, konnte ich nur Mitleid mit ihr haben.

3

Sie war nicht überzeugt. Ich hätte es mir denken können. Ich riech' sie dir an, sagte sie immer wieder. Darauf gab es keine Antwort. Also nahm ich sie in meine Arme u. schwor ihr, dass ich nicht ohne sie leben könne. Ich meinte es ernst, das will was heissen. Ja, ich bin sicher, dass ich es ernst meinte. Sie stiess mich nicht zurück.

[*fol. 18v*]

M (chor)

Ja[,] Friede – dachte man – alles aus – alle Qual –
alles wie [. . .] – nie [*erasure*] gewesen – es wird
kommen – Schluckauf [–] Verzeihung – dies hat
keinen Sinn – oh[,] ich weiss – immerhin –
dachte man – Friede [. . .] ich meine [. . .] – nicht nur –
alles vorbei – sondern wie [. . .] – nie gewesen

[Yes, peace, one assumed, all out, all the pain, all as if . . . never been, it will come – (*Hiccup.*) – pardon – no sense in this, oh I know . . . none the less, one assumed, peace . . . I mean . . . not merely all over, but as if . . . never been –]

Wir waren nicht lang zusammen – (chor)

[We were not long together –]

1

Wir waren nicht lang zusammen, als sie
Wind davon bekam. Gib die Hure auf,
sagte sie, oder ich schneide [schneid'] mir die Kehle
durch – Schluckauf – Verzeihung – so wahr
mir Gott helfe. Ich wusste, dass sie nichts
beweisen konnte. Also sagte ich zu ihr, ich
wüsste nicht, wovon sie redete.

[We were not long together when she smelled the rat. Give up that whore, she said, or I'll cut my throat – (*Hiccup.*) – pardon – so help me God. I knew she could have no proof. So I told her I did not know what she was talking about.]

2

Worüber kannst du dich eigentlich beklagen? sagte ich.
Hab' ich dich etwa vernachlässigt? Wie könnte
man so wie wir miteinander leben, wenn da
noch eine andere wäre? Da ich sie so liebte,
nämlich von ganzem Herzen, konnte ich nur
Mitleid mit ihr haben.

[What have you to complain of? I said. Have I been neglecting you? How could we be together in the way we are if there were someone else? Loving her as I did, with all my heart, I could not but feel sorry for her.]

Transcription continues on pp. 76–77.

ich könne ohne sie

3

Sie war nicht überzeugt. Ich hätte es mir
denken können. Ich riech' sie dir an, sagte
sie immer wieder. Darauf gab es keine Antwort.
Also nahm ich sie in meine Arme u. [und] schwor
ihr, dass ich nicht ohne sie leben könne {ich könne ohne sie (nicht leben)}.
Ich meinte es ernst, das will was heissen.
Ja, ich bin sicher, dass ich es ernst meinte.
Sie stiess mich nicht zurück.

[She was not convinced. I might have known. I smell her off you, she kept saying. There was no answer to this. So I took her in my arms and swore I could not live without her. I meant it, what is more. Yes, I am sure I did. She did not repulse me.]

will

Ruck

4

Sie hetzte einen Spürhund hinter mir her, aber er liess mit sich reden. Er war froh über den Nebenverdienst.

5.

Das nächste war die Szene zwischen ihnen. Ich mag nicht, sagte sie, dass sie hier hereinstürzt u. droht, mir das Leben zu nehmen. Ich muss ein ungläubiges Gesicht gemacht haben. Frag Gustav, sagte sie, wenn du mir nicht glaubst. Sie droht doch, sich ihr eigenes zu nehmen, sagte ich. Nich dir deines? sagte sie. Nein, sagte ich, sich ihres. Wir hatten Spass an dem Versuch, das klarzustellen.

6

Dann kriegte ich es mit der Angst u. gestand. Sie sah zusehends verzweifelter aus. Sie hatte ein Rasiermesser in ihrem Schminktäschchen. Ehebrecher, merkt euch eins, gebt es nie zu.

7

Als ich sie wiedersah, wusste sie Bescheid. Sie sah – Schmuckauf – jämmerlich aus. Beziehung. Irgendein Idiot mähte Gras. Ein rascher Druck, dann wieder einer. Es ging darum, sie davon zu überzeugen, dass kein ... Aufleben intimer Beziehungen damit verbunden war. Ich konnte es nicht. Ich hätte es mir denken können. Also nahm ich sie in meine Arme u. sagte, ich könne ohne sie nicht weiterleben. Ich glaube nicht, dass ich es gekonnt hätte.

[*fol. 19v*]

will

Ruck

[*fol. 20r*]

4

Sie hetzte einen Spürhund hinter mir her,
aber er liess mit sich reden. Er war froh über
den Nebenverdienst.

[She put a bloodhound on me, but I had a little chat with him. He was glad of the extra money.]

5

Das nächste war die Szene zwischen [*erasure*] ihnen.
Ich mag {will} nicht, sagte sie, dass sie hier
hereinstürzt u. [und] droht, mir das Leben
zu nehmen. Ich muss ein ungläubiges
Gesicht gemacht haben. Frag Gustav, sagte
sie, wenn du mir nicht glaubst. Sie droht
doch, sich ihr eigenes zu nehmen, sagte ich.
Nich [*recte* Nicht] dir deines? sagte sie. Nein, sagte ich,
sich ihres. Wir hatten Spass an dem Versuch,
das klarzustellen.

[The next thing was the scene between them. I can't have her crashing in here, she said, threatening to take my life. I must have looked incredulous. Ask Erskine, she said, if you don't believe me. But she threatens to take her own, I said. Not yours? she said. No, I said, hers. We had fun trying to work this out.]

6

Dann kriegte ich es mit der Angst u. [und] {ge}stand.
Sie sah zusehends verzweifelter aus. Sie
hatte ein Rasiermesser in ihrem [*erasure*]
Schminktäschchen. Ehebrecher, merkt euch
eins [lernt daraus], gebt es nie zu!

[Then I got frightened and made a clean breast of it. She was looking more and more desperate. She had a razor in her vanity-bag. Adulterers, take warning, never admit.]

7

Als ich sie wiedersah, wusste sie Bescheid.
Sie sah – Schuckauf (*recte* Schluckauf) – jämmerlich aus.
Verzeihung. Irgendein Idiot mähte Gras.
Ein rascher <Druck> {Ruck}, dann wieder einer. Es

Transcription continues on p. 83.

ging darum, sie davon zu überzeugen,
dass kein . . . Aufleben intimer Beziehungen
damit verbunden war. Ich konnte es nicht.
Ich hätte es mir denken können. Also nahm
ich sie in meine Arme u. [und] sagte, ich könne
ohne sie nich [*recte* nicht] weiterleben. Ich glaube nicht,
dass ich es gekonnt hätte.

[When I saw her again she knew. She was looking – (*Hiccup.*) – wretched. Pardon. Some fool was cutting grass. A little rush, then another. The problem was how to convince her that no . . . revival of intimacy was involved. I couldn't. I might have known. So I took her in my arms and said I could not go on living without her. I don't believe I could have.]

8

Zuhause alles ein Herz u. eine Seele, ein neues Blatt, das Alte tot u. begraben. Ich traf deine Ex-Kebse, sagte sie eines abends auf dem Kopfkissen, du bist gut davongekommen. Ziemlich unangebracht, dachte ich. Und ob, Herzchen, sagte ich, u. ob. Was für ein Geschmeiss, die Weiber. Dank dir, mein Engel, sagte ich.

9

Schliesslich wurde mir alles zuviel. Ich konnte einfach nicht länger –

10

Ich konnte einfach nicht länger –

Bei disem Wechsel – (chor)

1

Bei diesem Wechsel, dem ersten, drängte es mich, Gott zu danken. Ich dachte, es ist geschafft, es ist gesagt, nun geht alles aus –

2

aus, ja, alles aus, alles unter, ins Dunkel. Frieden wird kommen, dachte ich, trotz allem, endlich, ich hatte recht, trotz allem, Gott sei Dank, bei diesem Wechsel, dem ersten.

3

Dachte ich.

4

Frieden, ja, nehme ich an, eine Art Frieden, u. alle Qual wie ... nie gewesen.

5

Es wird kommen. Muss kommen. Dies hat keine Zukunft.

[*fol. 20v*]

[*erasure*] ?

?

?

8

Zuhause alles ein Herz u. [und] eine Seele, ein neues Blatt,
das (Alte) tot u. [und] begraben. Ich traf deine Ex-Kebse,
sagte sie eines Abends auf dem Kopfkissen, du
bist gut davongekommen. Ziemlich unangebracht,
dachte ich. Und ob, Herzchen, sagte ich, u. [und] ob.
Was für ein Geschmeiss, die Weiber. Dank dir,
mein Engel, sagte ich.

[At home all heart to heart, new leaf and bygones bygones. I ran into your ex-doxy, she said one night, on the pillow, you're well out of that. Rather uncalled for, I thought. I am indeed, sweetheart, I said, I am indeed. God what vermin women. Thanks to you, angel, I said.]

9

Schliesslich wurde mir alles zuviel. Ich konnte
einfach nicht länger –

[Finally it was all too much. I simply could no longer –]

10

Ich konnte einfach nicht länger –

[I simply could no longer –]

Bei diesem Wechsel – (chor)

[When first this change –]

1

Bei diesem Wechsel, dem ersten, drängte es mich, {?}
Gott zu danken. Ich dachte, es ist geschafft,
es ist gesagt, nun geht alles aus –

[When first this change I actually thanked God. I thought, It is done, it is said, now all is going out –]

2

Aus, ja, alles aus, alles unter, ins Dunkel,
Frieden wird kommen, dachte ich, trotz
allem, endlich, ich hatte recht, trotz allem,
Gott sei Dank, bei diesem Wechsel, dem ersten. {?}

Transcription continues on p. 89.

[Down, all going down, into the dark, peace is coming, I thought, after all, at last, I was right, after all, thank God, when first this change.]

3

Dachte ich.

[I thought.]

4

Frieden, ja, nehme ich an, eine Art Frieden,
u. [und] alle Qual wie . . . nie gewesen.

[Peace, yes, I suppose, a kind of peace, and all that pain as if . . . never been.]

5

Er wird kommen. Muss kommen. Dies hat
keine Zukunft.

[It will come. Must come. There is no future in this.]

ganze
Tröpfchen

"

persönlich

selig

6

O gewiss, ich weiss jetzt –

7

Ich weiss jetzt, all das war nichts anderes als … Spiel. Und all dies? Wann wird all dies –

8

all dies, wann wird all dies nichts anderes gewesen sein als … Spiel?

9

Vielleicht sind sie Freundinnen geworden. Vielleicht hat der Gram –

10

Vielleicht hat der Gram sie zusammengebracht.

11

Vielleicht treffen sie sich u. sitzen bei einer Tasse jenes grünen Tees, den beide so liebten, keine Milch, keinen Zucker, nicht mal ein Scheibchen Zitrone –

12

Nicht mal ein Scheibchen Zitrone –

13

Treffen sich u. sitzen bald in dem einen lieben alten Haus, bald in dem anderen, u. grämen sich zusammen, u. vergleichen – Schluckauf – Verzeihung – glückliche Erinnerungen.

14

Ich trank immer am liebsten Liptons.

15

Bedaure sie auf jeden Fall, ja, vergleiche mein Los mit ihrem, wie gesegnet es auch sein mag, u. –

[*fol. 21v*]

squeeze
Tröpfchen

”

6

O gewiss, ich weiss jetzt –

[Oh of course I know now –]

7

Ich weiss jetzt, all das war nichts anderes
als . . . Spiel. Und all dies? Wann wird all
dies –

[I know now, all that was just . . . play. And all this? When will all this –]

8

All dies, wann wird all dies nichts anderes
gewesen sein als . . . Spiel?

[All this, when will all this have been . . . just play?]

9

Vielleicht sind sie Freundinnen geworden.
Vielleicht hat der Gram –

[Perhaps they have become friends. Perhaps sorrow –]

10

Vielleicht hat der Gram sie zusammengebracht.

[Perhaps sorrow has brought them together.]

11

Vielleicht treffen sie sich und sitzen bei einer
Tasse jenes grünen Tees, den beide so liebten,
keine Milch, keinen Zucker, nicht mal ein
Scheibchen {Tröpfchen} Zitrone –

[Perhaps they meet, and sit, over a cup of that green tea they both so loved, without milk or sugar not even a squeeze of lemon –]

12

Nicht mal ein Scheibchen {Tröpfchen} Zitrone –

[Not even a squeeze of –]

Transcription continues on pp. 94–95.

persönlich

selig

13

Treffen sich u. [und] sitzen bald in dem einen
lieben alten Haus, bald in dem anderen,
u. [und] grämen sich zusammen, u. [und] vergleichen –
Schluckauf – Verzeihung – glückliche Erinnerungen.

[Meet, and sit, now in the one dear old place, now in the other, and sorrow together, and compare – (*Hiccup.*) – pardon – happy memories.]

14

Ich {persönlich} trank immer {lieber} am liebsten Liptons.

[Personally I always preferred Lipton's.]

15

Bedaure sie auf jeden Fall, ja, vergleiche mein Los mit ihrem,
wie {selig} gesegnet es auch sein mag, u. [und] –

[I pity them in any case, yes, compare my lot with theirs, however blessed, and –]

91

ver- /
nach-
dämmern
verdunkeln
nachlassen

16

Ich bedaure sie.

17

Verheimliche ich irgend etwas? Verlor ich –

18

Verlor ich … das, was du verlangst? Warum erlöschen? Warum/ –

19

Warum das Dämmerlicht? Warum mich nicht –

20

rastlos

Warum mich nicht (unverwandt u.) unablässig anstrahlen? Ich könnte schliesslich irrereden u. – Schluckauf – damit herausrücken. Ver-

21

-Zeitung

22

Wenn man bedenkt, dass wir nie zusammen waren.

23

Nie zusammen erwachten, an einem Morgen im Mai, wer zuerst erwacht, weckt die beiden anderen. Dann in einer kleinen Jolle –

24

Eine kleine Jolle –

25

Eine kleine Jolle, auf dem Fluss, ich ruhend an meinen Rudern, sie lässig auf Luftkissen, achtern. Treibend. Solche Phantastereien.

[*fol. 22v*]

ver – /
nach –

dämmern,
verdunkeln
nachlassen

[*fol. 23r*]

[*erasure*]

16

<Ich> bedaure sie.

[Pity them.]

17

Verheimliche ich irgend etwas? Verlor ich –

[Am I hiding something? Have I lost –]

18

Verlor ich . . . das, was du verlangst? Warum
erlöschen? Warum {ver– *or* nach–, *i.e., depending on the word chosen in fragment 19*}

[Have I lost . . . the thing you want? Why go out? Why go –]

19

Warum das Dämmerlicht? {dämmern, verdunkeln, or nachlassen} Warum mich nicht –

[Why go down? Why not –]

20

Warum mich nicht (unverwandt u. [und]) {rastlos?} unablässig
anstrahlen? Ich könnte schliesslich irrereden [irre reden]
u. [und] – Schluckauf – damit herausrücken [es für dich herausbrechen]. Ver–

[Why not keep on glaring at me without ceasing? I might start to rave and – (*Hiccup.*) – bring it up for you. Par –]

21

– zeihung.

[– don.]

22

Wenn man bedenkt, dass wir nie zusammen waren.

[To think we were never together.]

Transcription continues on p. 101.

23

[*erasure*] Nie zusammen erwachten, an einem Morgen
im Mai, wer zuerst erwacht, weckt die beiden
anderen. Dann in eine[*erasure*] kleine[*erasure*] Jolle –

[Never woke together, on a May morning, the first to wake to wake the other two. Then in a little dinghy –]

24

Eine kleine Jolle –

[A little dinghy –]

25

Eine kleine Jolle, auf dem Fluss, ich ruhend
an meinen Rudern, sie lässig auf Luftkissen,
achtern. Treibend. Solche Phantastereien.

[A little dinghy, on the river, I resting on my oars, they lolling on air-pillows in the stern . . . sheets. Drifting. Such fantasies.]

Sich über mir öffnend u. schliessend. !

26

wir hatten keine Lebensart.

27

Solche Phantastereien. Einst. Und nun –

28

und nun – dass du ... bloss Auge bist. Nur schauend. In mein Gesicht. ab u. zu.

29

Schauend nach etwas. In meinem Gesicht. Nach irgendeiner Wahrheit. In meinen Augen. Nicht einmal.

30

Bloss Auge. Kein Verstand. Das sich über mir öffnet u. schliesst. Werde ich überhaupt –

31

Werde ich überhaupt ... gesehen?

—

wir waren nicht lang zusammen

[*fol. 23v*]

Sich über mir öffnend u. [und] schliessend. /

26

Wir hatten keine Lebensart.

[We were not civilized.]

27

Solche Phantastereien. Einst. Und nun –

[Such fantasies. Then. And now –]

28

Und nun, dass du . . . bloss Auge bist. Nur
schauend. In mein Gesicht. Ab u. [und] zu.

[And now, that you are . . . mere eye. Just looking. At my face. On and off.]

29

Schauend nach etwas. In meinem Gesicht.
Nach irgendeiner Wahrheit. In meinen
Augen. Nicht einmal.

[Looking for something. In my face. Some truth. In my eyes. Not even.]

30

Bloss Auge. Kein Verstand. Das sich über
mir öffnet u. [und] schliesst. Werde ich überhaupt – {Sich über
mir öffnend und schliessend –}

[Mere eye. No mind. Opening and shutting on me. Am I as much –]

31

Werde ich überhaupt . . . gesehen?

[Am I as much as . . . being seen?]

Wir waren nicht lang zusammen –

[We were not long together –]

II

Not being seen unseen

F1 1 ... mich nicht gesehen

" 24 ... Wirst es sehen

M 30 ... Werde ich überhaupt gesehen?

Not being heard unheard

F1 12 ... alles gefallen ins Leere

F2 11 Hörst du mir zu?

What demanded?

F1 5, 6 .. Wahrheit?

" 7, 8 .. Something she must say?

" 9, 10 .. " other than speech? Weep? → 12 Nothing

" 20 - Repent?

M 17 .. Something he is hiding?

" 18 .. " " has lost?

" 29 .. Some truth in his face, eyes?

~~Senselessness~~ Meaninglessness

F1 11-14 Wenn ich nur denken könnte ...

F2 9 ... nach Sinn zu suchen wo .. keiner ist

M 8 ... nichts anderes als Spiel

~~M 31 Cf. above~~.

Loss of reason

F1 7, 10 Mind still working, erstaunlich

" 14 Er (Verstand) würde weichen (~~scheitern~~) müssen

F2 6 mich ~~um~~ meinen Verstand ~~bringen~~ ausbrennen

" 21-25 .. aus dem Lot

~~Will light weary~~? M irrereden

F1 2 .. Wirst meiner müde

" 24-25 .. müde des Spiels mit mir

F2 3-4 .. Wirst meiner müde .. mich aufgeben

Nothing being demanded?

F1 12 ... gar nichts verlangt

Dark

F1 21, 23 . Stille u. Dunkel

M 2 . alles unter ins Dunkel

Hellish game

F1 25 Cf above

M 8 " "

[*fol. 24v*]

II^3

Not being seen <unseen>

F1 1 . . . mich nicht gesehen [haven't seen me]

" 24 . . . wirst es sehen [staring you in the face]

M 31 . . . Werde ich überhaupt gesehen [Am I as much as being seen]

Not being heard unheard

F1 12 . . . alles gefallen ins Leere. [all fallen on empty air]

F2 11 [*recte* 10] Hörst du mir zu? [Are you listening to me?]

What demanded?

F1 5, 6 . . . Wahrheit? [Truth]

" 7, 8 . . . Something she must say?

" 9, 10 . . . " other than speech? Weep?

——————→ 12 Nothing

" 20 – Repent?

M 17 . . . Something he is hiding?

" 18 . . . " " has lost?

" 29 . . . Some truth in his face, eyes?

M [*illegible*]

Senselessness

F1 11–14 . . . Wenn ich nur denken könnte . . . [If only I could think . . .]

F2 9 . . . nach Sinn zu suchen wo . . . keiner ist [looking for sense where there is none]

M 8 . . . nichts anderes als Spiel [have been just play]

<M 31 cf. above.>

Loss of reason

F1 7, 10 . . . Mind still working, erstaunlich [to be sure! *i.e.*, amazing]

" 14 . . . Er (Verstand) würde weichen <(scheitern)> müssen [It (mind) would have to go]

F2 6 . . . mich <um> meinen Verstand <bringen> ausbrennen [blaze me clean out of my wits]

F2 21–25 . . . aus dem Lot [unhinged]

<Will light weary?> M irrereden [to rave]

F1 2 . . . wirst meiner müde [weary of me]

" 24–25 . . . Müde des Spiels mit mir [Weary of playing with me]

F2 3–4 . . . wirst meiner müde . . . mich aufgeben [Give me up]

Transcription continues on p. 111.

<Nothing being demanded?>
<F1 12 . . . gar nichts verlangt> [Nothing being asked]

Dark
F1 21, 23 – Stille u. [und] Dunkel [Silence and darkness]
M 2 . . . alles unter, ins Dunkel [all going down, into the dark]

Hellish game
F1 25 . . . Cf. above
M 8 . . . " "

I

Duo

F1/F2	~~[illegible]~~ F2 – 1, 2, 3 F2 – 6	}	4 – 2 meetings
F1/M	F1 – 1 M – 1, 2, 3 F1 – 3 M–6 F1 – 5 M – 8	}	8 – 3 "
F2/M	F2 – 4, 5 M–5 F2 – 7, 8, 9 M – 7	}	7 – 3 "
			19

Solo

F1	2, 4, 6, 7, 8, 9, 10, 11	}	13
F2	10, 11		
M	4, 9, 10		
			32

I	F1	F2	M
1	F1 – ~~[illegible]~~ M 1	F2 – F1 1. F1's appearance.	M – F1 1. Suicide 1. Denial.
2	Alone. assiduity 1. Sleuth. Plato 1.	Do contd. Smell 1.	Do. assiduity 2. Love/pity.
3	F1 – M 2. Confession 1	Do contd. Gustav 1	Do. Smell 2. Need/embrace 1.
4	Alone. Wonderment	F2-M 1. Desert.	alone. Sleuth 2.
5	F1 – M 3. Journey 1.	Do. contd. Plato 2	M – F2 1. Suicide 2. Gustav 2.
6	~~[illegible]~~. F1 - F2 2. F2's appearance.	F2 – F1 2. Gustav 3	M – F1 2. Confession 2.
7	Appearance contd.	F2 – M 2. Confession confessed.	M – F2 2. F2 knows. Mower 1 – Need/embrace 2.
8	Appearance contd.	~~[illegible]~~ Do. Mower 1.	M – F1 3. Home. Exchange pillow.
9	Home bliss.	Do. Journey 2.	Alone. Can't go on.
10	Smell 3	Alone. M gone 1.	Do.
11	Alone. M gone 2. F1 gone. Accident on way home?	Alone. Bonfire. Night.	

[*fol. 26v*]

I

Duo

F1/F2
<F1 – 1>
F2 – 1, 2, 3
F2 – 6
<5> 4–2 meetings

F1/M
F1 – 1
M – 1, 2, 3
F1 – 3
M – 6
F1 – 5
M – 8
<7> 8–3 "

F2/M
F2 – 4, 5
M – 5
F2 – 7, 8, 9
M – 7
7–3 "

19

Solo

F1 2, 4, 6, 7, 8, 9, 10, 11
F2 10, 11
M 4, 9, 10
13

32

I[4]	F1	F2	M
1	F1 – [*erasure*] M 1	F2–F1 1. F1's appearance.	M–F1 1. Suicide 1. Denial.
2	Alone. Assiduity 1. Sleuth. Plato 1	Do [ditto] contd. Smell 1.	Do. Assiduity 2. Love/pity.
3	F1–M2 Confession 1	Do contd. Gustav 1	Do. Smell 2. Need/embrace 1.
4	Alone. Wonderment	F2–M1 Desert.	Alone. Sleuth 2.
5	F1–M3 Journey 1.	Do. contd. Plato 2.	M–F2 1. Suicide 2 Gustave 2.
6	[*erasure*] F1–F2 2. F2's appearance.	F2–F1 2. Gustav 3.	M–F1 2. Confession 2.
7	Appearance contd.	F2–M 2. Confession confessed.	M–F2 2. F2 knows. Mower 1. Need/ embrace 2.
8	Appearance concld.	[*erasure*] Do. Mower 1.	M–F1 3. Home. Exchange pillow.
9	Home bliss.	Do. Journey 2.	Alone. Can't go on.
10	Smell 3	Alone. M gone 1.	Do.
11	Alone. M gone 2. F1 gone. Accident on way home?	Alone. Bonfire. Night.	

Ich sagte
lieb u. teuer – Eines morgens
vorzog – Wir waren
redete – Wovon
Luder – Obgleich
Beschuldiste ja – Worüber
mit ihr haben – Da ich
derzeit – Sie war
ernst meinte – Man stelle
beichtete – Sie legte
Nebenverdienst – Warum
Oder doch? – Ich gebe
Kerl – Was zwischen
Zusammelebte – Das nächste
klarzustellen – Dann verzieh
Verpflichtungen – Sie kam
Gustav – Dann kriegte
nie zu – Als ich klein

---

mich doch hatte – Als er wieder
zu so was – Pudding
dass man – Er redete
zu denken – Waden
Seltpullen – Als ich sie
gekommt hätte – Es gab
wir könnten – Er war also
die Welt – Zuhause
mein Engel, sagte ich – Dann roch
Ja – Als er nicht
mehr u. weniger – Schliesslich
nicht länger – Ehe ich
Rotland – Ich konnte
nicht länger – Ich packte

I

1 | F1 First exchange with M. No dialogue.
1 | F2 First visit to ~~F2.~~ ~~[illegible]~~ from F1. F's physique.
1 | M First exchange with F1.
2 | F2 F1's first visit contd. Smell.
2 | F1 Solo. Sleuth. Plato.
2 | M First exchange with F1 contd.
3 | F2 F1's first visit concld. Gustav.
3 | M First exchange with F1 concld. Smell.
3 | F1 Second exchange with M. Confession. No dialogue.
4 | M Solo. Sleuth.
4 | F2 First exchange with M.
4 | F1 Solo. Wonderment.
5 | F2 First exchange with M concld. Plato.
5 | M Second exchange with F2. F1's first visit evoked. Gustav.
5 | F1 Second exchange with M concld. (Assuming pardon immediate.)
6 | F2 Second visit of F1. ~~Solo~~ Gustav. — Visit 2
6 | M Second exchange with F1. Confession. No dialogue. — Conf. 2
6 | F1 Second visit to F2. Solo. — Visit 2
7 | F2 Third exchange with M.
7 | F1 Solo. F2's ~~appearance~~ physique.
8 | F2 Third exchange with M contd. Mower.
8 | F1 Solo. F2's appearance concld.
7 | M Third exchange with F2. (~~Assuming part of showdown.~~) Mower
9 | F2 Third exchange with M concld. (" " " ")
9 | F1 Solo. ~~Home bliss.~~
Home bliss
8 | M Third exchange with F1. Pillow.
10 | F1 Solo. Smell.
10 | F2 Solo. M gone.
9 | M Solo. Enough.
11 | F1 Solo. M gone Third visit to F2. F2 gone.
10 | M Solo. Enough.
11 | F2 Solo. Bonfire.

[*fol. 270v*]

[*Whole page in pencil*]

	Ich sagte [I said]
lieb u. [und] teuer [I held most sacred]	– Eines Morgens [One morning]
vorzog [preferred me]	– Wir waren [We were]
redete [talking about]	– Wovon [What . . . about]
Luder [bitch]	– Obgleich [Though]
beschuldigte. Ja [accusing. Yes]	– Worüber [What . . . of]
mit ihr haben [feel sorry for her]	– Da ich [Fearing she was]
derzeit (seinerzeit) [at the time]	– Sie war [She was not]
ernst meinte (Sie stiess mich nicht zurück) [I am sure I meant it. (She did not repulse me.)]	– Man stelle [Judge then]
beichtete [confessed]	– Sie hegte (hetzte) [She put]
Nebenverdienst [extra money]	– Warum [Why]
Oder doch? [Or is there?]	– Ich gebe [I confess]
Kerl! [male!]	– Was zwischen [Anything between]
zusamme[n]lebte [living with]	– Das nächste [The next thing]
klarzustellen [work this out]	– Dann verzieh [Then I forgave him]
Verpflichtungen [commitments]	– Sie kam [She came]
Gustav [Erskine]	– Dann kriegte [Then I got]
nie zu [never admit]	– Als ich keinen [When I was]

---

mich doch hatte [when he had me]	– Als er wieder{kam} [When he came again]
zu so was! [(Back) to that!]	– Pudding (Puddinggesicht) [Pudding face]
dass man [you could]	– Er redete [He went on]
zu denken [thought that ever]	– Waden [Calves]
Sektpullen [flunkey]	– Als ich sie [When I saw her]
gekonnt hätte [I could have]	– Es gab [The only solution]
wir könnten [we could]	– Er war also [So he was mine]
die Welt [The world]	– Zuhause [At home]
mein Engel, sagte ich [angel, I said]	– Dann roch [Then I began to smell]
Ja [Yes]	– Als er nicht [When he stopped coming]
Mehr o. [oder] weniger [More or less]	– Schliesslich [Finally]
nicht länger [no longer]	– Ehe ich [Before I]
Rottland [Snodland]	– Ich konnte [I simply could]
nicht länger [no longer]	– Ich packte [I made a bundle]

I[5]

1	F1	First exchange with M. No dialogue.	
1	F2	First visit <to F2 of F1> from F1. F's physique.	
1	M	First exchange with F1.	
2	F2	F1's first visit contd. [continued] Smell.	
2	F1	Solo. Sleuth. Plato.	
2	M	First exchange with F1 contd.	
3	F2	F1's first visit concld. [concluded] Gustav.	
3	M	First exchange with F1 concld. Smell.	
3	F1	Second exchange with M. Confession. No dialogue.	
4	M	Solo. Sleuth.	
4	F2	First exchange with M.	
4	F1	Solo. Wonderment.	
5	F2	First exchange with M concld. Plato.	
5	M	Second exchange with F2. F1's first visit evoked. Gustav.	
5	F1	Second exchange with M concld. (Assuming pardon immediate.)	
6	F2	Second visit of F1. [*erasure*] Gustav.	visit 2
6	M	Second exchange with F1. Confession. No dialogue.	conf. 2
6	F1	Second visit to F2. Solo.	visit 2
7	F2	Third exchange with M.	
7	F1	Solo. F2's <appearance> physique.	
8	F2	Third exchange with M contd. Mower.	
8	F1	Solo. F2's appearance concld.	
7	M	Third exchange with F2. (<assuming part of showdown.>) Mower	
9	F2	Third exchange with M concld. (" " " ")	
9	F1	Solo. Home Bliss.	
8	M	Third exchange with F1. Pillow. {Home bliss}	
10	F1	Solo. Smell.	
10	F2	Solo. M gone.	
9	M	Solo. Enough.	
11	F1	Solo. {M gone} Third visit to F2. F2 gone.	
10	M	Solo. Enough.	
11	F2	Solo. Bonfire.	

5 { Hiccup: 1 Big chorus after "es wird kommen".
I { 2. M1 after <u>Kehle durch</u>.
3. M7 before <u>jämmerlich</u>. <u>Verzeihung</u> delayed.
II { 4. M13 after <u>vergleichen</u>
5. M20 before <u>damit herausrücken</u> " delayed & broken.

F1

1-14 <u>Present</u>

15-19 <u>Other two</u> Mediterranean. Evening.
M late.

20-25 <u>Present</u>

F2

1-10 <u>Present</u>

11-14 <u>Other two</u> House. Reconciled. Pitying F2.
Love kisses

15-25 <u>Present</u>

M

1-8 <u>Present</u>

9-16 <u>Other two</u> Become friends. Tea. Sharing
sorrows. Past happiness.

17-31 <u>Present</u>

Cut small chorus – straight from big (brief black) to strong individual spot

—

In terms of light big chorus belongs to II.
Regard as conclusion leading to the beginning

—

Strong spot I – curses inquisitive
Weak " II – " first visits

—

Fade up at beginning – cut close or snap?

—

Up curtain, up on general light, down do.

[*fol. 28v*]

5 Hiccup:[6] 1 Big chorus after "es wird kommen" [it will come]

I
2. M1 after Kehle durch [cut my throat]
3. M7 before jämmerlich [wretched]. Verzeihung [Pardon] delayed.

II
4. M13[7] after vergleichen [compare]
5. M20 before damit herausrücken [bring it up for you] "
[*i.e.*, Verzeihung] delayed and broken.[8]

F1[9]

1–14	Present	
15–19	Other two	Mediterranean. Evening. M late.
20–25	Present	

F2

1–10	Present	
11–14	Other two	House. Reconciled. Pitying F2. Sour kisses
15–25	Present	

M

1–8	Present	
9–16	Other two	Become friends. Tea. Sharing sorrows. Past happiness.
17–31	Present	

cut small chorus[10] – straight {from big} (brief black) to strong individual spot

——

In terms of light big chorus belongs to II.
Regard as conclusion leading to rebeginning.[11]

——

Strong spot I – urns invisible
Weak " II – " just visible

——

Fade up opening & out close as much?

——

If curtain, up on general light, down do [*i.e.*, ditto].

1 M bei diesem ... alles aus
1 F1 Grade ... wird sie kommen
1 F2 Ich sage mich ... etwas ruhiger
2 F1 Oder du wirst ... mich lassen
2 M [Ja aus] ... dem ersten
2 F2 Weniger verwirrt ... erträgliche Momente
3 M Dachte ich
3 F2 Wenn du erlischst ... endgültig
3 F1 Höllisches Halblicht
4 M Frieden ja ... nie gewesen
4 F2 Mich aufgeben ... andererseits
4 F1 Lass mich. Lass mich.
5 M Es wird kommen ... Keine Zukunft
5 F2 andererseits ... die Gefahr
6 M Oh gewiss ich weiss jetzt
5 F1 Sollte es sein ... für die Wahrheit
6 F2 Du könntest ... nicht wahr
7 M Ich weiss jetzt ... u. all dies
6 F1 Sollte es das sein
7 F2 Nicht wahr
8 M Wann wird all dies ... als Spiel
7 F1 Ich kann nichts ... noch funktioniert
8 F2 Aber ich glaube nicht ... oder nicht
9 M Vielleicht sind ... vielleicht hat der Gram
8 F1 aber ich habe ... alles was ich –
10 M Vielleicht hat der Gram ... zusammen gebracht.
9 F2 Ich nehme an ... womöglich keiner ist
11 M Vielleicht treffen ... Zitrone
10 F2 Hörst du ... um mich.
12 M Nicht mal ... Zitrone
9 F1 Sollte es etwas ... Weinen
11 F2 Ist mein Name ... ~~[illegible]~~ Ärmste
10 F1 Meine Zunge .. erstaunlich
13 M Treffen sich .. Erinnerungen
11 F1 Wenn ich nur ... Kann es nicht
12 F2 Die Ärmste ... armes Ding
14 M Ich persönlich ... Liptons
12 F1 u. das alles ... von mir verlangt
13 F2 Sie würden ... mit Ihnen

13 F1 Ich kann es nicht.
14 F2 Ihre saure Küsse Küssend
15 M Bedaure sie -- und
14 F1 Ich kann es nicht – Ja.
16 M bedaure sie.
15 F2 Was machst du – sondern
17 M Verheimliche · Warum
15 F1 Sie war wohl – wie eine Sau.
16 F2 Wie das Rollen – Schwung
17 F2 Stoß u. wieder die Mühe
18 M ~~[illegible]~~ –
18 F2 u. dabei ... etwas Ruhe
16 F1 Vielleicht – in der Sonne.
19 M ~~[illegible]~~ Warum ... mich nicht
19 F2 Ich weiss es nicht.
17 F1 Vielleicht .. die Oliven
20 M ~~[illegible]~~
20 F2 Nein.
21 M ~~Die zusammen ... Kleine Folter~~
18 F1 Weit hinab ... Ja.
22 M ~~Eine kleine Folter ... wenn ich denk~~
21 F2 · Bin ich nicht – aus dem Lot
19 F1 ~~Die~~ Ärmste. Die Ärmsten.
23 M ~~Eine kleine Folter ... Phantastereien~~
20 F1 ~~Die Ärmste. Die Ärmsten~~
22 F2 ~~Bin ich nicht ... aus dem Lot~~
24 M ~~Wir hatten keine Liebe [illegible]~~
21 F1 Stille .. mehr zu flehen
25 M ~~Solche Phantastereien ... und nun~~.
22 F1 Höllisches Halblicht
23 F2 ~~[illegible] ich glaube nicht~~.
26 M ~~[illegible]~~
23 F1 Dürstend – Seltsam
27 M Solche Phantastereien – und nun –
24 F2 Ich glaube nicht. (Lachen)
24 F1 Ja, u. alles .. Oder müde werden
28 M und nun .. ab u. zu
25 F1 Müde des Spiels – Ja
29 M Schauend – Nicht einmal

25 F2 Lachen
30 M Bloss auge ... überhaupt.
31 M Werde ich überhaupt ... gesehen

End of 1st 8 x 3	F1.7 F2.8. M.9
" " 2nd " "	" 17 " ~~16~~ " 17
" " 3rd " "	" 23 " 23 " 26
" " last 3 "	~~[illegible]~~ 25 " 25 " 31

Verlor ich – Warum

Warum mich nicht – Ver-

-Zeihung

Wenn man .. zusammen wären

~~Nie zusammen – Kleine Rolle~~
nie zusammen – Kleine Rolle
Büssen ... auch das nicht
Ich sagte .. Ich glaube nicht.
Eine Kleine Rolle –

eine Kl. Rolle – solche Phantastereien

Leicht ... ich glaube nicht
Wir ... Keine Lebensart

1	M	bei di[e]sem[12] [When first this] . . . alles aus [all is going out]
1	F1	Gnade [Mercy] . . . wird sie kommen [Then it will come]
1	F2	Ich sage nich [*recte* nicht] [To say I am not] . . . etwas ruhiger [More restful]
2	F1	Oder du wirst [Or you will weary] . . . mich lassen [Get off me]
2	M	Aus, ja [Down] . . . dem ersten [first this change]
2	F2	Weniger verwirrt [Less confused] . . . erträgliche Momente [endurable moments]
3	M	Dachte ich [I thought]
3	F2	Wenn du erlischst [When you go out] . . . endgültig [for good]
3	F1	Höllisches Halblicht [Hellish half-light]
4	M	Frieden ja [Peace, yes] . . . nie gewesen [never been]
4	F2	Mich aufgeben [Give me up] . . . andererseits [On the other hand]
4	F1	Lass mich. Lass mich. [Get off me.]
5	M	Es wird kommen [It will come] . . . keine Zukunft [no future in this]
5	F2	Andererseits [On the other hand] . . . die Gefahr [there is that danger]
6	M	Oh gewiss ich weiss jetzt [Oh of course I know now –]
5	F1	Sollte es sein [Is it that I] . . . für die Wahrheit? [for the truth?]
6	F2	Du könntest [You might] . . . nicht wahr [Mightn't you?]
7	M	Ich weiss jetzt [I know now] . . . u. [und] [Wann wird] all dies [When will all this]
6	F1	Sollte es das sein [Is that it?]
7	F2	Nicht wahr [Mightn't you?]
8	M	Wann wird all dies [When will all this] . . . als Spiel [just play?]
7	F1	Ich kann nichts [I can do nothing] . . . noch funzioniert [*recte* funktioniert] [works still!]
8	F2	Aber ich glaube nicht [But I doubt it] . . . oder nicht [Or don't you?]
9	M	Vielleicht sind [Perhaps they have] . . . Vielleicht hat der Gram [Perhaps sorrow –]
8	F1	Aber ich habe [But I have said] . . . alles was ich – [All I –]
10	M	Vielleicht hat der Gram . . . [sie] zusammengebracht. [Perhaps sorrow has brought them together.]
9	F2	Ich nehme an [No doubt I make] . . . womöglich [möglicherweise] keiner ist [possibly there is none]
11	M	Vielleicht treffen [Perhaps they meet] . . . Zitrone [lemon –]
10	F2	Hörst du [Are you listening to] . . . um mich [about me at all?]
12	M	Nicht mal [Not even] . . . Zitrone [a squeeze of (lemon)]

Transcription of fol. 29v and left side of fol. 30r continues on pp. 128 and 130; transcription of right side of fol. 30r appears on p. 131.

9 F1 Sollte es etwas [Is it something] . . . Weinen [Weep?]
11 F2 Ist mein Name [Is my name] . . . [*erasure*] Ärmste [poor creature]
10 F1 Meine Zunge [(Bite off) my tongue] . . . erstaunlich [to be sure! (*i.e.*, amazing)]
13 M Treffen sich [Meet] . . . Erinnerungen [happy memories]
11 F1 Wenn ich nur [If only I could] . . . kann es nicht [I can't]
12 F2 Die Ärmste [The poor creature] . . . armes Ding [Poor thing]
14 M Ich persönlich [Personally I] . . . Liptons [Lipton's]
12 F1 U. [und] das alles [And that all] . . . von mir verlangt [asking me]
13 F2 Sie würden [They might] . . . mit Ihnen [for them]
13 F1 Ich kann es nicht. [I can't.]
14 F2 Ihre saure[n] Küsse küssend [Kissing their sour kisses]
15 M Bedaure sie [I pity them] – und [and –]
14 F1 Ich kann es nicht [I can't] – Ja. [Yes.]
16 M bedaure sie. [Pity them.]
15 F2 Was machst du [What do you do?] – sondern [Sift?]
17 M Verheimliche [Am I hiding] . . . Warum[13] [Have I lost –]
15 F1 Sie war wohl [She had means] – wie eine Sau. [like a pig.]
16 F2 Wie das Rollen [Like dragging] – Schwung [momentum coming –]

17 F2 Stop u. [und] wieder die Mühe [Kill it – strain again.]
18 M [*erasure*] {Verlor ich [Have I lost] – Warum [Why go]}
18 F2 U. [und] dabei [And you] . . . etwas Ruhe [a rest]
16 F1 Vielleicht [Perhaps] – in der Sonne. [in the sun.]
19 M [*erasure*] Warum [Why] . . . mich nicht [Why not –]
19 F2 Ich weiss es nicht. [I don't know.]
17 F1 Vielleicht [Perhaps] . . . die Oliven [the olives]
20 M [*erasure*] {Warum mich nicht [Why not keep] – Ver– [Par–]}
20 F2 Nein. [No.]
21 M [*erasure*] {–Zeihung [–don, i.e., pardon]}
18 F1 Weit hinab [Gazing down] . . . Ja. [Yes.]
22 M [*erasure*] {Wenn man [To think we were] . . zusammen waren [never together]}
21 F2 Bin ich nicht [Am I not] – aus dem Lot? [unhinged already?]
19 F1 <Die> Ärmste. Die Ärmsten. [Poor creature. Poor creatures.] {[*erasure*]}
23 M [*erasure*] {nie zusammen [Never woke together] – kleine Jolle [little dinghy]}
20 F1 [*erasure*] {Büssen [Penitence] . . . auch das nicht [not . . . the point either]}
22 F2 [*erasure*] {Ich sagte [I say] . . Ich glaube nicht [I doubt it]}
24 M [*erasure*] {Eine kleine Jolle– [A little dinghy–]}

21 FI Stille [Silence] . . . mehr zu flehen [*recte* erflehen] [pray for more]

25 M [*erasure*] {eine kl. [kleine] Jolle [A little dinghy] – solche Phantastereien [Such fantasies]}

22 FI Höllisches Halblicht [Hellish half-light]

23 F2 [*erasure*] {Leicht [A shade] . . . ich glaube nicht [I doubt it]}

26 M [*erasure*] {Wir [We] . . . keine Lebensart [not civilized]}

23 FI Dürstend [Dying (*i.e.*, thirsting)] – Seltsam [Strange]

---

27 M solche Phantastereien [Such fantasies] – Und nun – [and now –]

23 F2 Ich glaube nicht. [I doubt it.] (Lachen) [*laugh*]

24 FI Ja, u. [und] alles [Yes, and the whole thing] . . . Oder müde werden [Or weary]

28 M Und nun [And now] . . . Ab u. [und] zu [On and off]

25 FI Müde des Spiels [Weary of playing] – Ja [Yes]

29 M Schauend [Looking] – Nicht einmal [Not even]

25 F2 Lachen [*Laugh*]
30 M Bloss Auge [Mere eyes] . . . überhaupt [as much]
31 M Werde ich überhaupt [Am I as much as] . . . gesehen [being seen?]

End of 1st 8 × 3	F1. 7	F2. 8.	M. 9
" " 2nd " "	" 17[14]	" 16	" 17
" " 3rd " "	" 23	" 23	" 26
" " last 3 "	" 25	" 25	" 31
	[*erasure*]		

EDITORIAL NOTES ON THE RED NOTEBOOK

The bulk of the Red Notebook (*Red Nb*) for *Spiel* (RUL MS 1976) is linguistic, devoted to Beckett's close re-examination of the German text, translated in collaboration with the author by Elmar and Erika Tophoven. Simultaneously, Beckett revised a copy of the trilingual German text (*Spiel* (SB)) published by Suhrkamp. The textual revisions in the *Red Nb* and in *Spiel* (SB) are not, however, identical, so comments on the *Spiel* (SB) revisions are included in the 'Linguistic Notes' to the *Red Nb* (below) and in a separate section of 'Cuts and Changes' (p. 197) as well.

In the *Red Nb* Beckett wrote out the whole of his play, not as printed, since that would have duplicated what he was simultaneously doing with the printed text, *Spiel* (SB). Instead, he grouped the speeches in consecutive order under each character's designation, beginning with the first female character, F1. (The *Red Nb* uses the German character names, F for Frau, instead of the English W for Woman. The male designation is, of course, the same, M for Man or Mann.)

Beckett has followed such a practice of regrouping fragmented speeches of a text before, in the composition of *That Time*, and he called that version of the play a 'continuity ms.'. The *Red Nb* then is Beckett's 'continuity ms.' for *Spiel*. This (near) fair copy of the text gave Beckett an alternative to the ordering of the printed text. The 'continuity' version allowed Beckett another way of looking at the thematic, structural and linguistic patterns of his play – and those patterns dominate the remainder of the *Red Nb* and are taken up again in the following Brown Notebook (RUL MS 1730).

After copying out the play, Beckett returned to the first two folios of the *Red Nb* to begin a series of structural outlines. That work then carried over to the end of the textual portion of the *Red Nb*. For some reason Beckett stopped work in the *Red Nb* on folio 30 (see the 'Note on the Manuscript', p. 5, as well) and began anew in another, brown notebook. The Brown Notebook (*Brown Nb*) then duplicates (and occasionally refines) many of the structural outlines of the *Red Nb*. 'Notes' to the *Brown Nb* follow its transcription.

The 'Notes' on Beckett's linguistic revisions, called below 'Linguistic Notes', follow Beckett's designation of speeches, F1 chorus, followed by her first speech, F1, 1. In the second part of the play, after the second chorus, however, Beckett resumes the numbering of speeches with 1. Since that is the system Beckett used in his outlines, the 'Linguistic Notes' follow it as well. Notes to the structural revisions, called 'Structural and Thematic Notes', follow the 'Linguistic Notes' and are designated in the transcription by superscript numbers.

Linguistic Notes

Fol. 8r

F1 **chorus** – Beckett brought the German closer to the English text, 'the thing is there'. Beckett included 'das Ding ist da' ('the thing is there') in his version as a revision of the original German text 'der Sinn ist da' ('the mind or sense is there'). This revision appears in *Spiel* (SB), p. 239.
F1, **2** – Beckett substituted 'Masche' where the German text has 'Tour'. 'Masche' is more negative than 'Tour'; it means to trick someone through oily flattery. 'Tour' is simply to take this route. This revision appears in *Spiel* (SB), p. 243.
F1, **4** – Beckett at first retains the word in the original German text 'Erstaunen', which means 'surprise' or 'amazement'. On the facing verso he suggests an alternative, 'Bewunderung', which means 'admiration'. This revision appears in *Spiel* (SB), p. 247.

Fol. 9r

F1, **5** – The original German text has 'verzieh'. On the facing verso Beckett suggests the change to 'vergab'. The two verbs mean roughly the same: 'to forgive', although one might say that 'verzeihen' has the element of 'to excuse' (one says 'Verzeihung' when one bumps into someone); 'vergeben' has more the sense of 'to pardon' or 'to forgive'. This change is *not* made in *Spiel* (SB), p. 247.

Beckett's 'Wozu sich Liebe nicht hergibt!' replaced the wording of the original German text: 'Wozu Liebe sich nicht hergibt!' This revision appears in *Spiel* (SB), p. 247.

The original German text has 'eine kleine Vergnügungsreise' which Beckett revised to 'einen kleinen Ausflug'. 'Vergnügungsreise' is more overtly for pleasure; 'Ausflug' is something more casual, something harmless. 'Vergnügung' has about it the satisfaction of the senses. This change appears in *Spiel* (SB), p. 247.

The original German text has 'Er sah blass aus, spitz', which Beckett revised to 'Er sah blass aus. Spitz.' This minor punctuation change does, however, emphasize 'spitz' a bit more. This change appears in *Spiel* (SB), p. 247.
F1, **11** – For the original German text 'Ich war wochenlang' Beckett's facing verso revision suggests 'Ich lag wochenlang'. The change from 'I was' to 'I lay' suggests

more the condition of 'erschlagen', someone down and out. This revision appears in *Spiel* (SB), p. 251.

Fol. 10r

FI, 7 – The original German translation has 'Wie der Kopf immer noch arbeitet', which Beckett revised to 'Wie der Kopf immer noch funktioniert'. While 'arbeitet' is, of course, fine, 'funktioniert' suggests Beckett's preference for the more colloquial expression ('Masche' vs. 'Tour', for example). Moreover, 'funktioniert' also implies mechanical functioning. Beckett, however, misspelled the word 'funktioniert' several times as 'funzioniert'. The revision appears in *Spiel* (SB) as 'funktionert', p. 257.

Beckett also circled 'was' and linked it to the circled 'das' in FI, 9 contemplating, perhaps, an echo. In *Spiel* (SB) Beckett revised the 'das' of FI, 9 to 'was' to echo this 'was', p. 259.

FI, 8 – The German translation has 'Aber ich hab''. In the *Red Nb* Beckett replaced the apostrophe with the missing 'e'. 'Hab'' is, of course, merely a contraction, which suggests greater informality. The original German translation 'Aber ich hab' alles gesagt' sounds a bit helpless, a bit touching. 'Aber ich habe alles gesagt' sounds more definite, more final. In *Spiel* (SB) Beckett retained the original German contractions (p. 257).

Fol. 11r

FI, 10 – Beckett again revised the 'arbeitet' of the original German translation to 'funzioniert'. See FI, 7 above.

FI, 11 – On the facing verso Beckett corrected his rendering of this line by noting the omitted 'nicht den geringsten'. The German translation contains the full phrase, 'auch dies nicht, nicht den geringsten'.

FI, 15 – Beckett revised the original German translation 'Sie war nicht mittellos' to 'Sie war wohl nicht mittellos'. The 'wohl' noted on the facing verso means 'probably' or 'quite likely' and is used here as a qualifier. This revision appears in *Spiel* (SB), p. 261.

Contemplating a revision Beckett placed parentheses around 'sag' ich mir'. Apparently no revision was made, however.

Fol. 12r

FI, 21 – Beckett revised the original German translation 'Stille und Dunkel war alles, was ich verlangte', substituting 'waren' for 'war'. This revision does *not* appear in *Spiel* (SB), p. 265.

Beckett also revised the 'was ich verlangte' in the German translation to 'wonach ich sehnte', which should perhaps be 'wonach ich mich sehnte'. The original German translation 'was ich verlangte', 'what I desired' or 'what I needed', was replaced by 'wonach ich mich sehnte', 'for which I longed'. There is much more need expressed in Beckett's version. The revision appears in *Spiel* (SB), p. 265.

In the original German translation 'Vielleicht ist es frevelhafter, um mehr zu bitten' ('Perhaps it is sinful to beg for more'), 'frevelhafter' has the connotation of something 'criminal'. Beckett's revision reads: 'Vielleicht ist es noch Sünde, um mehr zu flehen' ('Perhaps it is sinful to plead for more'). The revision appears in *Spiel* (SB), p. 265.

F1, 22 – Beckett corrected the omission of F1's speech 22 of part II on the facing verso, 'Höllisches Halblicht', and subsequently corrected the numeration of the remainder of F1's speeches.

Fol. 13r

F2, chorus – Beckett wanted to replace 'ernstlich' in the original German translation, 'nicht ernstlich', with 'ernst'. This would have to be, however, 'nicht im Ernst' and would be more serious than simply 'ernstlich'. The revision does *not* appear in *Spiel* (SB), p. 241.

F2, 1 – On the facing verso Beckett revised the original German translation 'gehört mir' to 'ist mein', a change from 'belongs to me' to 'is mine'. The revision does *not* appear in *Spiel* (SB), p. 243.

On the facing verso Beckett revised the original German translation 'Die Fotos von ihr waren schmeichelhaft' to 'Die Fotos von ihr waren schmeichlerish', which should be spelled 'schmeichlerisch', implying 'to be ingratiating', 'to reach a goal'. The 'schmeichelhaft' of the text means 'to flatter', 'to fawn'. The revision appears in *Spiel* (SB), p. 243.

On the facing verso Beckett added 'in Lebensgrösse' to the 'Fleisch und Blut sah' of the original German translation. Beckett's change, 'Fleisch und Blut in Lebensgrösse sah', adds 'as large as life' as an intensifier and perhaps picks up the English 'full length': 'Seeing her now for the first time full length . . .'. The revision in *Spiel* (SB) is 'und Lebengrösse'.

F2, 2 – On the facing verso Beckett noted the word 'Ihr' and underlined the German translation 'Jemand, der Ihnen gehört?' ('Someone who belongs to you?'). The English text reads, 'Someone yours?' Although Beckett made no indication where the 'Ihr' should be inserted, but only underlined 'der Ihnen gehört', to

parallel the English, the German should read, 'Ihr jemand?' The revision, however, does *not* appear in *Spiel* (SB), p. 243.
F2, 3 – On the facing verso Beckett suggests the deletion of the phrase 'sagte sie' and the replacement of 'kann' by 'könnte'. The sentence then should read: 'Beim Weggehen ['sagte sie' deleted], wie er bezeugen könnte [replacing 'kann'], wenn er noch lebt und es nicht vergessen hat, bei seinem Kommen u. [und] Gehen auf Erden, beim Leute-Hereinlassen u. [und] Leute-Hinausbringen, gab sie zu bestehen [replacing the original 'ungefähr'], dass sie mich kaltmachen würde.' The 'ungefähr' of the German translation is not in the *Red Nb* at all. Beckett's revisions tighten the syntax. 'Sagte sie' can be eliminated because of 'gab sie zu bestehen' ('she confessed'). The 'könnte' replacement of 'kann' is a switch to the conditional and agrees with 'wenn er noch lebt' ('if he is still alive'). In *Spiel* (SB) the 'sagte sie' is cut and 'könnte' replaced 'kann' as in the *Red Nb*, but it appears that Beckett wanted the 'gab sie zu verstehen' (that is, instead of 'zu bestehen') to replace the 'sagte sie'. The 'ungefähr' is deleted in *Spiel* (SB), p. 245, but no replacement is offered.

Fol. 14r

F2, 4 – Beckett's revision eliminated the first 'doch' in this speech. The German translation has 'es ist doch . . .' The revision (or omission), however, does *not* appear in *Spiel* (SB),p. 245.
F2, 5 – Beckett replaces the original German phrase 'keine Gefahr' ('no danger') with 'nicht die Gefahr' ('not danger'). The latter is just not as certain about the complete absence of danger. The 'für die' is eliminated in the *Red Nb* as well. The revision appears in *Spiel* (SB), p. 247.

Beckett again replaced the 'Tour' of the German translation with 'Masche' (see also F1, 2). The revision appears in *Spiel* (SB), p. 247.
F2, 6 – Beckett at first used the German translation in the *Red Nb*, 'Leckte sich die Lippen' ('licked her lips'), but then revised it to 'Sich die Lippen leckend' ('licking her lips') on the facing verso. This revision appears in *Spiel* (SB), p. 247.

Beckett noted on the facing verso the 'sagte sie' he omitted or missed from the German translation 'müssen, sagte sie'.
F2, 7 – Originally, Beckett had accepted the German translation for the *Red Nb*: 'Was bedeutete, dass er zu ihr zurückgekehrt war' ('Which meant that he had gone back to her'). On the facing verso, however, he suggested an alternate phrasing, 'Das hiess, er war zu ihr zurückgekehrt' ('That meant he had gone back to her'). This revision appears in *Spiel* (SB), p. 249.

F2, 8 – For the original German translation 'Grasmäher', Beckett substituted 'Rasenmäher' in the *Red Nb*. 'Rasen' suggests lawn and a residential area, which one would more likely cut with a handmower; 'grass' suggests more open country. *Spiel* (SB), however, retained 'Grasmäher', p. 249.

Beckett replaced the German translation 'Ich fiel ihm ins Wort' ('I interrupted him') with 'Ich schnitt ihm das Wort ab' ('I cut him off') in the *Red Nb*. This revision, however, does not appear in *Spiel* (SB), p. 249.

On the facing verso, Beckett marked a deletion sign to indicate that the 'dass ich' ('that I'), which he had previously put in parentheses, should be cut. The parenthesis around 'hätte' suggests that Beckett was uncertain about its revision from 'habe'. In *Spiel* (SB), p. 249, he cut the 'dass ich' and revised the 'habe' to 'hätte' so that the final 'hätte' could be cut.

Fol. 15r

F2, 11 – The German text has 'das Freudenfeuer', which Beckett revised in the *Red Nb* to 'das Müllfeuer'. The English text has 'bonfire', which is 'Freudenfeuer' in German, but bonfires burn brightly. It makes sense to throw old clothes on a 'Müllfeuer'. 'Müll' is rubbish. 'Das Müllfeuer schwelte', then, more accurately reflects that the rubbish fire smouldered. 'Schwelen' is to burn without flame. This revision, however, does not appear in *Spiel* (SB), p. 253.
F2, chorus – Beckett replaced the contraction in the German translation, 'Ich sag'', with 'Ich sagte'. This revision, however, does not appear in *Spiel* (SB), p. 253.
F2, 1 – As previous note.
F2, 3 – Beckett originally accepted the German translation, 'mich satt haben' ('to be filled up'). But on the facing verso he replaced it with 'meiner müde' ('tired of me'). The original German suggests a surfeit and tends towards the vulgar. On the other hand, 'meiner müde' is slightly poetic; it contains the feeling of weariness. This revision appears in *Spiel* (SB), p. 255.
F2, 4 – Beckett deleted 'Wirst du' ('you will') in both lines. The effect was to continue what F2 has just said. The deletion creates the effect of listing, of cataloguing. This revision appears in *Spiel* (SB), p. 255.

Beckett deleted the 'dir' in the German translation, 'um dir jemand'. This revision, however, does not appear in *Spiel* (SB), p. 255.

Fol. 16r

F2, 6 – In the *Red Nb* Beckett circled the word 'bringen' ('to bring') of the German translation. On the facing verso he seemed to have been searching for the German equivalent of 'blaze', as in the English colloquialism, 'blaze me clean out of my wits'. He seems to have settled on 'brennen' ('to burn'). *Spiel* (SB), p. 257, substitutes 'ausbrennen' ('to burn out' or 'scorch') and deletes the 'um' as well.

F2, 9 – Beckett replaced 'denselben' of the German translation with 'gleichen'. Both mean 'the same' but 'gleich' is closer to 'similar' or 'the same kind'. This revision appears in *Spiel* (SB), p. 259.

F2, 10 – A whole sentence, 'Sieht irgend jemand mich an?' ('Is anyone looking at me?'), is missing or was deleted from this speech. It, however, appears in the German text after the second sentence. This appears to be an omission rather than an excision since no change was made in *Spiel* (SB), p. 259.

F2, 11 – Beckett questioned the ellipsis in this section, but it remains in *Spiel* (SB), p. 259.

Fol. 17r

F2, 14 – Beckett at first accepted the German translation 'Die ihre sauren Küsse küssen' ('Those who kiss their sour kisses'). On the facing verso, however, he revised the sentence to 'Ihre sauren Küsse küssend' ('Their sour kisses kissing'). This revision appears in *Spiel* (SB), p. 261.

F2, 15 – Beckett at first accepted the German translation 'wenn du ausgehst?' but on the facing verso he suggested 'erlischst' as a replacement for 'ausgehst'. Beckett's change, 'wenn du erlischst?' ('erlöschen' – 'to die down', as a flame dies) is more poetic; it has the idea of ceasing to exist about it; 'ausgehen' is more pedestrian. Beckett also suggested that the change echoes an earlier use of 'erlöschen' in **F2, 3** of part II. This revision appears in *Spiel* (SB), p. 261, but uncharacteristically in the centre margin.

The German translation has 'sieben' ('to sift'), which Beckett replaced with 'sondern' ('to separate', as the good from the bad). This revision appears in *Spiel* (SB), p. 261.

F2, 16 – Of the German translation 'glühend heissen' Beckett noted on the facing verso 'one word', but 'glühendheissen' is rather clumsy German. By trying to make those two words one, Beckett seems to have wanted to increase the amount of 'glühen' ('glowing', from heat). The revision, however, does not appear in *Spiel* (SB), p. 263.

F2, 17 – On the facing verso Beckett replaces the German translation 'Halt' with the more colloquial and universal, at least after the Second World War, 'Stop'. The revision, however, does not appear in *Spiel* (SB), p. 267.

Fol. 19r

M, 1 – A minor adjustment as Beckett replaced the apostrophe with the 'e' in the German translation, 'ich schneid''. The *Red Nb* then reads, 'ich schneide'. The revision does not appear in *Spiel* (SB), p. 243.
M, 3 – The German translation and the *Red Nb* contain 'dass ich nicht ohne sie leben könne' ('that I could not live without her'). On the facing verso Beckett suggested an alternative, 'ich könne ohne sie nicht leben' ('I could not live without her'). The change seems simply to be less cumbersome German and more direct speech. He also deleted the 'ihr' just before the above phrase. Both revisions appear in *Spiel* (SB), p. 245.

Fol. 20r

M, 5 – The German translation and the *Red Nb* contain 'Ich mag nicht' ('I don't like it'). On the facing verso Beckett suggested the alternative 'Ich will nicht' ('I don't want it' or 'I won't have it'). Beckett's change made the pronouncement much more emphatic. *Spiel* (SB) contains this revision and another not in the *Red Nb*, p. 247.
M, 6 – Beckett replaced the German translation 'lernt daraus' ('take a lesson') with the less stuffy 'merkt euch eins' ('take note'). This change is included in *Spiel* (SB) as 'macht euch eins', p. 249.
M, 7 – Beckett at first rejected the wording of the German translation, replacing 'Ruck' with 'Druck' (which can be a pressing of something). He then scratched it out and returned to the wording of the German translation by adding 'Ruck' (which is a push, or intermittent pushing) on the facing verso. *Spiel* (SB) retains 'Ruck', p. 249.

Fol. 21r

M, 8 – Both German text and notebook have 'das Alte', which Beckett circled and queried on the verso. In *Spiel* (SB) 'Alte' is revised to 'Vergangene', p. 251.
M, 1 – Again Beckett queried the German phrasing without posing an alternative in the *Red Nb*. *Spiel* (SB) offers no alternative. In *Spiel* (WA), however, the following revision is made: 'drängte es mich, Gott zu danken' is revised to 'dankte ich sogar, Gott', p. 253.
M, 2 – As in previous note.

Fol. 22r

M, 11 – Both the German translation and the *Red Nb* have 'Scheibchen Zitrone' ('slice of lemon'). Beckett's English/German facing verso note reads, 'squeeze Tröpfchen' ('squeezed tiny drop'). The new version would read, 'nicht mal ein gepresstes Tröpfchen Zitrone'. The earlier version, 'Scheibchen Zitrone', doesn't connote the infinitesmal amount of 'gepresstes Tröpfchen'. The revision appears in *Spiel* (SB), p. 259.
M, 12 – As previous note.
M, 14 – Both the German translation and the *Red Nb* contain 'Ich trank immer am liebsten Liptons' ('I always preferred to drink Lipton's'). Beckett's two changes make the sentence 'Ich persönlich trank immer lieber Liptons' ('I, personally, liked to drink Lipton's more'). The 'ich persönlich' sets M apart from the two women, as in 'now I, myself . . .' The only change in *Spiel* (SB) is to add the 'persönlich', p. 261.
M, 15 – The German text and the *Red Nb* contain 'wie gesegnet' ('how blessed'). Beckett altered the phrase with a facing verso revision to 'wie selig' ('however holy'). Beckett's change was from the more formal 'gesegnet' ('blessed') to 'selig' (which is the state one gets into after drinking just a little, or, even without drink, as in 'selige Stimmung', a 'good mood' or even 'blissful'). This revision appears in *Spiel* (SB), p. 261.

Fol. 23r

M, 16 – On the facing verso Beckett cuts the 'Ich' from the German translation and *Red Nb* entry, 'Ich bedaure sie' ('I feel sorry for them'). Beckett's change produced the clipped 'Bedaure sie' ('Feel sorry for them'). The revision is apparently missed in *Spiel* (SB) but appears in *Spiel* (WA), p. 261.
M, 18 – In a facing verso notation Beckett contemplated adding a 'ver–' or a 'nach–' to the 'Warum' at the end of this speech. *Spiel* (SB), includes the 'ver–', p. 263.
M, 19 – On the facing verso Beckett contemplated a number of alternatives for dimness in 'Warum das Dämmerlicht?' The English is, simply, 'Why go down?' He contemplated 'Dämmern' or 'twilight'; 'redunkeln', 'to make dark'; and 'nachlassen', 'to make dark'. *Spiel* (SB) includes 'Dämmern', p. 263.
M, 20 – Again Beckett was unhappy about the translation for the quality of the light. The German text and the *Red Nb* read, 'Warum mich nicht unverwandt u. [und] unablässig anstrahlen?' ('Why not glare at me steadfast and without

interruption?'). Beckett would change 'unverwandt und' and replace it with 'rastlos' ('restless'), although Beckett has a '?' after his suggested change. 'Unverwandt' is 'steadfast and without change', whereas 'rastlos' suggests a hectic quality. Beckett may well have noticed that 'unverwandt und unablässig' are redundant. *Spiel* (SB) contains 'endlos' for the pair, p. 263.

The German translation has 'es für dich herausbrechen' ('to vomit it up for you'); Beckett's change in the *Red Nb* was 'damit herausrücken' ('to let it come out'). This revision appears in *Spiel* (SB), p. 263, where Beckett also added a 'Ver–' to the end of the speech to anticipate the '–zeihung' of M's next speech. This addition conforms with the broken 'Par–' '–don' of the English text.

M, 23 – Beckett corrected the 'erwachen' of the German text to 'erwachten'. This revision appears in *Spiel* (SB), p. 265.

Fol. 24r

M, 30 – Both the German text and the *Red Nb* have: 'Das sich über mir öffnet und schliesst' ('That opens and closes above me'). On the facing verso Beckett suggested, 'Sich über mir öffnend und schliessend' ('Opening and closing above me.') The change suggests a present that goes on forever. This revision appears in *Spiel* (SB), p. 267.

Structural and Thematic Notes

1 – After revising the German text of *Spiel* by writing it out entirely in the *Red Nb* and making revisions to a copy of the German text, *Spiel* (SB), Beckett returned to the empty pages at the beginning of the *Red Nb* to begin re-examining the patterns of dialogue in that material he had just copied out as a continuous narrative for each of his three characters, his 'continuity' manuscript. On the recto Beckett outlined the pattern of 32 speeches to part I and 81 speeches to part II. On the verso he broke the speeches down according to whether they discussed the character's present situation or focused on the other characters in this love (or lust) triangle. These diagrams are duplicated by Beckett in the *Brown Nb* (with only slight variation). (See also notes 3 and 8 to the *Red Nb*.)

2 – In the *Brown Nb* Beckett added a 'da' after 'Morgens' here and in F2's first individual speech which follows, to parallel the phrasing in **F1, 3**.

3 – Here Beckett began a series of thematic groupings, which he refined when he copies it into the *Brown Nb*. (See also note 19 to the *Brown Nb*.)

4 – An outline of part I of *Spiel* which allowed Beckett to work out the pattern of monologues and dialogues on the facing verso. (See also note 14 to the *Brown Nb.*)

5 – A further development of the structure of part I, which features monologues, dialogues and assorted themes. The opening and closing phrases of each of these speeches is outlined in German on the facing verso. (See also note 19 to the *Brown Nb.*)

6 – Here Beckett outlined the location and number of M's hiccups in the play.

7 – This is, of course, M's speech 13 in part II of the play.

8 – The original German text reads, 'dich herausbrechen', which Beckett revised in *Spiel* (SB). He also added the first syllable of 'Verzeihung' to the end of this speech so that the 'Pardon' could be broken as it was in the English text.

9 – This is an outline of part II of *Spiel.*

10 – The small chorus here is the one just after the first '*Blackout. Five seconds. Strong spots simultaneously on three faces.*' The short chorus introduced the first phrase in each of the characters' opening speeches simultaneously. It is not cut in *Spiel* (SB), which was devoted exclusively to textual changes as Beckett was rewriting the text into the *Red Nb*, but it is cut in Asmus's working copy of the text, *Spiel* (WA). In the *Brown Nb* Beckett suggested that the cut from the long chorus (with weak spots) directly to the first part of the play (which Beckett calls 'individual I') would be impossible. The problem may simply be the use of plural 'spots'. In the *Brown Nb* Beckett further noted as a technical feature, 'Provoke A & B not by triple spot but by general light on 3 [characters]?'

11 – Beckett's point here was that the big chorus that opens the play is actually an introduction to the next round of the canon. This suggests that the beginning we are watching is already a repetition.

12 – Outline of beginning and ending phrases of each speech in part II of *Spiel*, with revisions of dialogue. The heavy underscoring represents the division of part II into four subsections. In the *Brown Nb* Beckett combined the last two subsections so that part II is divided into three, not four, subsections.

13 – The German text has 'Verlor ich–' here.

14 – The number here apparently should be '15'.

SPIEL
CLAIREFONTAINE

FACSIMILE OF BECKETT'S PRODUCTION NOTEBOOK WITH TRANSCRIPTION AND TRANSLATION

Note on Manuscript II: The Brown Notebook

The second *Spiel* notebook is in a brown, 44 folio spiral notebook measuring 17 × 10.5 cm., on deposit at the University of Reading Samuel Beckett Archive, MS 1730. The front cover includes a small rectangular box for labelling in which Beckett wrote 'SPIEL'. The lower right-hand corner contains an inverted triangle with a stylized drawing of a water-bearer, above which is printed 'Clairefontaine'. The back cover bears this same logo, centred, but without the word 'Clairefontaine'. The *Spiel* notes begin on the verso of folio 1 and continue to the recto of folio 11.

Inverting the notebook, Beckett wrote three titles on the back cover: *Kommen u. Gehen* (*Come and Go*), *Eh Joe*, and *Happy Days*. Beckett began notes to *Kommen und Gehen*, which would be on the programme with *Spiel* in 1978 at the Schiller-Theater (the director of record, however, was Walter Asmus), on the recto of folio 1 if one were foliating from the back, and they continue to the recto of folio 4. The *Eh Joe* notes for the 1979 Süddeutscher Rundfunk remake begin on the recto of folio 5 and continue to midway down the verso of folio 7. The *Happy Days* notes for the Royal Court production of 1979 pick up just below the *Eh Joe* notes on the verso of folio 7. The *Happy Days* section is separately paginated, beginning on folio 8 with page 3; Beckett must, therefore, have considered the inside back cover as page 1 and the verso of folio 7 as page 2. Beckett's pagination continues from 3 to 55, or to the recto of folio 34, the verso of which contains the last notes to *Spiel* – upside down, of course, reading this way. (Thus the final *Spiel* notes on the recto of folio 11, counting from the front, are also on the verso of folio 34 if one counts from the rear.) Beckett also inserted two pieces of heavy red tape to divide the notes, one on folio 34 to separate *Happy Days* from *Spiel*, and one on folio 7 to separate *Eh Joe* from *Happy Days*. (For additional details see also *Happy Days: The Production Notebook of Samuel Beckett*, edited with an introduction and notes by James Knowlson [London: Faber and Faber Ltd, 1985]).

Interpolations, usually English translations, are bracketed. The bracketed English throughout the notebook, however, is not necessarily a literal translation of the German but the equivalent phrase from Beckett's English text. Variations from the trilingual German edition, *Samuel Beckett: Dramatische Dichtungen in drei Sprachen* (Suhrkamp Verlag, Frankfurt am Main, 1981), are also indicated within square brackets. Cancelled text is indicated by angle brackets, <>.

First ex. with M. No dialogue.
" visit from F1. F1's appearance.
" ex. with F1.
" visit from F1 contd. Smell.
Solo. Sleuth. Plato.
First ex. with F1 contd.
" Visit from F1 concld. Gustav.
" ex. with F1 ". Smell.
Second ex. with M. Confession. No dialogue.
Solo. Sleuth.
First ex. with M.
Solo. Wonderment
First ex. with M concld. Plato.
Second " " " F2. Gustav.
Second " " M concld (assuming pardon immediate).
" visit from F1. Gustav. No dialogue
" ex. with F1. Confession. No dialogue.
" visit to F2
Third ex. with M
Solo. F2's appearance.
Third ex. with M contd.
Solo. F2's appearance concld.
Third ex. with F2 (assuming part of showdown)
" " " " concld. (" " " ")
Solo. Home bliss.
Third exchange with F1. Pillow.
Solo. Smell.
Solo. M gone.
Solo. Enough.
Solo. M gone. Third visit to F2. F2 gone.
Solo. Enough.
Solo. Bonfire

I

1 F1 Ich sagte
1 F2 Eines Morgens
1 M Wir waren
2 F2 Woran
2 F1 obgleich
2 M Worüber
3 F2 Da ich
3 M Sie war nicht
3 F1 Man stelle
4 M Sie hegte
4 F2 Warum
4 F1 Ich gebe zu
5 F2 Was zwischen
5 M Das nächste
5 F1 Dann vergab
6 F2 Sie kam
6 M Dann kriegte
6 F1 als ich
7 F2 als er wiederkam
7 F1 Pudding
8 F2 Er redete
8 F1 Waden
7 M als ich sie
9 F2 Es gab nur
9 F1 Er war
8 M Zu Hause
10 F1 Dann roch
10 F2 als er nicht
9 M Schliesslich
11 F1 Ehe ich
10 M Ich konnte
11 F2 Ich packte

F1 11
F2 11
M 10

1300 approx

First[1] ex. [exchange] with M. No dialogue.
" visit from F1. F1's appearance.
" ex. [exchange] with F1.
" visit from F1 contd [continued]. Smell.
Solo. Sleuth. Plato.
First ex. [exchange] with F1 contd.
" visit from F1 concld [concluded]. Gustav.
" ex. [exchange] with F1 " . Smell.
Second ex. [exchange] with M. Confession. No dialogue.
Solo. Sleuth.
First ex. [exchange] with M.
Solo. Wonderment
First ex. [exchange] with M concld [concluded]. Plato.
Second " " " F2. Gustav.
Second " " M concld (assuming pardon immediate). No dialogue
" visit from F1. Gustav.
" ex. [exchange] with F1. Confession. No dialogue.
" visit to F2
Third ex. [exchange] with M
Solo. F2's appearance.
Third ex. with M cont [continued, *revised from* concld].
Solo. F2's appearance concld [concluded].
Third ex. [exchange] with F2 (assuming part of showdown)
" " " " concld. [concluded] (" " " ")
Solo. Home bliss.
Third exchange with F1. Pillow.
Solo. Smell.
Solo. M gone.
Solo. Enough.
Solo. M gone. Third visit to F2. F2 gone.
Solo. Enough.
Solo. Bonfire.

[fol. 2r]

I²

F1 11
F2 11
M 10

1 F1 Ich sagte [I said]
1 F2 Eines Morgens [One morning]
1 M Wir waren [We were not long]
2 F2 Wovon [What are you]
2 F1 Obgleich [Though]
2 M Worüber [What have you]
3 F2 Da ich [Fearing she was]
3 M Sie war nicht [She was not]
3 F1 Man stelle [Judge then]
4 M Sie hegte [*revised from* hetzte] [She put]
4 F2 Warum [Why]
4 F1 Ich gebe zu [I confess my]
5 F2 Was zwischen (uns) [Anything between us]
5 M Das nächste [The next thing]
5 F1 Dann vergab [*revised from* Dann verzieh] [Then I forgave]
6 F2 Sie kam [She came]
6 M Dann kriegte [Then I got frightened]
6 F1 Als ich [When I was satisfied]
7 F2 Als er wiederkam [When he came again]
7 F1 Pudding [*revised from* Puddinggesicht] [Pudding face]
8 F2 Er redete [He went on]
8 F1 Waden [Calves]
7 M Als ich sie [When I saw her again]
9 F2 Es gab nur [The only solution]
9 F1 Er war [So he was]
8 M Zu Hause [Zuhause] [At home]
10 F1 Dann roch [Then I began]
10 F2 Als er nicht [When he stopped coming]
9 M Schliesslich [Finally] 1300 approx
11 F1 Ehe ich [Before I]
10 M Ich konnte [I simply could]
11 F2 Ich packte [I made]

F1:	1 – 14 ·	Present 1	– 14
	15 – 19 ·	F2/M	– 5
	20 – 25 ·	Present 2	– 6
F2:	1 – 10	Present 1	– 10
	11 – 14	F1/M	– 4
	15 – 25	Present 2	– 11
M:	1 – 8	Present 1	– 8
	9 – 16	F1/F2	– 8
	17 – 31	Present 2	– 15

		Begins	ends
1st 8	1st 4	M Bei diesem	F1 Lass mich
	2nd "	" Es wird	M Vielleicht sind sie
2nd "	3rd "	F1 Aber ich	F2 Die Ärmste
	4th "	M Ich persönlich	F2 Wie das Rollen
3rd "	5th "	F2 Halt	M Wenn man bedenkt
	6th "	F2 Bin ich nicht	F1 Dürstend
Final 3		M Solche Ph.	M Werde ich überhaupt

II

1 M bei diesem	9 F1 sollte	21 F2 Bin ich
1 F1 Gnade	11 F2 ist mein	19 F1 Die Ärmste
1 F2 Ich sage	10 F1 Meine	23 M Nie zusammen
2 F1 Oder du	13 M Treffen	20 F1 Büssen.
2 M aus ja	11 F1 Wenn	22 F2 Ich sagte
2 F2 Weniger	12 F2 Die	24 M eine Kleine
3 M dachte	14 M Ich	21 F1 Stille
3 F2 Wenn du	12 F1 u. das	25 M eine Kleine
3 F1 höllisches	13 F2 Sie	22 F1 Höllisches
4 M Frieden	13 F1 Ich kann	23 F2 Leicht
4 F2 Mich	14 F2 Ihre	26 M Wir hatten
4 F1 Lass mich	15 M Bedaure	23 F1 Dürstend
5 M Es wird	14 F1 Ich kann	27 M Solche Ph.
5 F2 andererseits	16 M bedaure	24 F2 Ich glaube nicht
6 M oh gewiss	15 F2 Was	24 F1 Ja, u. alles
5 F1 Sollte es	17 M Verheim-	28 M Und nun
6 F2 Du könntest	15 F1 Sie war	25 F1 Müde des Spiels
7 M Ich weiss	16 F2 Wie	29 M Schauend
6 F1 Sollte es	17 F2 Halt	25 F2 Lachen 2
7 F2 nicht wahr	18 M Verlor	30 M Bloss auge
8 M all dies, wann wird	18 F2 u. dabei	31 M Werde ich
7 F1 Ich kann	16 F1 Vielleicht	
8 F2 aber ich	19 M Warum	
9 M Vielleicht	19 F2 Ich weiss	F1 12 openings
8 F1 aber ich	17 F1 Vielleicht	M 11 "
10 M Vielleicht	20 M Warum	F2 4 "
9 F2 Ich nehme	20 F2 Nein	
11 M Vielleicht	21 M Zeihung	1 Bei diesem M
10 F2 Hörst	18 F1 Weit	25 aber ich habe F1
12 M Nicht mal	22 M Wenn	49 Halt F2
1000 approx.	F1 25 F2 25 M 31	73 Solche M

[*fol. 2v*]

F1:[3]	1–14 –	Present 1	–	14
	15–19 –	F2/M	–	5
	20–25 –	Present 2	–	6
F2:	1–10 –	Present 1	–	10
	11–14 –	F1/M	–	4
	15–25 –	Present 2	–	11
M:	1–8 –	Present 1	–	8
	9–16 –	F1/F2	–	8
	17–31 –	Present 2	–	15

			Begins[4]		ends
1st 8	1st 4	M	Bei diesem [When first]	F1	Lass mich [Get off me]
	2nd "	"	Es wird [It will come]	M	Vielleicht sind sie [Perhaps they have]
2nd "	3rd "	F1	Aber ich [But I have]	F2	Die Ärmste [That poor creature]
	4th "	M	Ich persönlich[5] [Personally I]	F2	Wie das Rollen [Like dragging a great roller]
3rd "	5th "	F2	Halt [Kill it][6]	M	Wenn man bedenkt [To think we were]
	6th "	F2	Bin ich nicht [Am I not]	F1	Dürstend [Dying][7]
Final	3	M	Solche Ph. [Phantastereien] [Such fantasies]	M	Werde ich überhaupt [Am I as much as]

II[8]

1 M bei diesem 1	9 F1 sollte 11	21 F2 Bin ich 21
1 F1 Gnade	11 F2 ist mein	19 F1 Die Ärmste
1 F2 Ich sage	10 F1 Meine	23 M Nie zuzammen [*recte* zusammen]
2 F1 Oder du 2	13 M Treffen 12	20 F1 Büssen 22
2 M aus ja	11 F1 Wenn	22 F2 Ich sagte
2 F2 Weniger	12 F2 Die	24 M eine kleine
3 M dachte 3	14 M Ich 13	21 F1 Stille 23
3 F2 Wenn du	12 F1 U. [und] das	25 M eine kleine
3 F1 höllisches	13 F2 Sie	22 F1 Höllisches
4 M Frieden 4	13 F1 Ich kann	23 F2 Leicht 24
4 F2 Mich	14 F2 Ihre	26 M Wir hatten
4 F1 Lass mich	15 M Bedaure	23 F1 Dürstend
5 M Es wird 5	14 F1 Ich kann 15	27 M Solche Ph. [Phantastereien] 25
5 F2 andererseits	16 M bedaure	24 F2 Ich glaube nicht
6 M Oh gewiss	15 F2 Was	24 F1 Ja, u. [und] alles
5 F1 Sollte es 6	17 M Verheim– 16	28 M Und nun 26
6 F2 Du könntest [*erasure*]	15 F1 Sie war	25 F1 Müde des Spiels
7 M Ich weiss	16 F2 Wie	29 M Schauend
6 F1 Sollte es 7	17 F2 <stop> Halt 17	25 F2 Lachen 2 27
7 F2 nicht wahr	18 M Verlor	30 M Bloss Auge
8 M all dies Wann wird	18 F2 u. [und] dabei	31 M Werde ich
7 F1 Ich kann 8	16 F1 Vielleicht 18	
8 F2 aber ich	19 M Warum	
9 M Vielleicht	19 F2 Ich weiss	F1 12 openings[9]
8 F1 Aber ich 9	17 F1 Vielleicht	M 11 "
10 M Vielleicht	20 M Warum	F2 4 "
9 F2 Ich nehme	20 F2 Nein	
11 M Vielleicht 10	21 M Zeihung 20	1[10] Bei diesem M
10 F2 Hörst	18 F1 Weit	25 aber ich habe F1
12 M Nicht mal	22 M Wenn	49 Halt F2
		73 Solche M
	F1 25[11]	81
1000 approx[12]	F2 25	
	M 31	

Translation of transcription of fol. 3r appears on p. 155.

II[8]

1 M When first 1	9 F1 Is it 11	21 F2 Am I not 21
1 F1 Mercy	11 F2 Is my	19 F1 Poor creature
1 F2 To say I	10 F1 Bite off	23 M Never woke together
2 F1 Or you will 2	13 M Meet 12	20 F1 Penitence 22
2 M Down	11 F1 If only	22 F2 I say
2 F2 Less confused	12 F2 That	24 M A little
3 M I thought 3	14 M Personally 13	21 F1 Silence 23
3 F2 When you	12 F1 And that	25 M A little
3 F1 Hellish	13 F2 They	22 F1 Hellish
4 M Peace 4	13 F1 I can't	23 F2 A shade gone 24
4 F2 Give me up	14 F2 Kissing	26 M We were not
4 F1 Get off me	15 M I pity	23 F1 Dying
5 M It will come 5	14 F1 I can't 15	27 M Such fantasies 25
5 F2 On the other hand	16 M I pity	24 F2 I doubt it
6 M Oh of course	15 F2 What	24 F1 Yes and the
5 F1 Is it that 6	17 M Am I 16	28 M And now 26
6 F2 you might [*erasure*]	15 F1 She had	25 F1 Weary of playing
7 M I know	16 F2 Like	29 M Looking
6 F1 Is that it 7	17 F2 Kill it– 17	25 F2 *Laughter* 2 27
7 F2 Mightn't you	18 M Have I	30 M Mere eye
8 M All this when will all	18 F2 And you	31 M Am I as much
7 F1 I can 8	16 F1 Perhaps 18	
8 F2 But I doubt it	19 M Why	
9 M Perhaps	19 F2 I don't know	F1 12 openings[9]
8 F1 But I have 9	17 F1 Perhaps	M 11 "
10 M Perhaps	20 M Why	F2 4 "
9 F2 No doubt	20 F2 No	
11 M Perhaps 10	21 M –don 20	1[10] When first M
10 F2 Are you	18 F1 Gazing	25 But I doubt F1
12 M not even	22 M To think	49 Kill it F2
		73 Such M
		81

F1 25[11]
F2 25
M 31

1000 approx[12]

I

Duo

F1/F2	F2	1, 2, 3, 6	4 - 2 meetings
F1/M	F1	1, 3, 5	8 - 3 "
	M	1, 2, 3, 6, 8	
F2/M	F2	4, 5, 7, 8, 9	7 - 3 "
	M	5, 7	
			19

Solo

F1	2, 4, 6, 7, 8, 9, 10, 11	
F2	10, 11	13
M	4, 9, 10	
		32

[*fol. 3v*]

[*fol. 4r*]

I[13]

Duo

F1/F2	F2 [*erasure*]	1, 2, 3, 6	4 – 2 meetings
F1/M	F1	1, 3, 5	8 – 3 "
	M	1, 2, 3, 6, 8	
F2/M	F2	4, 5, 7, 8, 9	7 – 3 "
	M	5, 7	—
			19

Solo

F1	2, 4, 6, 7, 8, 9, 10, 11	
F2	10, 11	13
M	4, 9, 10	—
		32

F1

ja seltsam
lieber Dunkel
u. je dunkler
je schlimmer
bis alles Dunkel
dann alles gut
eine Zeitlang
doch es wird kommen
die Zeit wird kommen
das Ding ist da
du wirst es sehen
mich lassen
verlassen
alles dunkel
alles still
alles vorbei
ausgelöscht

F2

ja vielleicht
leicht verwirrt
nehm' ich an
könnte man sagen
armes Ding
leicht verwirrt
nur ganz leicht
im Verstand
Lachen
nur ganz leicht
aber ich glaube nicht
ich glaube nicht
nicht ernstlich
mir fehlt nichts
noch gar nichts
tu' mein Bestes
was ich kann

M

ja Frieden
dachte man
alles aus
alle Qual
alles wie
nie gewesen
es wird kommen
Schluckauf Verzeihung
dies hat keinen Sinn
oh ich weiss
immerhin
dachte man
Frieden ... ich meine
nicht nur
alles vorbei
sondern wie ...
nie gewesen

[*fol. 4v*]

[*fol. 5r*]

F1[14]
Ja seltsam
[Yes, strange,]
lieber Dunkel
[darkness best,]
u. [und] je dunkler
[and the darker]
je schlimmer
[the worse,]
bis alles Dunkel
[till all dark,]
dann alles gut
[then all well,]
eine Zeitlang
[for the time,]
doch es wird kommen
[but it will come,]
die Zeit wird kommen
[the time will come,]
das Ding ist da[15]
[the thing is there,]
du wirst es sehen[16]
[you'll see,]
mich lassen
[get off me,]
verlassen
[keep off me,][17]
alles dunkel
[all dark,]
alles still
[all still,]
alles vorbei
[all over,]
ausgelöscht
[wiped out–]

F2
Ja vielleicht
[Yes, perhaps,]
leicht verwirrt
[a shade gone,]
nehm' ich an
[I suppose,]
könnte man sagen
[some might say,]
armes Ding
[poor thing,]
leicht verwirrt
[a shade gone,]
nur ganz leicht
[just a shade,]
im Verstand
[in the head–]
Lachen
[*Faint wild laugh.*]
mir ganz leicht
[– just a shade,]
aber ich glaube nicht
[but I doubt it,]
ich glaube nicht
[*I* doubt it,]
nicht erns[t]lich
[not really,]
mir fehlt nichts
[I'm all right,]
noch gar nichts
[still all right,]
tu' mein Bestes
[do my best,]
was ich kann
[all I can–]

M
Ja Frieden [Friede]
[Yes, peace,]
dachte man
[one assumed,]
alles aus
[all out,]
alle Qual
[all the pain,]
alles wie
[all as if . . .]
nie gewesen
[never been,]
es wird kommen
[it will come–]
Schluckauf–Verzeihung
[*Hiccup.*–pardon,]
dies hat keinen Sinn
[no sense in this,]
Oh ich weiss
[oh I know . . .]
immerhin
[none the less,]
dachte man
[one assumed,]
Frieden . . . ich meine
[peace . . . I mean . . .]
nicht nur
[not merely]
alles vorbei
[all over,]
sondern wie . . .
[but as if . . .]
nie gewesen
[never been–]

Being seen?

F1 Chor: Das Ding ist da ... du wirst es sehen

1 Du hast mich nicht gesehen. Aber du wirst mich sehen

24 Alles ist da ... Du wirst es sehen

F2 10 Sieht irgend jemand mich an?

M 29 Schauend nach etwas. Nicht einmal

31 Werde ich überhaupt gesehen

Being heard?

F1 12 alles fällt ... ins Leere

F2 10 Hörst du mir zu? Hört irgend jemand mir zu?

M 28-30 Bloss Auge ... nur schauend

What being demanded?

F1 5 Wahrheit?

7 etwas, was ich sagen muss?

9 " anderes als sprechen. Weinen?

12 Nichts?

20 Büsse? Sühne?

M 17/18 Something he his hiding? Has lost?

20 Some truth in his face? Eyes

Will eye weary?

F1 2 Du wirst meiner müde ...
mich lassen

24/5 Du wirst müde werden. Müde
des Spiels mit mir.

F2 3/4 Wirst meiner müde u. erlöschen..
endgültig. Mich aufgeben.

Meaninglessness

F1 11 Wenn ich nur denken könnte, dies hat
keinen Sinn.

F2 9 den Fehler, nach Sinn zu suchen,
wo möglicherweise keiner ist

M chor: dies hat keinen Sinn

5 " " " " (Zukunft)

8 nichts anderes als Spiel

Loss of reason

F1 7/10 Mind still working. Erstaunlich

14 Er (Verstand) würde weichen müssen.

F2 Chor. Verwirrt - 23

2 weniger verwirrend

6 meinen Verstand ausbrennen

21/5 aus dem Lot

M 20 Könnte schliesslich irrereden (cf. F1 6)

[*fol. 5v*]

Being seen?[18]

F1	chor:	Das Ding ist da . . . du wirst es sehen [the thing is there . . . you'll see it]
	1	Du hast mich nicht gesehen. Aber du wirst mich sehen [You haven't seen me. But you will.]
	24	Alles ist da . . . Du wirst es sehen [The whole thing is there . . . You'll see it.]
F2	10	Sieht irgend jemand mich an? [Is anyone looking at me?]
M	29	Schauend nach etwas. Nich [*recte* Nicht] einmal [Looking for something . . . Not even.]
	31	Werde ich überhaupt . . . gesehen [Am I as much as . . . being seen]

Being heard?

F1	12	alles fällt . . . ins Leere [all is falling . . . on empty air]
F2	10	Hörst du mir zu? Hört irgend jemand mir zu? [Are you listening to me? Is anyone listening to me?]
M	28–30	Bloss Auge . . . Nur schauend [mere eye . . . Just looking.]

What being demanded?

F1	5	Wahrheit? [Truth?]
	7	etwas, was ich sagen muss? [something I have to say?]

Transcription continues on p. 168.

[*fol. 6r*]

Will eye weary?

F1 2 Du wirst meiner müde . . .
Mich lassen.
[you will weary of me . . . Get off me.]

24/5 Du wirst müde werden. Müde
des Spiels mit mir.
[You'll weary of me. Weary of playing with me.]

F2 3/4 Wirst meiner müde u. [und] erlöschen . . .
endgültig. Mich aufgeben.
[You will tire of me and go out.]

Meaninglessness

F1 11 Wenn ich nur denken könnte, dies hat
keinen Sinn
[If only I could think, There is no sense in this]

F2 9 den [denselben] Fehler, nach Sinn zu suchen, wo möglicherweise
keiner ist.
[looking for sense where possibly there is none.]

M chor: Dies hat keinen Sinn
[no sense in this]

5 " " " " (Zukunft)
[There is no future in this]

8 nichts anderes als Spiel
[when will all this have been . . . just play]

Loss of Reason

F1 7/10 Mind still working. Erstaunlich [to be sure]

14 Er (Verstand) würde weichen müssen.
[It (the mind) would have to go.)

F2 Chor. Verwirrt – 23 [a shade gone]

2 Weniger verwirrend
[Less confusing.]

Transcription continues on p. 169.

9 " anderes als sprechen.
[other than utter]
Weinen?
[Weep?]

12 Nichts?
[Nothing?]

20 Büsse? Sühne?
[Penitence? Atonement?]

M 17/18 Something he is hiding? Has lost?
20 Some truth in his face? Eyes

6 meinen Verstand ausbrennen
[blaze me clean out of my wits]

21/5 aus dem Lot
[unhinged already]

M 20 könnte schliesslich irrereden (cf. F2 6)
[I might (finally) start to rave]

I

1 F1 1st ex. with M. No dialogue.
1 F2 1st visit F1. F1 described.
1 M 1st ex. with F1. Suicide threat.
2 F2 1st visit F1 contd. Smell.
2 F1 Solo. Sleuth. Plato.
2 M 1st ex. with F1 contd.
3 F2 1st visit F1 concld. Gustav. Threat to F2.
3 M 1st ex. with F1 concld. Smell. Embrace
3 F1 2nd ex. with M. Confession. No dialogue.
4 M Solo. Sleuth.
4 F2 1st ex. with M.
4 F1 Solo. Wonderment.
5 F2 1st ex. with M concld. Plato.
5 M 2nd ex. with F2. F1's threats. Gustav.
5 F1 2nd ex. with M concld. (assuming pardon immediate)
6 F2 2nd visit F1. M's confession. Gustav.
6 M 2nd ex. with F1. Confession. No dialogue.
6 F1 Solo. 2nd visit to F2. No dialogue.
7 F2 3rd exchange with M. His confession.
7 F1 Solo. F2 described.
8 F2 3rd ex. with M contd. Mower. ~~[illegible]~~.
8 F1 Solo. F2 described concld.
7 M 3rd ex. with F2. Mower. Embrace.
9 F2 3rd ex. with M concld. (assuming same occasion)
9 F1 Solo. Home bliss
8 M 3rd ex. with F1. Home bliss. Pillow.
10 F1 Solo. Smell.
10 F2 Solo. M gone.
9 M Solo. Enough.
11 F1 Solo. M gone. 3rd visit to F2. F2 gone
10 M Solo. Enough.
11 F2 Solo. Bonfire

[*fol. 6v*]

[*fol. 7r*]

I[19]

1 F1 1st ex. [exchange] with M. No dialogue.

1 F2 1st visit F1. F1 described.

1 M 1st ex. with F1. Suicide threat.

---

2 F2 1st visit F1 contd. [continued] Smell.

2 F1 Solo. Sleuth. Plato.

2 M 1st ex. with F1 contd.

---

3 F2 1st visit F1 concld [concluded]. Gustav. Threat to F2.

3 M 1st ex. with F1 concld. Smell. Embrace.

3 F1 2nd ex. with M. Confession. No dialogue.

---

4 M Solo. Sleuth.

4 F2 1st ex. with M.

4 F1 Solo. Wonderment.

---

5 F2 1st ex. with M. concld. Plato.

5 M 2nd ex. with F2. F1's threats. Gustav.

5 F1 2nd ex. with M concld. (assuming pardon immediate).

---

6 F2 2nd visit F1. M's confession. Gustav.

6 M 2nd ex. with F1. Confession. No dialogue.

6 F1 Solo. 2nd visit to F2. No dialogue.

---

7 F2 3rd exchange with M. His confession.

7 F1 Solo. F2 described.

8 F2 3rd ex. with M contd. Mower. [*erasure*]

---

8 F1 Solo. F2 described concld.

7 M 3rd ex. with F2. Mower. Embrace.

9 F2 3rd ex. with M concld. (assuming same occasion)

---

9 F1 Solo. Home bliss

8 M 3rd ex. with F1. Home bliss. Pillow.

10 F1 Solo. Smell.

---

10 F2 Solo. M gone.

9 M Solo. Enough.

11 F1 Solo. M gone. 3rd visit to F2. F2 gone.

---

10 M Solo. Enough.

11 F2 Solo. Bonfire

or possibly:

A
C Ich sagte ...
A
C Ich sagte ...
* A reduced
C Wir waren ...
or
1st 3 normal order reduced, e.g.
F1 Ich sagte zu ihm, Gib sie auf —
F2 Eines morgens ... schrie sie —
M Wir waren nicht lang zusammen —

* Cut on { dann alles gut / nur ganz leicht / nie gewesen

Is transition C1 – C2 possible without short chorus? No. But short ch. before C1 dispensable.

Finally

Long ch. Dim.
Indiv. 1. Strong.
Short ch. Dim.
Indiv. 2. "
Long ch. "
Indiv. 1. Strong
Short ch. Dim
Indiv. 2 "
Long ch. " (abridged)
Wir waren " (?)
→ geht aus

as if single gaze widening for 3

Cut short chorus. Straight from long chorus with faint (shots) (same intensity as individual II) to individual I, with strong spot.

(impossible)

A - Long chorus
B - Short "
C - Indiv. 1 - 2.

A
B
C - Ich sagte
A
B
C - Ich sagte
B
C - M: Wir waren . . .

I.e. change after repeat whereas normally repeat again.

Change: Long chorus cut, order of indiv. changed.

Question:
author decides to go no further?
Interrogator " " " " i.e. Kaufmann granted = Dark/silence?

Technical Provoke A + B not by triple shot but by general light on 3? Why? Because if 3 spots available why single pinpointing for indiv.?

[fol. 7v]

or possibly:[20] ←

A
C Ich sagte . . . [I said . . .]
A
C Ich sagte . . . [I said . . .]
*A reduced[21]
C Wir waren . . . [We were . . .]
or
1st 3 normal order reduced, e.g.
F1 Ich sagte zu ihm, Gib sie auf– [I said to him, Give her up.]
F2 Eines Morgens . . . schrie sie– [One morning . . . she screamed]
M Wir waren nicht lang zusammen– [We were not long together]

* cut on { dann alles gut [then all well]
nur ganz leicht [a shade gone]
nie gewesen [never been][22] }

Is transition C1–C2 possible without
short chorus? No. But short ch. [chorus] before
C1 dispensable.[23]

Finally[24]

long ch. [chorus]	Dim. [Diminished][25]
Indiv. [Individual] 1	Strong.
Short ch. [chorus]	Dim. [Diminished]
Indiv. 2	"
Long ch. [chorus]	"
Indiv. 1	Strong
Short ch. [chorus]	Dim [Diminished]
Indiv. 2	"
{ Long ch. [chorus]	" (abridged)
{ Wir waren [We were]	" (?)
→ geht (alles) aus [all is going out]	

as if single gaze widening for 3[26]

[*fol. 8r*]

<Cut short chorus. Straight from long chorus
with faint spots (same intensity as individual II)[27]
to individual I, with strong spot.>

impossible

A – Long chorus
B – Short "
C – Indiv. [Individual] 1–2

A
B
C – Ich sagte [I said]
A
B
C – Ich sagte [I said]
B
C – M: Wir waren . . . [We were . . .]

i.e. change after repeat whereas normally
repeat again.[28]

change: Long chorus cut, order of indiv. [individual]
changed.[29]

question:[30]
Author decides to go no further?
Interrogator " " " " " i.e. mercy
granted = Dark/silence?

Technical Provoke A & B not by triple spot
but by general light on 3? Why? Because
if 3 spots available why single [*erasure*] pivoting for indiv. [individual]?

Chor
Ebene

Iop.

M Nicht einmal ein Tröpfchen 220/1 ✓
because of nicht einmal 225

M warum mich nicht dauernd 223 ✓

F2 Nur ganz leicht 224 because of chor F2 ✓

F2 ~~eine~~ eines morgens, da ~~[illegible]~~ 213 ✗
because of F1 eines schönen morgens, da 215

M. chorus Frieden twice because of Frieden
twice individual 219 ✓

M dies hat keinen Sinn author ✓

M Ja, bestimmt 215 ✓

Chor
Ebene

[*fol. 8v*]

Chor.
Ebene [level or even]

Top. [Tophoven][31]

Nicht einmal ein Tröpfchen[32] [not even a squeeze of (lemon)] 220/1

M because of nicht einmal 225 √

M Warum mich nicht dauernd[33] [Why not keep on glaring] 223 √

F2 Nur ganz leicht[34] [just a shade] 224 because of chor F2 √

F2 <one> eines Morgens, da[35] [One morning, as] [*erasure*] 213 ×

because of F1 eines schönen Morgens, da [one fine morning, as] 215

M. Chorus Frieden[36] [Peace] twice because of Frieden

twice individual 219 √

M dies hat keinen Sinn[37] [there is no sense in this]. Author √

M ja, bestimmt [certainly] 215 √

Chor

Ebene [level or even]

Dann verzieh

Sie Kam wieder

A To light change (short chords)
B Thence to long chorus

A1 To dann verzieh ich ihn 15
A2 Thence to end (qualenden) 17

B1 To Vielleicht sind sie .. 24
B2 Thence to Wie das Rollen 24
B3 " " end (gesehen) 33

F1 F2 M
F2 F1 M
15 F2 M F1
M F2 F1
F2 M F1

F2 M F1
F2 F1 F2
17 F1 M F2
F1 M F1
F2 M F1
M F2

M F1 F2
F1 M F2
M F2 F1
M F2 F1
M F2 M 24
F1 F2 M
F1 F2 M
F1 F2 M Vielleicht

F1 M F2 Aber ich habe
M F2 M
F1 F2 F1
M F1 F2 24
M F1 F2
F1 F2 M
F1 M F2
M F1 F2 Wie das Rollen

F2 M F2 Halt
F1 M F2
F1 M F2
M F1 M
F2 F1 M 33
F1 F2 M
F1 M F1
F2 M F1 Dürstend.

M F2 F1
M F1 M
F2 M M

1 2
A A B
Rehearse 1 15 + 17
II 24 + 24 + 33
B A B C
1 2 3

[*fol. 9v*]

Dann verzieh[38]
[Then I forgave]

Sie kam wieder
[She came again]

A[39] To light change (short chorus)
B Thence to long chorus

A1	To dann verzieh ich ihm [Then I forgave him]	15[40]
A2	Thence to the end (qualmten) [smouldering]	17
B1	To Vielleicht sind Sie [Perhaps they have . . .]	24
B2	Thence to Wie das Rollen [like dragging a great roller]	24
B3	" " end (gesehen) [being seen]	33

	F1 F2 M	M F1 F2[41]	
	F2 F1 M	F1 M F2	
15	F2 M F1	M F2 F1	
	M F2 F1	M F2 F1	
	F2 M F1	M F2 M	24
	F2 M F1	F1 F2 M	
	F2 F1 F2	F1 F2 M	
17	F1 M F2	F1 F2 M	Vielleicht [Perhaps]
	F1 M F1	F1 M F2	Aber ich habe [But I have (said)]
	F2 M F1	M F2 M	
	M F2	F1 F2 F1	
		M F1 F2	
		M F1 F2	24
		F1 F2 M	
		F1 M F2	
		M F1 F2	Wie das Rollen [Like dragging a great roller]
		F2 M F2	Halt [Kill it (i.e., light)]
		F1 M F2	
		F1 M F2	
		M F1 M	
		F2 F1 M	
		F1 F2 M	33
		F1 M F1	
		F2 M F1	Dürstend . . . [Dying (for dark) . . .]
		M F2 F1	
		M F1 M	
		F2 M M	

		1		2		
	A	<A>[42]		<B>		
Rehearse	<I>	15	+	17		
	<II>	24	+	24	+	33
	B	<A>		<B>		<C>
		1		2		3

Voices

ein rascher Ruck, dann wieder einer

Broken, breathless – extorted

Ich sagte zu ihm . . . Gib sie auf . . . ich schwor bei allem . . . was ich lieb u. teuer –

etc.

increasingly so da capo

finally: wir waren . . . nicht lang . . . zusammen

from indiv. 1 to 2 simply lower

Light

1. General. Invariable. Dim
2. 3 faces. " "
3. ~~[illegible]~~ Spot. 2 intensities.

2. Not  but  or 

[*fol. 10v*]

Voices — ein rascher Ruck, dann wieder einer[43]
[A little rush, then another]

Broken, breathless – exhorted

Ich sagte zu ihm . . . Gib sie auf . . . ich schwor
bei allem . . . was ich lieb u. [und] teuer–

[I said to him, Give her up. I swore
by all I held most sacred–]

etc.

increasingly so da capo

finally: wir waren . . . nicht lang . . . zusammen
[We were not long together–]

from indiv. [individual] 1 to 2 simply lower[44]

<u>light</u>[45]

1. General. Invariable. Dim
2. 3 faces ” ”
3. [*erasure*] Spot. 2 intensities.

2. Not o o o but o o o or o o o[46]

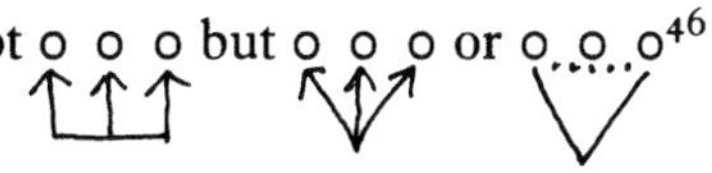

EDITORIAL NOTES
ON THE BROWN NOTEBOOK

After completing the linguistic revision of the German text in the *Red Nb* (RUL MS 1976), Beckett returned to the opening pages of that notebook to begin outlining the structure of the play. After filling the opening two pages of the *Red Nb* with structural outlines, Beckett continued that process after the completion in holograph of *Spiel* on folio 30 of the *Red Nb*. Beckett then began a second, brown notebook (RUL MS 1730), *Brown Nb*, to continue his notes and outlining.

Although most of the textual references in the *Brown Nb* are in German as well, the two notebooks provide an astonishing record of Beckett's directorial and compositional method. Perhaps more than any other of his theatrical notebooks, the two *Spiel* notebooks vividly demonstrate Beckett's obsession with structure. Moreover, as he outlined his play over and over again, obsessively, marking each section with the opening or key phrase, the outlines become virtually a motif index to the play, suggesting key themes and the pattern of their presentation, both elements being equally important to Beckett's dramaturgy.

The bracketed English here and throughout the transcription of the notebook is not necessarily a literal translation of the German but the equivalent phrase in Beckett's English text.

1 – Beckett outlined part I of *Play* here on the verso and recto (folio 2). On the recto outline, he labelled I (for part I, of course), and he indicated speaker and opening German phrase. On the verso the outline indicates the dramatic situation and recurring motifs. Beckett also began to divide the verso outline into triplets but stopped after speech 21.

2 – This is Beckett's outline of the first portion of *Play* keyed to the first words of each character's speech. Beckett outlined as well the number of times each character speaks in the upper right-hand corner, and in the lower right he gave a word count for this section, approximately 1,300 words. This number seems very approximate and must include the opening, long chorus.

3 – Here Beckett outlined the eighty-one speeches of part II of the play. The outline corresponds to the facing recto and is keyed to this outline of part II. On the verso Beckett first grouped each character's speeches and divided them according to dramatic chronology: the first group of each focuses on the dramatic present, the second imagines a union of the other two, and the last returns to the

dramatic present. In M's case, for instance, the first eight speeches after the second chorus (that is, the first eight speeches of part II) focus on the present. The second eight focus on real or imagined meetings of the two women. And the third group, fifteen speeches, returns to the present of the light and a fantasy.

4 – This outline of the second part of the play with speeches grouped in sets of four (the final three excepted) is keyed to the motif index outlining all the eighty-one speeches of the second part on the following recto. The opening and closing lines of each of those sections (themselves containing three speeches) is here noted. The ending of the first set of four threes, 'Lass mich', is Beckett's revision of the original German translation, 'Mich lassen' ('Get off me').

5 – Beckett added the 'Persönlich' to the 'Ich trank immer am liebsten Liptons' to correspond to the English 'Personally I always preferred Lipton's'.

6 – This is a reference to the light. Beckett later revised the German 'Halt' to 'Stop'.

7 – Again a reference to the light, 'Dying for dark–'.

8 – Here Beckett outlined the eighty-one speeches of part II according to the opening phrase. The three heavy black lines, one in each column, divide part II of the play into four sections, a pattern that Beckett did not change until the very last pages of this notebook. See also notes 38, 40, and 41 below.

9 – These are references to the number of times each character opens a set of three speeches. Woman 2 (F2) opens only four sets of speeches.

10 – These numbers refer to the speech number in this section. 'Aber ich habe', for example, begins speech 25 in part II (8 F1 above, i.e. the eighth speech of Woman 1).

11 – This breakdown corresponds to that on the previous, facing verso.

12 – This was apparently Beckett's estimate of the number of words of dialogue in the second half of the play, *i.e.*, in the eighty-one speeches outlined on this page. The actual count in the German text is closer to 1,057.

13 – Yet another outline, this of the thirty-two speeches in part I grouped according to how many people were present in the scene described and in what combinations.

14 – Another outline of the fifty-one fragments in the opening chorus.

15 – Beckett's revision of 'der Sinn ist da'.

16 – Beckett's revision of 'du wirst ihn sehen'.

17 – The German text misprints the line as 'keep of me'.

18 – On these two facing pages Beckett outlined the speeches that deal with the six, underlined themes.

19 – Another thematic or motif index listing the speeches of part I in the order of

presentation. Essentially a duplicate of the opening outline of this notebook but with speakers labelled and speeches numbered.

20 – In order of composition this alternative outline of the choral patterns on folio 7 verso is the successor to the following outline on folio 8 recto. Beckett was here entertaining the possibility of eliminating the 'short chorus', 'B'. (The 'short chorus' is not the chorus between parts I and II of *Spiel*, but the chorus after the first blackout.) Here the two complete runthroughs of the play and the abbreviated third are marked with 'C'. 'A' indicates the opening chorus, at least to the first blackout. The truncated 'closing repeat', the third 'C', then begins with a different order of speakers, as it does in all printed versions of the play. M's 'Wir waren' is the final line of the play and the signal of a new round.

21 – The point of reduction of the opening chorus is indicated below with 'cut on'.

22 – This represents the point of the cut in the shortened version of the opening chorus. It is also marked in *Spiel* (WA), p. 239.

23 – This chorus is indeed cut in *Spiel* (SB), p. 243.

24 – As usual Beckett was working backwards in the notebook, that is, from recto to facing verso. This version of the pattern of choruses and individual examination apparently eliminated the short chorus immediately after the long chorus, that is, after the first blackout, but retained a short chorus between parts I and II of the play. For the 'closing repeat' Beckett suggested here an abridged version of the long chorus, detailed in 'cut on' above. After several alternatives Beckett apparently settled on the pattern in the London and Paris productions and published in the revised texts of *Play* as 'Repeat'. See also *CDW*, p. 320. This note is not included in the first American edition, *Cascando and Other Short Dramatic Pieces* (Grove Press, New York, 1968), p. 63.

25 – This is a reference not to the abridgement of the chorus (see below) but to diminished lighting.

26 – Here again Beckett emphasized his preference for a single source of light rather than three separate lights. During the chorus the narrow spotlight becomes a 'single gaze widening for 3'.

27 – This deletion holds an important clue to the lighting of *Play*. Evidently the faint lighting of the opening chorus should be the same for the individual interrogation in the repeat, i.e. 'individual II'.

28 – After the repeat the long chorus, 'A', was to be eliminated, at least in this version. Beckett changed his mind several times on this issue.

29 – This describes the 'closing repeat'. 'A', the long chorus, is cut and the order of individual responses is altered.

30 – The question here seems to be Beckett's justification to himself for why the cycles of *Play* end at all: the Author decides to go no further or the Interrogator decides to grant mercy, that is, darkness and silence.

31 – This note, 'Top', for Tophoven, suggests that these are notes Beckett had planned to send to his German translator Elmar Tophoven.

32 – Beckett's revision of 'Nicht mal ein Scheibchen Zitrone–' (M, part II, 12). The change of 'mal' to 'einmal' is made to prepare for the echo at the end of M's speech 29 in part II.

33 – Beckett's revision of 'Warum mich nicht unverwandt und unablässig . . .' (M, part II, 20). In the *Red Nb* he had proposed 'rastlos' for 'unverwandt'.

34 – Beckett added the 'Nur' to the 'Ganz leicht' of F2's speech 23 of part II to echo the same phrase in F2's opening (long) chorus.

35 – Beckett added the 'da' to F2's choral fragment and opening line to prepare for the echo in F1's speech 3 of part I.

36 – Beckett added the 'n' to 'Friede' of M's opening (long) chorus to be consistent with 'Frieden' in the 'individual' interrogation.

37 – This is a line from F1's speech 11 of part II. Beckett (Author?) may have thought of adding a parallel phrase for M.

38 – Beckett's notes at the top of the page indicate the division of part I into two sections after speech 15. The sections are called A1 and A2 in the chart below. See also notes 39, 40, and 41 below for additional details.

39 – This pattern of As and Bs introduces a new system of referring to the play's structure, one evidently worked out during rehearsals and not while Beckett was revising the German text. The system is not keyed to Beckett's revised script, *Spiel* (SB), but to Walter Asmus's photocopy of Beckett's revised German text, *Spiel* (WA). Part I of the play is divided into two sections, A1 and A2. A1 runs through the first fifteen speeches to, as Beckett noted at the top of this page, F1's 'Dann verzieh'; the seventeen speeches of A2 begin with F2's 'Sie kam wieder', a phrase again that Beckett jotted at the top of this page, and run to the second chorus. B1 begins immediately after the second chorus and runs for twenty-four speeches to M's speech beginning, 'Vielleicht sind sie'. B2 begins immediately thereafter, with F1's 'Aber ich hab'', and also continues for twenty-four speeches to F2's 'Wie das Rollen'. B3 then comprises the remaining thirty-two speeches in the play and M's final 'Wir waren nicht lang zusammen–', which Beckett counted as the thirty-third speech in this section and which signals a repeat of the cycle but in a new order.

40 – These numbers to the right of the outline indicate the number of speeches in these sections: fifteen speeches in the section called A1 and seventeen in the section called A2. See also notes 38, 39, and 41 for additional details.

41 – Here again the play is outlined according to speakers. The column on the left represents what was earlier called 'part I' but which Beckett revised at the bottom of the page to A. It is divided, as the chart on the facing verso suggests, after speech 15. The column on the right was earlier called 'part II', but it too was revised at the bottom of the page to B. The B section then was first divided into four parts, but as the number '33' indicates, Beckett changed his mind and combined the final two parts, dividing the B section into three parts, B1, B2, and B3, the final section comprising thirty-three speeches.

42 – These cancellations indicate Beckett's changing his system of notation. To break each part down further, at least for rehearsal purposes, he apparently divided part I into A and B, and part II into A, B, and C. He then changed his mind and reversed the pattern of numbers subdivided by letters to letters subdivided by numbers. This A and B designation for the two parts of the play is the one used on the facing verso.

43 – This image within the play of a hand lawnmower is also Beckett's central dramaturgical method in this play. The speeches, he told his actors in rehearsals, should follow the pattern of this lawnmower, a short burst of energy, then a pause. As he noted shortly after citing the line, the speeches should all be 'broken, breathless – exhorted'. He then outlined an example of this style of presentation by breaking up F1's first speech after the chorus. This intensity and breathlessness should then increase until the da capo or repeat.

44 – The difference between the first runthrough and the repeat, i.e. between what Beckett called 'indiv. 1' and 'indiv. 2', is that the repeat, 'indiv. 2', is lower.

45 – Beckett here outlined the three lighting possibilities for *Play*. First, the dim lighting of all three urns. Second, the lighting of all three faces, as outlined below, from a single source. Beckett asked himself earlier in his notebook as a 'Technical' matter: 'Provoke A & B not by triple spot but by general light on 3?' The affirmative answer to that question is given here. And finally two intensities of spot-lighting individual faces are offered. The entire play then is performed with these four lighting possibilities, two of which differ only in intensity.

46 – See note 26 above.

CUTS AND CHANGES TO THE SCHILLER-THEATER PRODUCTION TEXT

Page references are to the text Beckett used to prepare for the Berlin Production, *Spiel* (SB), and to the text his assistant, Walter Asmus, used during rehearsals, *Spiel* (WA). The page numbers follow that trilingual (with facing English and German texts) Suhrkamp edition.

Page 239

In F1's final fragment on the page, 'das Ding' replaced 'der Sinn'.

Page 241

In F1's first fragment, 'es' replaced 'ihn' in 'du wirst ihn sehen'.

Page 243

Chorus atop the page, what Beckett called the 'short chorus', was cut, but only in *Spiel* (WA), the working copy of the text. This and the revision of the 'closing repeat' below were Beckett's principal textual revisions to *Spiel*.
F2, 1 – Beckett revised 'schmeichelhaft' to 'schmeichlerisch', and added 'und Lebensgrösse' after 'Fleisch und Blut'.
F1, 2 – 'Masche' replaced 'Tour'.

Page 245

F2, 3 – 'Beim Weggehen sagte sie, wie er bezeugen kann . . .' was revised to 'Beim Weggehen gab sie zu verstehen, wie er bezeugen könnte . . .', and 'ungefähr' was cut in 'Leute-Hinausbringen, ungefähr'. In the *Red Nb*, however, Beckett offered no replacement for the deleted 'sagte sie', but replaced 'ungefähr' with 'gab sie zu bestehen'.
M, 3 – 'ihr' was cut and the syntax of 'dass ich nicht ohne sie leben könne' was revised to 'ich könne ohne sie nicht leben'.

Page 247

F1, 4 – 'Reaktion' replaced 'Regung' and 'Bewunderung' replaced 'Erstaunen'.
F2, 5 – 'Und natürlich bestand bei ihm keine Gefahr für die . . . rein seelische Tour' was revised to 'Und natürlich bestand bei ihm nicht die Gefahr den . . . seelischen Masche'.
M, 5 – 'zwischen ihnen' was revised to 'zwischen den beiden' in the first sentence, and 'Ich mag nicht' became 'Ich will nicht' in the second.

The typography of the German text is askew in this paragraph and so Beckett moved the widowed 'klarzustellen' to the last word in the speech.

F1, 5 – Beckett revised 'Wozu Liebe sich' to 'Wozu sich Liebe' and 'Ich schlug eine kleine Vergnügungsreise vor . . .' to 'Ich schlug einen kleinen Ausflug vor . . .'

In 'Er sah blass aus, spitz', 'spitz' was set off as a separate sentence: 'Er sah blass aus. Spitz.'

F2, 6 – 'Leckte sich die Lippen' was revised to 'Sich die Lippen leckend'.

Page 249

M, 6 – 'lernt daraus' was revised to 'macht euch eins.'
F2, 7 – 'Er redete noch' was revised to 'Er redete immer noch'.

'Was bedeutete, dass er zu ihr zurückgekehrt war' was revised to 'Dass heist er war zu ihn zurückgekehrt'.

F2, 8 – 'Drohungen parat habe – dass ich aber auch nicht viel Lust auf ihre Abfälle hätte' was revised to 'Drohungen parat hätte – aber auch nicht viel Lust auf ihre Abfälle'.

Page 251

F1, 9 – 'Er war also wieder mein' was revised to 'Er gehörte mir also wieder', and 'Ganz mein' to 'Ganz und gar'.
M, 8 – 'Alte' was revised to 'Vergangene'.
F1, 11 – 'Ich war' was revised to 'Ich lag . . .'

Page 253

The chorus separating parts I and II of *Spiel* was extended in Beckett's production. F1's chorus became 'Gnade, Gnade, die Zunge lechzt noch nach

Gnade'. F2's was now 'Ich sag' nicht, dass ich nicht enttäuscht sei–'; and M's was now 'Bei diesem Wechsel, dem ersten dankte ich sogar Gott'. This change does not appear in *Spiel* (SB) but only in *Spiel* (WA) and so it was evidently made in rehearsals.
M, 1 – 'drängte es mich, Gott zu danken' was revised to 'dankte ich sogar Gott'. This change was not made in *Spiel* (SB) but in *Spiel* (WA). In the *Red Nb*, however, Beckett underlined the passage and inserted a pair of question marks on the facing verso.

Page 255

F2, 3 – 'meiner müde' replaced 'mich satt haben'.
F2, 4 – Beckett cut the opening 'Wirst du' from both sentences in this speech.

Page 257

F2, 6 – Beckett revised 'Du könntest böse werden und mich um meinen Verstand bringen' to 'Du könntest böse werden und mir meinen Verstand ausbrennen'.
F1, 7 – 'funktionert' replaced 'arbeitet'.

Page 259

F2, 9 – 'dass ich denselben' was revised to 'dass ich dengleichen', and Beckett added 'nämlich' before 'nach Sinn'.
M, 11 – 'Tröpfchen' replaced 'Scheibchen'.
M, 12 – 'Tröpfchen' replaced 'Scheibchen'.
F1, 9 – 'was' replaced 'das'.
F1, 10 – 'funktionert' replaced 'arbeitet'.

Page 261

M, 14 – 'persönlich' was added between 'Ich' and 'trank'.
F2, 14 – 'Die ihre sauren Küsse küssen' was revised to 'Ihre sauren Küsse küssend'.
M, 15 – 'selig' replaced 'gesegnet'.
M, 16 – the 'Ich' in 'Ich bedaure sie' was cut not in *Spiel* (SB) but in *Spiel* (WA) only. The revision did appear, however, in the *Red Nb*.
F2, 15 – 'Alles sieben?' was revised to 'Alles sondern?'

F1, 15 – 'Sie war nicht mittellos, sag' ich mir' was revised to 'Sie war wohl nicht mittellos'. The 'sag' ich mir' was deleted.

Page 263

M, 18 – 'Warum–' revised to 'Warum Ver–'.
M, 19 – 'Warum das Dämmerlicht?' revised first by Beckett to 'Warum dämmern?' and then in Walter Asmus's hand to'Warum verdammern?'.
M, 20 – 'Warum mich nicht unverwandt und unablässig . . .' revised first by Beckett to 'Warum mich nicht endlos . . .' and the in Walter Asmus's hand to 'Warum mich nicht dauernd . . .'.
M, 20 – 'es für dich herausbrechen' revised to 'damit herausrücken. Ver–'.

Page 265

M, 23 – 'erwachen' revised to 'erwachten'.
F1, 21 – 'was ich verlangte' revised to 'wonach ich mich sehnte'.
F1, 21 – 'Vielleichtistes frevelhafter, um mehr zu bitten' revised to 'Vielleicht ist es wieder sündhaft, noch mehr zu erflehen'.

Page 267

M, 30 – 'Das sich über mir öffnet und schliesst' revised to 'sich über mir öffnend und schliessend'.

Page 269

The ending was severely revised and simplified in Beckett's production. The final chorus and almost all of the chorus for the 'closing repeat' were cut: F1's 'Ja, seltsam', F2's 'Ja, vielleicht', and M's 'Ja, Friede' were cut. The repeat was retained, '*Spiel wiederholen bis.*' The 'closing repeat', M's 'Werde ich überhaupt . . . gesehen?', was cut, as was the following blackout: '*Scheinwerferlicht auf M erlischt. Finsternis. Fünf Sekunden. Grelles Scheinwerferlicht gleichzeitig auf allen drei Gesichtern. Stimmen normale Lautstärke.*' The fragment of the opening chorus was also cut: F1's 'Ich sagte zu ihm, Gib sie auf–'; F2's 'Eines Morgens, als ich im Zimmer', and M's 'Wir waren nicht lang zusammen–' were cut to simplify the ending. M's final 'Wir waren nicht lang zusammen–', however, was retained as the play's ending. None of these changes appeared in *Spiel* (SB), but only in *Spiel* (WA), which generally contained the changes made during rehearsals.

PART II

Come and Go

Revised Text

TYPOGRAPHICAL NOTE

Text between square brackets [ ] has been added to the original English text.
Text between pointed brackets {} has been revised.
A pair of angle brackets <> indicates that a section of text has been cut from the original English text.
All changes indicated by the above brackets are explained in the Textual Notes.

PUBLISHER'S NOTE

The publisher has taken this opportunity to make a number of minor adjustments to the layout and typographical style adopted for earlier editions of *Come and Go.*

COME AND GO

A dramaticule

For John Calder

CHARACTERS

FLO

VI

RU

(Ages undeterminable)

Sitting centre side by side stage right to left FLO, VI *and* RU.
Very erect, facing front, hands clasped in laps.
Silence.

[VI: Ru. 4
RU: Yes. 5
VI: Flo. 6
FLO: Yes.] 7
VI: When did we three last meet? 8
{FLO}: Let us not speak. 9
(*Silence.*
Exit VI *right.*
Silence.)
<> Ru. 13
RU: Yes.
FLO: What do you think of Vi?
RU: I see little change.
(FLO *moves to centre seat, whispers in* RU's *ear.*)
(*Appalled*) Oh!
(*They look at each other.* FLO *puts her finger to her lips.*)
Does she not realize?
FLO: God grant not.
(*Enter* VI. FLO *and* RU *turn back front, resume pose.* VI *sits right.*
Silence.)
Just sit together as we used to, in the playground at Miss Wade's.
RU: On the log.
(*Silence.*
Exit FLO *left.*
Silence.)
Vi.
VI: Yes.
RU: How do you find Flo?

VI: She seems much the same.
(RU *moves to centre seat, whispers in* VI*'s ear.*)
(*Appalled*) Oh!
(*They look at each other.* RU *puts her finger to her lips.*)
Has she not been told?
RU: God forbid.
(*Enter* FLO. RU *and* VI *turn back front, resume pose.* FLO *sits left.*
39 [*Silence.*])
Holding hands . . . that way.
41 {VI}: Dreaming of . . . love.
(*Silence.*
Exit RU *right.*
Silence.)
45 <> Flo.
FLO: Yes.
VI: How do you think Ru is looking?
FLO: One sees little in this light.
(VI *moves to centre seat, whispers in* FLO*'s ear.*)
(*Appalled*) Oh!
(*They look at each other.* VI *puts her fingers to her lips.*)
Does she not know?
VI: Please God not.
(*Enter* RU. VI *and* FLO *turn back front, resume pose.* RU *sits right.*
Silence.)
May we not speak of the old days?
(*Silence.*)
Of what came after?
(*Silence.*)
Shall we hold hands in the old way?
(*After a moment they join hands as follows:* VI*'s right hand with* RU*'s right hand,* VI*'s left hand with* FLO*'s left hand,* FLO*'s right hand with* RU*'s left hand,* VI*'s arms being above* RU*'s left arm and* FLO*'s right arm. The three pairs of clasped hands rest on the three laps.*
Silence.)

FLO: [Ru. 66

(*Silence.*) 67

Vi. 68

(*Silence.*)] 69

I can feel the rings.

(*Silence.*)

CURTAIN

NOTES

Successive positions

1	FLO	VI	RU
2	FLO		RU
		FLO	RU
3	VI	FLO	RU
4	VI		RU
	VI	RU	
5	VI	RU	FLO
6	VI		FLO
		VI	FLO
7	RU	VI	FLO

Hands

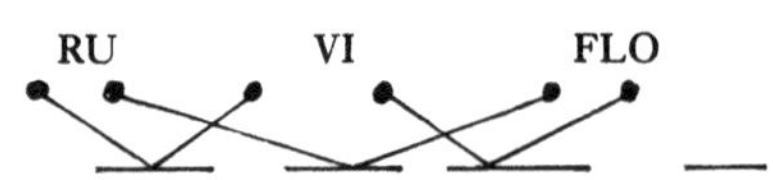

Lighting

Soft, from above only and concentrated on playing area. Rest of stage as dark as possible.

Costume

Full-length coats, buttoned high, dull violet (RU), dull red (VI), dull yellow (FLO). Drab nondescript hats with enough brim to shade faces. Apart from colour differentiation three figures as alike as possible. Light shoes with rubber soles. Hands made up to be as visible as possible. No rings apparent.

Seat

Narrow benchlike seat, without back, just long enough to accommodate three figures almost touching. As little visible as possible. It should not be clear what they are sitting on.

Exits

The figures are not seen to go offstage. They should disappear a few steps from lit area. If dark not sufficient to allow this, recourse should be had to screens or drapes as little visible as possible. Exits and entrances slow, without sound of feet.

Ohs
Three very different sounds.

Voices
As low as compatible with audibility. Colourless except for three 'ohs' and two lines following.

4–7 – These opening lines were not part of the first edition, *Come and Go: A Dramaticule* (Calder and Boyars, London, 1967), p. 7, but they were part of the first American edition, *Cascando and Other Short Dramatic Pieces* (Grove Press, New York, 1968), p. 67, and all translations, particularly the French and German. More important, they were part of the final text which Beckett revised for the Schiller-Theater production in 1978 which was directed by Walter Asmus, *KuG*(WA). Subsequent English texts by Faber and Faber were, however, based on the Calder and Boyars text of 1967, and both the *Collected Shorter Plays of Samuel Beckett* and *CDW*, projects initiated by Faber and Faber and photo-offset by Grove Press, reprint the incomplete Calder and Boyars edition. These opening lines are included in the text Breon Mitchell published in the journal *Modern Drama* in 1976 (pp. 245–60), but his text introduces a new set of anomalies.

Thematically, these opening lines not only establish character names, but they create a motif which is echoed in the first two lines following each character's departure and in the addition to FLO's final speech. Cf. lines 66–69.

8 – Numerous critics have commented on the allusion in this line to the opening query of the three witches in *Macbeth.*

9 – 'FLO' replaced 'RU'. This is one of the most significant changes Beckett developed in the *Kommen und Gehen* notebook and made for the German production of the work which was to accompany his direction of *Spiel* (*Play*). In his notebook Beckett called this change, 'perhaps more correct psychologically'. In addition, the revision creates an irony in that it is now FLO who says, 'Let us not speak', but it is she who shortly thereafter initiates the conversation at VI's departure.

13 – With the revision above (line 9) the demarkation 'FLO' here would be redundant (cf. line 45).

39 – This *Silence* was part of the first English edition by Calder and Boyars and the first American edition by Grove Press.

41 – 'VI' replaced 'FLO', and so the line is spoken as a coda to the exchange and secrets between VI and RU, and not as an intrusion by the recently returned FLO. This is the second major revision of the *Kommen und Gehen* notebook, and it was also included in the Schiller production and in *KuG*(WA). Cf. line 9.

45 – With the revision above (line 41) the demarkation 'VI' here would be redundant (cf. line 13).

66–69 – The addition of the two names to FLO's final lines for the French translation appears in English only in the Mitchell text (p. 258), but more important the addition is part of the printed German text that Beckett reviewed for the Schiller production, *KuG*(WA).

Structurally, this addition echoes the four added lines at the opening of the play, but without the responses, 'Yes'. Cf. lines 4–7. Beckett's own note on the play's final line is 'No rings apparent', which is different from saying 'No rings'.

Costume – In the *Kommen und Gehen* notebook Beckett modified the costumes considerably to create a more etherial quality: 'Hats: flimsy, broad brimmed, beflowered – ribboned – feathered, to stir in draught. Dress: loose, light, for same effect.'

Samuel Beckett's Production Notebook for *Kommen und Gehen* (*Come and Go*) at the Schiller-Theater Werkstatt, Berlin, October 1978

Kommen u. Gehen
Eh Joe
HAPPY DAYS

FACSIMILE OF BECKETT'S PRODUCTION NOTEBOOK WITH TRANSCRIPTION AND TRANSLATION

Note on the Manuscript

The *Kommen und Gehen* (*Come and Go*) notebook is contained within the second *Spiel* notebook, a brown, 44-folio spiral notebook measuring 17 × 10.5 cm., on deposit at the University of Reading Samuel Beckett Archive, MS 1730. For a full description of this notebook, see page 145.

Inverting the notebook, Beckett wrote three titles on the back cover: *Kommen u. Gehen* (*Come and Go*), *Eh Joe*, *Happy Days*. Beckett began notes to *Kommen und Gehen*, which would be on the programme with *Spiel* in 1978 at the Schiller Theater (the director of record, however, was Walter Asmus), on the recto of folio 1 if one were foliating from the back of the inverted notebook, and they continue to the recto of folio 4; the figures in square brackets at the top of each page of transcription accord with this foliation. (Foliating from the front of the notebook, the *Kommen und Gehen* notes occupy folios 41 verso to 44 verso.)

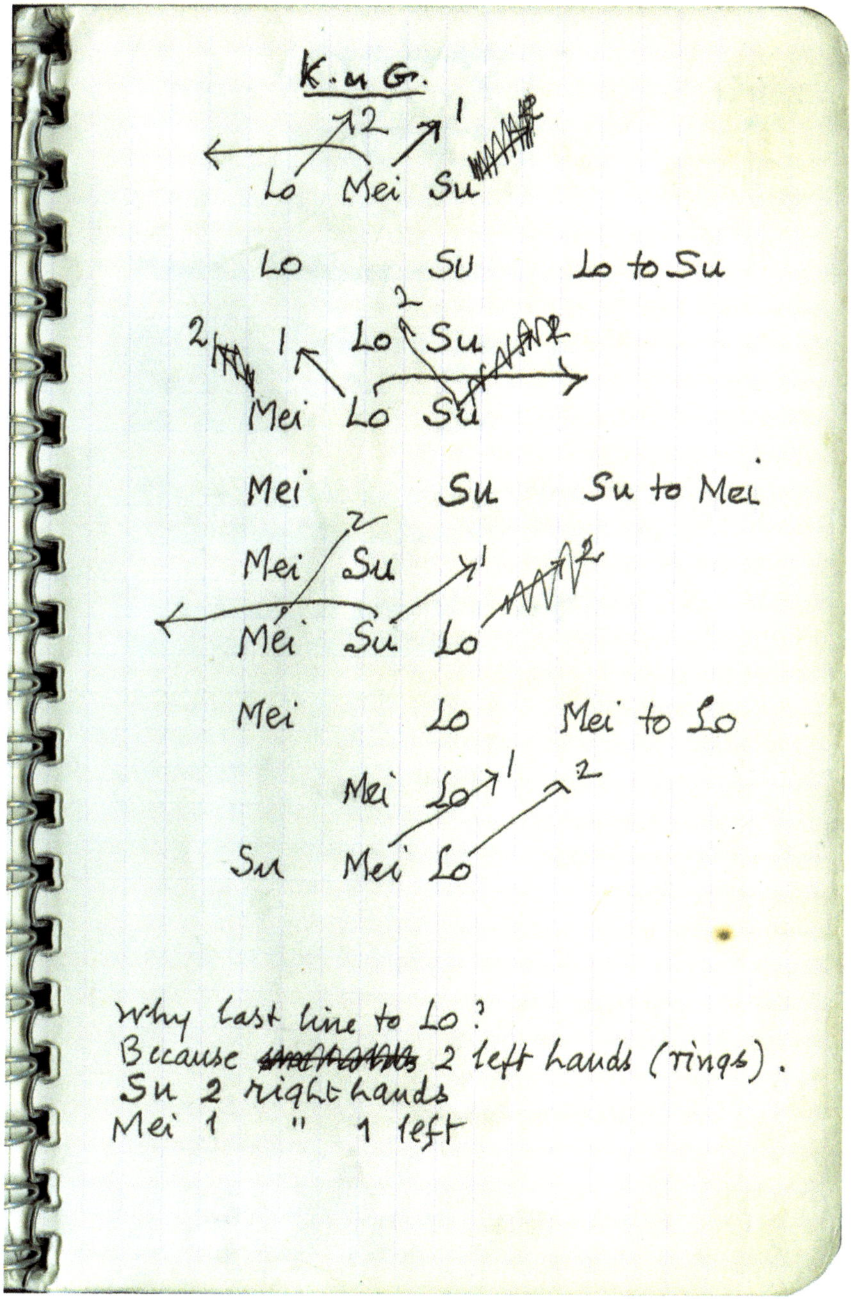
K. u. G.
Lo Mei Su
Lo Su Lo to Su
Lo Su
Mei Lo Su
Mei Su Su to Mei
Mei Su
Mei Su Lo
Mei Lo Mei to Lo
Mei Lo
Su Mei Lo
Why last line to Lo?
Because 2 left hands (rings).
Su 2 right hands
Mei 1 " 1 left

K. [Kommen] u. [und] G. [Gehen]

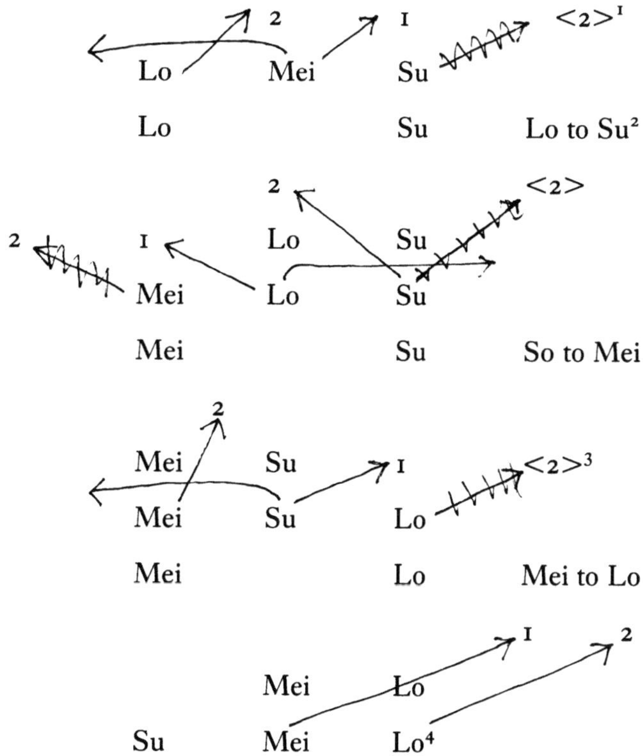

Why last line to Lo?
Because <she holds> 2 left hands (rings).[5]
Su 2 right hands
Mei 1 " 1 left

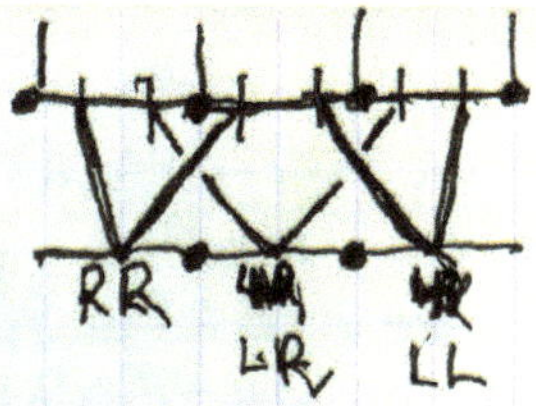

Hands holding & held

Mei's L	holding	Lo's L
Su's R	"	Mei's R
Lo's R	"	Su's L

Hands taken in air at top of gesture
sink gently plumb together

Raised all 6 together ~~at~~ first
Mei's in invitation

[*fol. 1v*]

[Sketch]

Hands holding & held

Mei's L holding Lo's L
Su's R " Mei's R
Lo's R " Su's L

Hands taken in air at top of gesture
sink gently plumb together

Raised all 6 together or first
Mei's in invitation

When 3 each in turn opens & responds

1. Mei - Su   Mei - Lo   perhaps more
4. Lo - Mei   or   Lo - Su   correct
7. Su - Lo   Su - Mei   psychologically

Opener always one to go

2. Mei
5. Lo
8. Su

When 2 always [illegible] responder opens (confides) to non-responder [illegible]

2. Lo to Su
5. Su " Mei
8. Mei " Lo

10. Normal that Mei should open as she did at 1. But why last words given to Lo? Because she touches both left hands (wedding rings). Su both right hands. Mei one right - one left.

When 3 together always central opens

1 Lo Mei Su

2 Lo Su } Lo to Su re Mei

3 Lo Su

4 Mei Lo Su

5 Mei Su } Su to Mei re Lo

6 Mei Su

7 Mei Su Lo

8 Mei Lo } Mei to Lo re Su

9 Mei Lo

10 Su Mei Lo

<u>Continuation</u>

Su Lo } Su to Lo re Mei

Su Lo

Mei Su Lo

Mei Lo } Lo to Mei re Su

Mei Lo

Mei Lo Su

Mei Su } Mei to Su re Lo

Mei Su

Lo Mei Su

mathematically desirable

Logically { inacceptable / impossible

[*fol. 2v*]

When 3 each in turn opens & responds

<1.[6] Mei – Su		Mei – Lo	perhaps more
4. Lo – Mei	or	Lo – Su	correct
7. Su – Lo>		Su – Mei	psychologically

Opener always one to go

2. Mei
5. Lo
8. Su

When 2 always [*erasure*] responder opens
(confides) to non-responder <or convene[?]>

2. Lo to Su
5. Su " Mei
8. Mei " Lo

10. Normal that Mei should open as she did at 1.[7] But why last words given to Lo? Because she touches both left hands (wedding rings). Su both right hands. Mei one right – one left.

When 3 together always central opens

[*fol. 3r*]

← [*erasure*]

1	Lo	Mei	Su[8]	
2	Lo		Su	Lo to Su re [regarding] Mei
3		Lo	Su	→
4	Mei	Lo	Su	
5	Mei		Su	Su to Mei re [regarding] Lo
6	Mei	Su		←
7	Mei	Su	Lo	
8	Mei		Lo	Mei to Lo re [regarding] Su
9	<Su>	Mei	Lo	
10	Su	Mei	Lo	(←)

Continuation[9]

Su		Lo	
	Su	Lo	→ Su to Lo re [regarding] Mei
Mei	Su	Lo	
Mei		Lo	Lo to Mei re [regarding] Su
Mei	Lo		←
Mei	Lo	Su	
Mei		Su	Mei to Su re [regarding] Lo
	Mei	Su	
Lo	Mei	Su	

Mathematically desirable
logically [inacceptable
impossible

Top

wie damals 229

Lo	Mei	Su
Red hat	Violet hat	Yellow hat
Yellow dress	red dress	violet dress
violet shoes	yellow shoes	red shoes

Hats: flimsy, broadbrimmed, beflowered - ribboned - feathered, to stir in draught.

Dress: loose, light, for same effect

Shoes: genre ballerina, exits silent.

—

If ventilator(s) then screens L & R.

—

For heads same level if necessary each her cushion. To be taken with her or moved by confider to future place. Same colour as dress.

[*fol. 3v*]

Top[10]

wie damals 229

Lo	Mei	Su
Red hat	Violet hat	Yellow hat
Yellow dress	red dress	Violet dress
Violet shoes	yellow shoes	red shoes[11]

Hats: flimsy, broad brimmed,
beflowered – ribboned – feathered,
to stir in draught.[12]

Dress: Loose, light, for same effect

shoes: genre ballerine, exits
silent.[13]

—

If ventilator(s) the screens L & R.[14]

—

For heads same level[,] if necessary
each her cushion. To be taken with
her or moved by confider to future place.[15]
Same colour as dress.

1 – Beckett has here altered the pattern of respondents and has given Su's line 'Nicht sprechen' ['Let us not speak'] to Lo. This, of course, creates another irony in that now Lo says 'Let us not speak' and yet she is the first to break the silence after Mei's departure. This revision was made by Walter Asmus in his director's script (*vide* 'Cuts and Changes' to *Kommen und Gehen* (*Come and Go*)). This revision, however, appears in no previous English text.
2 – That is, after Mei's departure Lo initiates the conversation about the absent Mei and moves towards Su, thus occupying the centre seat.
3 – Beckett has here altered the pattern of respondents and has given Lo's line 'Träumend . . . von Liebe' ['Dreaming of . . . love'] to Mei. This revision was made by Walter Asmus in his director's script (*vide* 'Cuts and Changes' to *Kommen und Gehen* (*Come and Go*)). This revision, however, appears in no previous English text.
4 – This initial drawing in the *Brown Nb* emphasizes the centrality of pattern in the play. At the end of the play Mei has reclaimed her central position, but Lo and Su have traded places. Beckett elaborated on this drawing later in the *Brown Nb* and considered adding a second round of departures and whispered secrets so that after the second runthrough the three characters would return to their original positions: Lo – Mei – Su.
5 – Although Beckett answered his own question here, he repeated the answer a few pages later: 'Because she touches both left hands (wedding rings).'
6 – These numbers refer to the outline of ten scenes on the facing recto. The pattern of speaking in three of the four scenes where all three characters are together, scenes 1, 4 and 7, is here revised. Beckett cancelled the initial pattern of, in scene 1, Mei's opening and Su's responding to Mei's opening and Lo's responding. This diagram also explains the revisions to the first outline on folio 1 recto. There Beckett drew an arrow from Mei and called that '1'. She is the opener. He then drew an arrow from Su and called that '2', that is, responder. But he cancelled that and designated Lo as '2'. In Walter Asmus's director's copy of the text, the responder is revised from Su to Lo (*vide* the revisions for page 9 in 'Cuts and Changes' to *Kommen und Gehen* (*Come and Go*)). The revisions on folio 1 recto correspond to the revisions in this outline, of which Beckett said finally, 'perhaps more correct psychologically'. But these revisions appear in no previous English text.

7 – Here Beckett referred to the second outline called 'continuation' on the facing recto. Although Su and Lo have changed places by the end of the play, scene 10, if the cycle played through another loop it would be 'normal', Beckett noted, 'that Mei should open [the conversation] as she did at [scene] 1'.
8 – This pattern repeats the outline on folio 1 recto with the exception that in the final episode, labelled '10' here, Beckett contemplated the departure of Mei for a second round of confidences, which he detailed after 'continuation' but which he finally rejected as 'impossible'. The numbering of scenes in this outline is used by Beckett on the facing verso.
9 – Beckett seems to have considered a second round to this play of repeated confidences so that, at the end of the second loop, the characters would be restored to their original places, Lo, Mei, Su, but Beckett noted shortly thereafter, 'Mathematically desirable [but] logically impossible.'
10 – 'Top' is Beckett's shorthand for 'Tophoven', and the note is for German translator Elmar Tophoven to revise 'früher' to 'damals' to be echoed by Su's 'Hand in Hand . . . wie damals.' *Damals* is, of course, the German title of Beckett's play *That Time*. The revision appears on page 9 of Walter Asmus's director's text (*vide* 'Cuts and Changes' to *Kommen und Gehen* (*Come and Go*)).
11 – Such cross-dressing is a visual pattern Beckett developed in his productions to emphasize the interconnections among his characters. Here the three women are visually connected by colour as they are physically related by the pattern of their linking hands and psychologically by their shared intimacies. Compare this to Beckett's costuming of Didi and Gogo for his Schiller-Theater production of *Waiting for Godot*.
12 – The somewhat ornate costuming here recalls the excesses of costume in Beckett's other major plays featuring women, *Happy Days* and *Rockaby*.
13 – Although the visuals for this play are colourful, the emphasis on the diaphanous quality of the costumes and the silent movement suggests something ethereal, other-worldly, ghostly.
14 – These ventilators designed to stir the characters' costumes were much discussed in rehearsals but never used.
15 – These cushions were used in the production but they were not carried off by the exiting character. Instead Beckett's alternate solution was adopted, 'moved by confider to future place'.

CUTS AND CHANGES TO THE SCHILLER-THEATER PRODUCTION TEXT

This is Walter Asmus's director's copy, *KuG* (WA), and so includes some of his own comments on the play. The few textual revisions in this short play were initiated by Beckett. This, then, is the final script that Beckett revised, and so it provides the model for the revised English text. Moreover, the play's division into four parts and the specific notations on the duration of pauses make this a fascinating document.

Page 9

Three lines written above the title, 'Die Erstarrung Anfang in Tonlosigkeit + Unsicherheit übersteigen.' [Roughly: 'The freeze at the beginning should surpass speechlessness and insecurity.'] This is Walter Asmus's note to himself about the mood of the opening tableau.

At the end of the first stage directions, '20″' (i.e., 20 seconds) is noted. To the right 'Lo', 'Mei', and 'Su' were added by hand and their patterns of movement, departures and returns, noted with arrows.

Mei's, Su's, and Lo's subsequent lines were followed by arrows indicating an up and down movement and '4″' was noted beside each line.

At the end of Mei's third line an arrow connected it with Lo's fourth line. Next to the line, an illegible word.

Second printed 'SU' was revised to 'LO'. This was Beckett's principal revision to the German text. See note to line 9 of the revised English text, p. 212. 'Sprechen' was underlined, and '4″' added at the end of the line.

In the second set of stage directions 'MEI' was boxed, and an arrow pointing left showed the direction of her departure.

Next to '*Schweigen*', '8″' was added. Near the right margin the pattern of movement for 'Lo – Su' and the departed 'Mei' were noted.

In Lo's fourth line the word 'unsere' was emphasized with a box.

In the third set of stage directions 'LO' was boxed, and in the right margin '– Lo Su' was noted to continue the outline of the movements.

After Lo's 'Gott bewahre!' a line is drawn across the page indicating the end of the play's first part.

In the fourth set of stage directions 'MEI' was boxed and 'rechts' underlined. In the right margin 'Mei', 'Lo', and 'Su' were noted with an arrow indicating Mei's return.

In Lo's sixth line 'damals' replaced 'früher'.

In Su's fourth line 'dem Balken' replaced 'der Kiste'.

In the fifth set of stage directions '20″' was noted after the first '*Schweigen*'. 'LO' was boxed in the next line, and an arrow to the right pointed to the outline of movement ('Mei – Su') and indicated the direction of Lo's departure.

After '*Schweigen*', '8″' was noted.

After Mei's last line '4″' was written in.

Page 10

Illegible markings after Su's first line.

After Mei's first line, '8″' was noted.

To the right of the first stage directions 'Mei Su –' indicates the absence of Lo; 'nicht gesagt?' replaced 'erzählt?'

A line was drawn across the page under 'Gott behüte!' to indicate the end of the second part of the play.

'LO' was boxed in the second set of stage directions. 'Links' was underlined, and '8″' added at the end of the line. In the right margin 'Mei', 'Su', and 'Lo' were noted with an arrow indicating the direction of Lo's return.

The printed 'LO' was revised to 'MEI'. This was Beckett's second major revision to the German text. See note to line 41 of the revised English text, p. 212. A barely legible mark ('7″'?) was noted next to the line.

'20″' was added after '*Schweigen*'.

'SU' was boxed with an arrow pointing left to indicate the direction of her departure.

'8″' followed the second '*Schweigen*'. To the right was another drawing, 'Mei – Lo', and an arrow indicating the direction of Su's departure.

'Was hältst du von Su?' was revised to 'Wie erscheint dir Su?' '4″' was written in at the end of the line.

'8″' was added to Lo's next line. In the left margin 'Ausrede' [Excuse] is noted beside Flo's 'One sees little in this light.'

In the fourth set of stage directions 'MEI' was boxed. At the end of the line '– Mei Lo' was noted.

A line drawn across the page after 'Gott möge es ihr ersparen' indicated the end of part 3.

In the fifth set of stage directions 'SU' was boxed, and 'rechts' [right] underlined. To the right 'Su Mei Lo' was noted with an arrow indicating the direction of Su's return.

In Mei's first speech of part 4, 'sprechen' was underlined.

Following several lines pauses were noted.

After '*Schweigen*', '10″'. Although the copy is blurred, '10″' was probably noted beside every '*Schweigen*' until the final one, which is marked '20″'.

'Warum sollen wir nicht von den alten Zeiten sprechen?' [roughly, 'Why shouldn't we speak of the old times?'] was written at the bottom of the page by Walter Asmus to reinforce the subtext of the play. It is a slight variation and possible revision of the first sentence in Mei's final speech, 'Sollen wir nicht von den alten Zeiten sprechen?' [in Beckett's English: 'May we not speak of the old days?'].

PART III

Eh Joe

Samuel Beckett's Production Notebook for *He Joe* (*Eh Joe*) at Süddeutscher Rundfunk, Stuttgart, January 1979

FACSIMILE OF BECKETT'S PRODUCTION NOTEBOOK WITH TRANSCRIPTION AND TRANSLATION

Note on the Manuscript

Samuel Beckett's production notes for his 1979 remake of *He Joe* (*Eh Joe*) in Stuttgart are contained in the second *Spiel* notebook, a brown, 44-leaf spiral notebook measuring 17 × 10.5 cm., on deposit at the University of Reading Samuel Beckett Archive, MS 1730. For a full description of this notebook, see page 145.

Inverting the back cover, Beckett wrote three titles: *Kommen und Gehen* (*Come and Go*), *Eh Joe*, *Happy Days*. The *Eh Joe* notes for the 1979 Süddeutscher Rundfunk remake begin on the recto of folio 5 (counting from the back of the inverted notebook) and continue to midway down the verso of folio 7; the figures in square brackets at the top of each page of transcription follow this foliation. (Foliating from the front of the notebook, the *Eh Joe* notes occupy folios 38 recto to 40 verso.) The *Happy Days* notes for the Royal Court production of 1979 begin just below the *Eh Joe* notes on the verso of folio 7; they are separated by a piece of heavy red tape.

Eh Joe

"Du Narr ... deine Seele"

–

Gleichnis des reichen Narren
Lukas XII. 16

.. es war ein reicher Mensch, des Feld hatte wohl getragen.

Und er gedachte bei sich selbst u. sprach: Was soll ich tun? Ich habe nicht, da ich meine Früchte hin sammle.

Und sprach: Das will ich tun: ich will meine Scheunen abbrechen u. grössere bauen u. will drein sammeln alles, was mir gewachsen ist, u. meine Güter;

u. will sagen zu meiner Seele: Liebe Seele, du hast einen grossen Vorrat u. viele Jahre; habe nun Ruhe, iss, trink, u. habe guten Mut!

aber Gott sprach zu ihm: Du Narr! diese Nacht wird man deine Seele von dir fordern; u. wes wird es sein, das du bereitet hast?

also geht es, wer sich Schätze sammelt u. ist nicht reich in Gott.

"Dreck bist du"

Gen. III. 19

Im Schweisse deines Angesichts sollst du dein Brot essen, bis dass du wieder zu Erde werdest, davon du gekommen bist. Denn du bist Erde, u. sollst zu Erde werden.

Eh Joe

"Du Narr . . . deine Seele"[1] ['Thou fool thy soul']

Gleichnis des reichen Narren [Parable of the rich fool]
Lukas [Luke] XII.16 [–21]

. . es war ein reicher Mensch, des [dessen] Feld
hatte wohl [gut] getragen.
Und er gedachte bei sich selbst u. [und] sprach:
Was soll ich tun? Ich habe nicht [nichts], da ich [wohin]
meine Früchte hin sammle.
Und sprach: Das will ich tun: ich
will meine Scheunen abbrechen u. [und] grössere
bauen u. [und] will drein [darin] sammeln alles, was
mir gewachsen ist, u. [und] meine Güter;
[all mein Korn und meine Vorräte]
u. [und] will sagen zu meiner Seele: Liebe
Seele, du hast einen grossen Vorrat [für] u. [und]
viele Jahre; habe nun Ruhe, iss, trink
u. [und] habe guten Mut!
Aber Gott sprach zu ihm: Du Narr!
diese Nacht wird man deine Seele von dir
fordern; u. [und] was wird es sein, das du
bereitet hast? [und wem wird dann gehören, was du angehäuft hast?]
Also geht es, wer sich Schätze sammelt
u. [und] ist nicht reich in Gott.
[So geht es dem, der sich Schätze sammelt und ist nicht reich bei
Gott]

[The King James version (Luke 12:16–20) is as follows:
The ground of a certain rich man brought forth plentifully:
And he thought within himself, saying, What shall I do, because I have no room where to bestow my fruits?
And he said, This will I do: I will put down my barns, and build greater; and there will I bestow all my fruits and my goods.
And I will say to my soul, Soul, thou has much goods laid up for many years; take thine ease, eat, drink *and* be merry.
But God said unto him, *Thou* fool, this night thy soul shall be required of thee: then whose shall those things be, which thou hast provided?]

Transcription continues on p. 251

"Dreck bist du"
['Mud thou art']

Gen. [Genesis] III.19
Im Schweisse deines Angesichts
sollst du dein Brot essen, bis (dass)
du wieder zu Erde werdest davon du
gekommen bist. Denn du bist Erde,
u. [und] sollst zu Erde werden

[The King James version (Genesis 3:19) is as follows:
In the sweat of thy face shall thou eat bread, till thou return unto the ground; for out of it wast thou taken: for dust thou *art*, and unto dust shall thou return.]

1	17	
2	9	
3	24	
4	17	
5	55	
6	20	
7	16	
8	22	
9	23	3
10	101	(54+47)

5 Du hattest ihr ewig
ehe wir aus dem letzten L

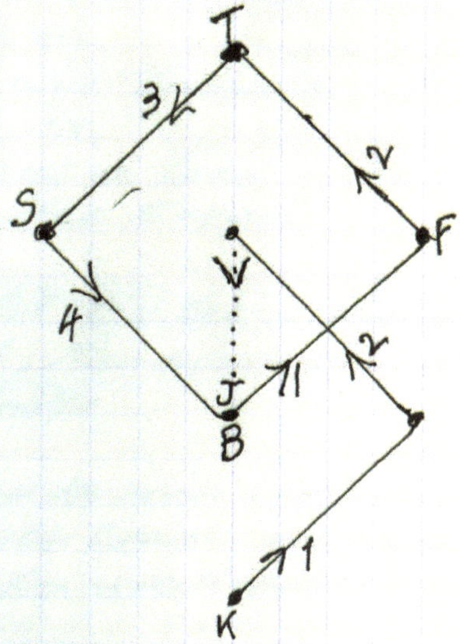

T
3
2
S
F
V
4
2
J
1
B
1
K

[*fol. 5v*]

1[2] 17
2 9
3 24
4 17
5 55
6 20
7 16[3]
8 22
9 23 3
10 101 (5<4> + 47)[4]

5[5] Du hattest ihr ewig
ehe wir aus dem letzten L . .

[Du hättest ihr ewig lauschen können . . .]

[You could have listened to it for ever]

[Diagram][6]

From Bed to Window }
" Window " Door } Same distance
" Door " Cupboard }
" Cupboard " Bed } " No. steps

—

Opening } Window, door, cupboard,
closing } same gesture
But how then [illegible] inwards?

South & East open

Window }
Door } Push open

Cupboard } Pull "
Bed }
(quilt hanging to floor)

1. Out of sight. Reach. Fear of dark.

2. Recitative formula – "Best to come" (1)

3. Voices in head – behind the eyes. Mental struggle.

4 Present voice last, then lessons to still, then silence till God's, unstillable

5. Clues for voice – Heaven. Worse when nearly home. What if final whisper unarticulable?

6. God to him 1.

7. Deficient in kindness, strength, intelligence, looks, cleanliness, sexuality.

8. Green one. "Best to come" 2. Subst'd.

9. Same as 4.

10. Voice falling to whisper.

[*fol. 6v*]

From	Bed	to Window	Same distance
"	Window	" Door	
"	Door	" Cupboard	" No. steps
"	Cupboard	" Bed	

Opening / Closing	Window, door, cupboard. Same gestures[7]

But how open C [cupboard] inward?

[Diagram]

South & East open[8]

Window / Door	push open / [*erasure*]
Cupboard / Bed	pull "

(quilt hanging to floor)

[*erasure*]

1.[9] Out of sight, reach. Fear of dark.
2. Rupture formula – "Best to come"[10] (1)
3. Voices in head – behind the eyes.
Mental thugee.[11]
4 Present voice last, then his own to
still, then silence till God's, un-
stillable[12]
5. Clues for voice & hearer. Worse when
nearly home. What if final
whisper unstillable?
6. God to him 1.
7. Deficient in kindness, strength,
intelligence, looks, cleanliness,
normality.
8. Green one. "Best to come" 2.
Duly laid.
9. Same as 4.
10. Voice falling to whisper

—

Voices always at night:
Sennenacht (father)
eines Nachts
Schwarzige Winternacht } Gr

—

well preserved for his age

—

---

3. Division
4. W's voices
5. To Wm. A
7. Eyes to Wm. B
9. To bag A – objects
11. Défaillances
13. Happy day
14. Bell
15. Those - that
17/19. Quotes
21. Song
22. Time
23. Old style
25. and now
27. Strange
28. Something, reason
29. Wonderful
30. Understandable
33. Mercies
35. No
36, 37. A I
38, 39. A II
40. A III

41, 42. A IV
43. A V
44. A VI
45. A VII
46 A VIII
47 Tidying
48 B I
49 B II
50 B III
51 B IV
52 From bag (with glasses or not)
53, 54. Props
55 Main events
6 Brief dream
8 Willie B IV
12 W in - out of hole
10 + ... —
18 Calendar

Happy Days Royal Court June 79

A

I To "Old eyes."
II Thence to "Hog's setae."
III " " "If."
IV " " Laugh.
V " " Opening of parasol.
VI " " Musical box
VII " " End of filing.
VIII " " " " act

B

I To "The face."
II Thence to "Gently Winnie."
III " " "Sing fr. old song, W."
IV " " end of act.

[*fol. 7v*]

Voice always at night? [*red tape*]

Juninacht (father)[13] [June night]

eines Nachts[14] [i.e., Bis eines Nachts . . . (Till one night)] schmutzige[n] Winternacht[15] [i.e., In einer schmutzigen Winternacht . . . (One dirty winter night . . .)]	God

---

Well preserved for his age.

[Beginning of *Happy Days* outline]

[Continuation of *Happy Days* outline]

1 – Beckett's first preparation for the refilming of *Eh Joe* was to establish the German version of two central biblical quotations. These are the two 'voices of God', that is, biblical quotations that are introduced by some version of 'And God said'. Beckett wrote out the complete German text, essentially from the Lutheran Bible. Bracketed material is from the 1984 revised edition from Deutsche Bibelgesellschaft, Stuttgart.

2 – The left-hand column of numbers here indicates not the play's camera moves, for there are nine of those, but the ten sections defined by the nine moves. The corresponding right-hand column indicates the number of lines of dialogue in each of those ten sections.

3 – Originally this section contained 17 lines but Beckett cut one, 'Schliesslich . . .'

4 – The tenth section is divided by the stage direction 'Stimme wird schwächer bis zu einem gerade noch hörbaren Flüstern, das Kursivgesetzte etwas lauter' ['Voice drops to whisper, almost inaudible except words in italics']. Part 1 contains 54 lines but Beckett evidently cut one, 'Zu dieser unziemlichen Zeit . . .', hence the revision of 54 to 53. He failed, however, to revise the total, 101. (See also 'Cuts and Changes' to the text of *He Joe* (*Eh Joe*), p. 61 in the German text and pp. 269–70 in this volume.)

5 – This potential revision then occurs in the fifth section of the teleplay. The original German version reads, 'Du hättest ihr ewig lauschen können . . .' ['You could have listened to it (i.e., Voice like flint glass) for ever . . .']. The revision was not made, however, in *He Joe* (RC). See also 'Cuts and Changes to the Text of *He Joe* (*Eh Joe*)'.

6 – This diagram traces the pattern of Joe's movement with the trailing camera (K, Kamera). It apparently includes the preaction of Joe's and the camera's entering the room and moving to the bed (B, Bettrand). It then traces the anti-clockwise pattern of room inspection: to the window (F, Fenster), to the door (T, Tür), to the cupboard (S, Schrank), and finally back to the bed.

7 – Beckett's preoccupation with symmetries in movement and gesture is again evident here. He would have liked all the openings to be inward, that is, away from Joe, but that was impossible with the cupboard, so Beckett devised another pattern of movement through the room, with a new drawing. The bed then will be

the last item inspected and can be paired with the cupboard as an outward (towards himself) gesture.

8 – That is, the bed in the revised diagram. Since the cupboard must open outward, Beckett wanted an action to pair with this outward gesture. He chose the examination beneath the bed with its floorlength quilt. The final pattern then is two gestures inward (push), two outward (pull).

9 – A thematic outline of the ten sections. The first item is the dramatic spine. It establishes what passes for plot for this teleplay. Once out of sight, Joe believes he will be out of reach of any potential perceiver, and so be still, at peace. The corresponding problem is that Joe is afraid of the dark. Much of the dramatic action of this teleplay, then, is built around this Scylla and Charybdis conflict of pursuing the lesser danger, in this case, the dark.

10 – This is the first mention of Joe's brush-off line. It is a version of the opening to Robert Browning's 'Rabbi Ben Ezra'. In his textual revisions to the German text for the production of *He Joe* at the Studios of Süddeutscher Rundfunk, Beckett revised the line 'Immer Kavalier, bis zum Schluss . . .' to 'Soviel hattest du noch für mich übrig'. On the English side of the text Beckett drew an arrow from the English version of this line, 'Last I was favoured with from you', to the first line of this section, 'The best's to come, you said, that last time . . .', and so identifying the reference to 'Last', i.e., 'The best's to come' were the last words the voice was favoured with from Joe. (See also 'Cuts and Changes' to the text of *He Joe* (*Eh Joe*), p. 47 in the German text and p. 267 in this volume.)

11 – This the technique of stilling the tormenting, assailing voices in the head.

12 – The voice of 'God' here also suggests something of the idealist philosopher George Berkeley (Bishop of Cloyne) and his notion of God as the ultimate perceiver validating all life. Beckett used Berkeley's famous dictum, 'esse est percipi' (being is being perceived), in his notes to an earlier experiment with film called simply *Film* (see also S. E. Gontarski, '*Film* and Formal Integrity' in Gontarski, 1985). The voice of 'God' also suggests the ending of the short story 'Dante and the Lobster' from *More Pricks than Kicks.*

13 – That is, the father's voice, 'Started in on you one June night'. Beckett revised the German 'Juniabend' ['June evening'] to 'Juninacht' ['June night'], and the change brings the German text closer to the original English text.

14 – This then is the first 'voice of God': 'Thou fool thy soul.' (See also note 1 above.)

15 – This is the second 'voice of God': 'Mud thou art.' (See also note 1 above.)

CUTS AND CHANGES TO THE SÜDDEUTSCHER RUNDFUNK PRODUCTION TEXT

Page references are to the text Beckett used to prepare for the Stuttgart production in 1979, *He Joe* (RC). The autograph presentation reads, 'for Rick [Cluchey] / affectionately / from Sam / Stuttgart / January 1979'. The page numbers follow those of the trilingual (with facing English and German texts) Suhrkamp edition of *Film* and *He Joe*. On the author's page Mr Cluchey has written the following note: 'Sam gave me his personal "work book" on the first occasion of my visit w/him at SDR [Süddeutscher Rundfunk] studios (T.V.) at Stuttgart W. Germany as it is dated and signed by Mr Beckett. [S.] Rick Cluchey. P.S. All notations and changes are in Sam Beckett's hand.'

Page 43

'Zehn' replaced 'fünfzig'.

'neunzig' replaced 'fünfzig'.

Page 45

'Zehn' replaced 'fünf'.

Page 47

'Hast dir ein anderes besorgt, nicht? . . .' was revised to 'Hast dir doch ein anderes besorgt, nicht?'

'Hilft auch nichts? . . .' was revised to 'Half auch nichts? . . .'.

'Als du mir nicht schnell genug in den Mantel helfen konntest . . .' was revised to 'Als du mir nicht schnell genug in meinen Mantel helfen konntest . . .'.

'Immer Kavalier, bis zum Schluss . . .' was revised to 'Soviel hattest du noch für mich übrig'. On the English side of the text Beckett drew an arrow from the English version of this line, 'Last I was favoured with from you', to the first line of this section, 'The best's to come, you said, that last time . . .', identifying the references to 'Last', i.e., 'The best's to come' were the last words Voice was favoured with from Joe.

'Daher kommt es, denkst du, nicht? . . .' was revised to 'Daher kommt dies, denkst du, nicht? . . .'.

'An einem Juniabend fing er an, auf dich einzureden' was revised to 'In einer Juninacht fing er an, auf dich einzureden . . .', to bring the German text closer to the English 'June night'.

'Immerzu' replaced 'Immer wieder . . .'.

Page 49

'Nicht daran zu rühren' was revised to 'Der kommt nichts gleich . . .'.

'Lebt jetzt irgendjemand, der dich liebt, Joe? . . .' was revised to 'Lebt noch irgendjemand, der dich liebt, Joe? . . .'.

'Lebt irgendjemand, der dich bemitleidet? . . .' was revised to 'Lebt noch irgendjemand, der dich bemitleidet? . . .'.

'Die Schlampe' replaced 'Das Weib'.

Beckett bracketed 'Was dann' in 'Was dann, wenn du zu kurz kämst, keine mehr von uns hättest . . .' and 'keine' was replaced by 'niemand'.

'Keine Seele mehr zu beschwichtigen . . .' was revised to 'Zum Schweigen zu bringen . . .'.

Page 51

'Auch meine Stimme' replaced 'Meine Stimme'.

'Wenn du die Worte nicht mehr verstehst . . .' was revised to 'Wenn du die Worte nicht mehr vernimmst'.

'Da' replaced 'Wenn' in 'Wenn du beinahe am Ziel . . .'.

Page 53

Beckett contemplated replacing 'gebracht' with 'beschwichtigt' in 'Wieder jemand zum Schweigen gebracht . . .' The number '49' next to 'beschwichtigt' suggests that Beckett was establishing a parallel to the phrase 'Keine Seele mehr zu beschwichtigen . . .' on page 49. But since he revised the 'Keine Seele mehr zu beschwichtigen . . .' to 'Zum Schweigen zu bringen . . .' he cancelled the 'beschwichtigt' here and relied on 'Schweigen' to establish the audio parallel.

Beckett revised 'dasitzt' to 'da' in 'Und du dasitzt in deinen schmutzigen alten Klamotten . . .'.

Page 55

Top right, Beckett noted the source in the Lutheran Bible for the allusion 'Du Narr, deine Seele . . .' ['Thou fool thy soul'] as follows: 'Gleichnis vom reichen Narren / Luke 12 20. Rich fool. / Du Narr! diese Nacht / wird man deine Seele / von dir fordern / (Luther)'.

'Ich fand jedoch etwas Besseres . . .' was revised to 'Ich aber fand etwas Besseres . . .'.

'Schliesslich . . .' was cut.

Page 57

'Du hast von ihr gehört, nicht? . . .' was revised to 'Die hast du geschafft, nicht?'

'Du hast sie erledigt' was revised to 'Die hast du erledigt . . .'

'Vor langer Zeit . . .' was revised to 'Die hast du erledigt . . .'

'das Weib' was revised to 'die arme Schlampe'.

Page 59

Top right, Beckett noted the source in the Lutheran Bible for the allusion 'Dreck bist du' ['Mud thou art'] 'Genesis III 19' and he wrote out the quotation as follows: 'Den[n] du bist Erde / u. [und] sollst zu Erde werden / (Luther)'.

'W. M. Harfenspieler / 83' in the right margin.

Beckett contemplated an alternative to 'ihrer Bettkante' ['on the edge of her bed']: 'ihrem Bett(e)'. This is, of course, the position of Joe as well at the opening of the play. He also drew an arrow from 'ihrem Bett(e)' to a phrase at the top of the page which is only partly legible, '. . . weinend sass' ['sat weeping'].

'Ah, sie kannte euch, himmlische Mächte! . . .' was revised to 'Ah, sie kannte euch, ihr himmlischen Mächte! . . .'.

'Geht weiter runter an den Rand und legt sich mit dem Gesicht ans Wasser . . .' was revised to 'Geht weiter runter an den Rand und legt sich nieder mit dem Gesicht ans Wasser'.

'klappte' was revised to 'klappt' twice.

Page 61

A comma was deleted in the first sentence, between 'rauf' and 'zurück'.

'Zu dieser unziemlichen Zeit' was bracketed for possible cut. According to the

He Joe notebook, one line from this section was cut, and this is the likely candidate. See editorial note 4 to the *He Joe* notebook, p. 265.

Beside 'Der Mond versinkt hinterm Hügel . . .' Beckett wrote 'bleibt ein W. [Weilchen] stehen' but the phrase is actually a possible revision of the following line, 'Sie steht ein Weilchen . . .' ['Stands a bit looking . . .'].

'Legt sich schliesslich hin' was revised to 'Legt sich schliesslich nieder'.

Page 63

'Kein Licht' was revised to 'Kein Licht mehr . . .'

'Juni . . . / Welches Jahr Deines Herrn? . . .' was bracketed.

Page 65

The stage direction at the top of the page, '(*Bild verschwindet, Stimme wie zuvor*)', was cut. The corresponding English phrase on page 64, ('*Image fades, voice as before.*)', was also cut.

'Nicht, Joe' bracketed, followed by note: 'Hold image to end of voice + 5″ before fade', which replaced the stage direction above. This change was the only substantive revision to the English text that Beckett made in his two German productions of *He Joe.*

Beckett wrote 'Gottab' beside 'Seiner' in 'Verglichen mit Seiner'. 'Gottab' further suggests Beckett's preoccupation with the voice of God in *He Joe.* The 'Gottab' here may suggest simply the difficulty of alluding to the deity through punctuation in German as he had in English where the 'Him' in Voice's penultimate line clearly refers to the deity in the English: 'Compared to Him'. The 'Gottab' may, however, suggest the exit or departure of God and so Joe's success at suppressing this voice as well.

PART IV

Footfalls

Revised Text

TYPOGRAPHICAL NOTE

Text between square brackets [ ] has been added to the original English text.
Text between pointed brackets {} has been revised.
A pair of angle brackets <> indicates that a section of text has been cut from the original English text.
All changes indicated by the above brackets are explained in the Textual Notes.

PUBLISHER'S NOTE

The publisher has taken this opportunity to make a number of minor adjustments to the layout and typographical style adopted for earlier editions of *Footfalls*.

MAY (M), *dishevelled grey hair, worn grey wrap hiding feet, trailing.*
WOMAN'S VOICE (V) *from dark upstage.*
Strip: downstage, parallel with front, length {nine} steps, width one metre, a little off centre audience right.

r l r l r l r l r ←
{L ———————————— R}
→ l r l r l r l r l

Pacing: starting with right foot (r), *from right* (R) *to left* (L), *with left foot* (l) *from* L *to* R.
Turn: rightabout at L, *leftabout at* R.
Steps: clearly audible rhythmic {tread}.
Lighting: dim, [*cold,*] *strongest at floor level, less on body, least on head.* [*Dim spot on face during halts at* R *and* L.
Upstage left, a thin vertical beam (B) *3 metres high.*]
Voices: both low {and slow} throughout.

Curtain. Stage in darkness.
Faint single chime. Pause as echoes die.
Fade up to dim on strip[*, including* B]. Rest in darkness.
M *discovered pacing {towards}* L. *Turns at* L, *paces three more lengths, halts, facing front at* R.
Pause.

M: Mother.
(*Pause*)
(*No louder*) Mother. (*Pause.*)
V: Yes, May.
M: Were you asleep?
V: Deep asleep. (*Pause.*) I heard you in my deep sleep. (*Pause.*) There is no sleep so deep I would not hear you there.
(*Pause.* M *resumes pacing. Four lengths.*)
(*After first length, synchronous with steps*) {. . .} <> seven [eight nine] wheel {. . .} <> seven [eight nine] wheel. (*Free.*) Will you not try to snatch a little sleep?

(M *halts facing front at* R. *Pause.*)

M: Would you like me to inject you [. . .] again?

V: Yes, but it is too soon.

(*Pause.*)

M: Would you like me to change your position [. . . again]?

V: Yes, but it is too soon.

(*Pause.*)

M: Straighten your pillows?

(*Pause.*)

Change your drawsheet?

(*Pause.*)

Pass you the bedpan?

(*Pause.*)

The warming-pan?

(*Pause.*)

Dress your sores?

(*Pause.*)

Sponge you down?

(*Pause.*)

Moisten your poor lips?

(*Pause.*)

Pray with you?

(*Pause.*)

For you?

[(*Pause.*)

Again.]

(*Pause.*)

V: Yes, but it is too soon.

(*Pause.* [M *resumes pacing. After one length halts facing front at* L. *Pause.*])

M: What age am I now?

V: And I?

(*Pause.*)

(*No louder*) And I?

M: Ninety.

V: So much?

M: Eighty-nine, ninety.

V: I had you late. (*Pause.*) In life. (*Pause.*) Forgive me [. . .] again.

(*Pause.*)

(*No louder*) Forgive me [. . .] again.
[(*Pause.*)]
M: {What age am I now?}
V: In your forties.
M: So little?
V: I'm afraid so.
(*Pause.* M *resumes pacing.*)
(*After first turn at* {R}) May.
(*Pause.*)
(*No louder*) May.
M: (*Pacing*) Yes, Mother.
V: Will you never have done?
(*Pause.*)
Will you never have done . . . revolving it all?
M: ({*Halting*}) It?
V: It all. (*Pause.*) In your poor mind. (*Pause.*) It all. (*Pause.*) It all.
(M {*resumes*} *pacing. Five seconds. Fade out on strip*[, *except* B].
All in darkness. Steps {*cease*}.
<> *Pause.*
Chime a little fainter. Pause for echoes.
Fade up to a little less on strip. Rest in darkness.
M *discovered facing front at* R.
Pause.)
I walk here now. (*Pause.*) Rather I come and stand. (*Pause.*) At nightfall. (*Pause.*) <> She fancies she is alone. (*Pause.*) See how still she stands, how stark, with her face to the wall. (*Pause.*) How outwardly unmoved. (*Pause.*) She has not been out since girlhood. (*Pause.*) <> Not out since girlhood. (*Pause.*) Where is she, it may be asked. (*Pause.*) {Why, in} the old home, the same where she – (*Pause.*) The same where she began. (*Pause.*) Where it began. (*Pause.*) It all began. (*Pause.*) But this, this, when did this begin? (*Pause.*) When other girls of her age were out at . . . lacrosse she was already here. (*Pause.*) At this. (*Pause.*) The floor here, now bare, once was –
(M *begins pacing. Steps a little slower.*)
But let us watch her move, in silence.
(M *paces.*)
(*Towards end of second length*) Watch how feat she wheels.
(M *turns, paces.*)
(*Synchronous with steps third length*) {Seven, eight, nine, wheel.}

(M *turns at* L, *paces one more length, halts facing front at* R.)
I say the floor here, now bare, this strip of floor, once was carpeted, a deep pile. Till one night, while still little more than a child, she called her mother and said, Mother, this is not enough. The mother: Not enough? May – the child's given name – May: Not enough. The mother: What do you mean, May, not enough, what can you possibly mean, May, not enough? May: I mean, Mother, that I must hear the feet, however faint they fall. The mother: The motion alone is not enough? May: No, Mother, the motion alone is not enough, I must hear the feet, however faint they fall.
(*Pause.* M *resumes pacing.*)
(*With pacing*) Does she still sleep, it may be asked? Yes, some nights she does, in snatches, bows her poor head against the wall and snatches a little sleep. (*Pause.*) Still speak? Yes, some nights she does, when she fancies none can hear. (*Pause.*) Tells how it was. (*Pause.*) Tries to tell how it was. (*Pause.*) It all. (*Pause.*) It all.
(M *continues pacing. Five seconds. Fade out on strip* [, *except* B].
All in darkness. Steps {*cease*}.
<> *Pause.*
Chime a little fainter still. Pause for echoes.
Fade up to a little less still on strip. Rest in darkness.
M *discovered facing front at* R.
Pause.)

M: Sequel. [(*Pause. Begins pacing. Steps a little slower still. After two lengths halts facing front at* R. *Pause.*) Sequel.] A little later, when she was quite forgotten, she began to – (*Pause.*) A little later, when as though she had never been, it never been, she began to walk. (*Pause.*) At nightfall. (*Pause.*) Slip out at nightfall and into the little church by the {north} door, always locked at that hour, and walk, up and down, up and down. {H}is poor arm. (*Pause.*) Some nights she would halt, as one frozen by some shudder of the mind, and stand stark still till she could move again. But many also were the nights when she paced without pause, up and down, up and down, before vanishing the way she came. (*Pause.*) No sound. (*Pause.*) None at least to be heard. (*Pause.*) The semblance. (*Pause.* {*Resumes*} *pacing.* <> *After two lengths halts facing front at* R. <>) [The semblance.] Faint, though by no means invisible, in a certain light. (*Pause.*) Given the right light. (*Pause.*) Grey rather than white, a pale shade of grey. (*Pause.*) Tattered. (*Pause.*) A tangle of tatters. (*Pause.*) A faint tangle of pale grey tatters. (*Pause.*) Watch it pass – (*Pause.*) – watch her pass before the candelabrum, how its flames, their light . . . like moon through

passing rack. (*Pause.*) Soon then after she was gone, as though never there,
began to walk, up and down, up and down, that poor arm. (*Pause.*) At
nightfall. (*Pause.*) That is to say, at certain seasons of the year, during
Vespers. (*Pause.*) Necessarily. (*Pause.* {*Resumes*} *pacing. After one length halts* 150
facing front at L. Pause.) Old Mrs Winter, whom the reader will remember,
old Mrs Winter, one late autumn Sunday evening, on sitting down to supper
with her daughter after worship, after a few half-hearted mouthfuls laid down
her knife and fork and bowed her head. What is it, Mother, said the
daughter, a most strange girl, though scarcely a girl any more . . . (*Brokenly*)
. . . dreadfully [un – . . .] (*Pause. Normal voice*) What is it, Mother, are you 156
not feeling yourself? (*Pause.*) Mrs W. did not at once reply. But finally, raising
her head and fixing Amy – the daughter's given name, as the reader will
remember – [raising her head and] fixing Amy full in the eye she said – 159
(*Pause.*) – she murmured, fixing Amy full in the eye she murmured, Amy did
you observe anything . . . strange at Evensong? Amy: No, Mother, I did not.
Mrs W: Perhaps it was just my fancy. Amy: Just what exactly, Mother, did
you perhaps fancy it was? (*Pause.*) Just what exactly, Mother, did you perhaps
fancy this . . . strange thing was you observed? (*Pause.*) Mrs W: You yourself
observed nothing . . . strange? Amy: No, Mother, I myself did not, to put it
mildly. Mrs W: What do you mean, Amy, to put it mildly, what can you
possibly mean, Amy, to put it mildly? Amy: I mean, Mother, that to say I
observed nothing . . . strange is indeed to put it mildly. For I observed
nothing of any kind, strange or otherwise. I saw nothing, heard nothing, of
any kind. I was not there. Mrs W: Not there? Amy: Not there. Mrs W: But I
heard you respond. (*Pause.*) I heard you say Amen. (*Pause.*) How could you
have responded if you were not there? (*Pause.*) How could you possibly have
said Amen if, as you claim, you were not there? (*Pause.*) The love of God,
and the fellowship of the Holy Ghost, be with us all, [now, and for] 174
evermore. Amen. (*Pause.*) I heard you distinctly. (*Pause.* {*Resumes*} *pacing.* 175
After {*five*} *steps halts without facing front. Long pause. Resumes pacing, halts* 176
facing front at R. *Long pause.*) Amy. (*Pause. No louder*) Amy. (*Pause.*) Yes,
Mother. (*Pause.*) Will you never have done? (*Pause.*) Will you never have done
. . . revolving it all? (*Pause.*) It? (*Pause.*) It all. (*Pause.*) In your poor mind.
(*Pause.*) It all. (*Pause.*) It all.

(*Pause. Fade out on strip* [, *except B*]. *All in darkness.* 181

Pause.

Chime even a little fainter still. Pause for echoes.

Fade up to even a little less still on strip.

No trace of MAY.
186 *Hold* {*ten*} *seconds.*
187 *Fade out* [, *including B*].)

CURTAIN

3, 5–7 – '*Nine*' replaced '*seven*', and in *Footfalls* (CI) Beckett noted beside the diagram, 'extend to 9'. This change was made in all post-production editions (see below) and is evident in the English notebook for *Footfalls*.

The principal change in both of Beckett's productions was the increase in the number of May's steps from seven to nine. Unfortunately, none of the previously published texts for this play is accurate and consistent on this revision. The original publication of *Footfalls* (Faber and Faber, London, 1976) antedated the première production. Preparing for his direction of the play for the Royal Court Theatre's celebration of his seventieth birthday in the spring of 1976, however, Beckett extended May's pacing from the seven steps of the original publication (1976) to nine steps. This revision was no minor adjustment to stage space since, as the notebooks confirm, the number of steps and the points of turning and pause are minutely detailed by Beckett and affect the tempo of this very musical composition which Beckett has called 'chamber music'. In Berlin Beckett told his technical directors that the basic unit of time in *Footfalls*, however, 'should be seven seconds each time . . . The bell at the beginning of *Footfalls* dies away in seven seconds; then the light comes up during seven seconds and one can see May walking. At the end of the three parts, the light fades out each time inside seven seconds, the bell dies away in seven seconds, and the light comes on again in seven seconds' (Asmus, 'Rehearsal Notes', p. 336). See the German notebook for *Footfalls* (*Tritte*) under the categories 'Light' and 'Bell' for Beckett's exact pattern.

Beckett subsequently prepared a revised text for his publisher, *Footfalls* (SB), but it contains a number of internal inconsistencies which house editors failed to query or correct. While the stage directions called for nine steps, for instance, May still counted only to seven in the dialogue. The publication of (unacknowledged) a revised text in *Ends and Odds: Plays and Sketches by Samuel Beckett* (Faber and Faber, London, 1977), a text subsequently reprinted in *Collected Shorter Plays of Samuel Beckett* (Faber and Faber, London, 1984) and *Samuel Beckett: The Complete Dramatic Works* (Faber and Faber, London, 1986), failed to include all of Beckett's revisions. The Grove Press editions, which photo offset first the Faber *Ends and Odds*, subtitling it first *Eight New Dramatic Pieces* (1976) and then, with the addition of . . . *but the clouds* . . ., *Nine Dramatic Pieces* (1981), and then *Collected Shorter Plays of Samuel Beckett*, which Grove retitled *Collected*

Plays of Samuel Beckett, simply repeated the omissions and inconsistencies of the Faber texts (see Gontarski, 1983).

Much of the textual confusion results from the fact that Beckett revised at least two separate texts which were not identical, *Footfalls* (SB) and *Footfalls* (CI). The former is much less comprehensive than the latter. The following notes refer to both of these revised texts. Changes made to the first printing of *Footfalls* (1976) are noted in this text as revisions as well even though they already appear in the various collected editions.

11 – '*Tread*' replaced '*pad*'.

12–14 – Although Beckett made very few notes on lighting in either of the *Footfalls* notebooks, he did confront a problem with the lighting as published in the English text in both of his productions. Beckett originally suggested the following, 'Lighting: dim, strongest at floor level, less on body, least on head.' Such lighting, however, left May's face almost invisible, a problem Beckett subsequently corrected in the French translation which was completed only after he had directed the play twice, once in English and once in German. The French text describes the light as 'Eclairage: faible, froid' ['Lighting: dim, cold'] and adds the sentence, 'Faible spot sur le visage le temps des haltes à D et G' ['Dim spot on face during halts at R and L'].

In rehearsals for the German production Beckett proposed, according to Walter Asmus, another revision to the lighting which would also solve the problem that the play's tailpiece, the fade-up on an empty stage, might be missed by the audience: 'In order to avoid the impression that the piece was over with the second-last fade-out, a vertical strip of light should be visible in the background, which would give the impression that the light was falling through the crack of a door. Then it would add a vertical accent to the horizontal light on the strip that would remain lit after each part. At the very end of the play, the empty strip will be faded out first, then, after seven seconds, the vertical strip of light' (Asmus, 'Rehearsal Notes', p. 341). Beckett then wrote this lighting change into the French translation, 'Au fond à gauche, un mince rai vertical (R) 3 mètres de haut' ['Upstage left, a thin vertical beam (B) 3 metres high']. That revision, with the change from R to B, to avoid confusion with Beckett's English symbol for 'right', R, is adopted here.

15 – '*and slow*' added.

18 – '*including* B' added from the French translation.

19 – '*Towards*' replaced '*approaching*'. May's posture during her pacing was central to Beckett's conception of the character. It is also connected with May's voice: 'The position of the body will help you find the right voice'; and 'When you walk,' noted Beckett, 'you slump together; when you speak you straighten up a bit.' 'If the play is full of repetitions,' he continued, 'then it is because of these life-long stretches of walking. That is the centre of the play; everything else is secondary.' May's posture expresses not fear exactly; 'It expresses that May is there exclusively for herself. She is isolated. The costume will look like a ghost costume. It is described in the play: "Tattered . . . A tangle of tatters . . . A faint tangle of pale grey tatters". It is the costume of a ghost.' For the German production Beckett even produced a photograph of Billie Whitelaw from the London production (Asmus, 'Rehearsal Notes', p. 338).

26 – 'Were you asleep?' Not so much an interested question as a routine statement, according to Beckett (Asmus, 'Rehearsal Notes', p. 337).

30–31 – '. . .' replaced 'one two three four five six', and 'eight nine' was added after 'seven' – twice. This revision was not made in *Footfalls* (SB) and so was not made in any of the post-production editions, but it was clearly made in *Footfalls* (CI) and is consistent with the change in the number of May's paces.

34 – Ellipsis added between 'you' and 'again' in *Footfalls* (CI) only, and so it was not included in any of the post-production editions.

37 – 'again' added after 'position' in both *Footfalls* (SB) and *Footfalls* (CI) but only the latter includes the ellipsis before 'again'. The 'again' reinforces the routine nature of May's ministrations. Beckett told his actress Hildegard Schmahl in Berlin that the scene could be played without feeling, except for the mention of the 'bedpan', which can generate some feeling, some warmth (Asmus, 'Rehearsal Notes', p. 337).

57–8 – '(*Pause.*) Again.' added in both *Footfalls* (SB) and *Footfalls* (CI).

61 – Beckett added 'M *resumes pacing. After one length halts facing front at* L. *Pause.*)' here and after the 'Forgive me again' on line 71 in *Footfalls* (CI) only. The second addition was then cancelled. All post-production texts printed this addition on line 71 and not on line 61 and delete the '*Pause*' of the original publication, which is reinserted here on line 72 following the revision of *Footfalls* (CI).

73 – 'What age am I now?' replaced 'Well?'

78 – 'R' replaced 'L' in *Footfalls* (CI) but not in *Footfalls* (SB), and consequently none of the post-publication editions made this revision.

78–84 – Beckett's direction of the play was tightly orchestrated. According to Beckett's assistant, Walter Asmus, 'The first "May" comes on the fourth step while May is walking from right to left, the second "May" comes on the eighth step. May says her "Yes, Mother" on the fourth step when she is walking from left to right, and on the sixth step of the same stretch the Mother begins with,

"Will you never have done?" The sentence ends immediately before the turn' (Asmus, 'Rehearsal Notes', p. 338; see also *Footfalls Nb*).

85 – 'Halting' replaced 'Pacing' in both *Footfalls* (SB) and *Footfalls* (CI).

87 – 'resumes' replaced 'continues', and 'except B' added from the French translation.

88 – 'cease' replaced 'silent'.

89 – 'Long' before 'Pause' deleted in *Footfalls* (SB) only, and the deletion is made in all post-production editions.

94 – This begins the second part of the play, V, the mother, speaking about May. This and the third part, May speaking about the mother, ll. 131ff., should be exactly parallel. 'One must sense the similarities of both narratives,' according to Beckett; 'Not so much from the text as from the style, from the way the text is spoken' (Asmus, 'Rehearsal Notes', p. 338).

95 – 'My voice is in her mind' deleted in *Footfalls* (SB) and *Footfalls* (CI), and this sentence was deleted in all post-production editions.

97 – 'She hears in her poor mind, she has not been out since girlhood. (*Pause.*)' deleted, as above.

98 – 'Why, in' replaced 'In' in both revised texts. The interruption at the end of this sentence suggests the mother's reluctance to say that her daughter, May, was ever *born*. Instead she says, 'where she began'. Beckett associated the mother's reluctance with a lecture he heard in 1935 by C. G. Jung at the Tavistock Clinic in London about a girl Jung could not treat because she had never been fully born. She existed but she wasn't actually living (Asmus, 'Rehearsal Notes', p. 338). Beckett evidently alluded to the same lecture by Jung in the 'Addenda' to his 1953 novel *Watt*: 'never been properly born'.

May should move her lips twice during the mother's text, murmuring to herself from 'she has not been out since girlhood' to the mother's reluctance to use the word 'born': '. . . the same where she –'. And again from '. . . till one night, while still little more than a child' to 'May: Not enough.' At the end of the lip movements she closes her eyes and drops her head for a moment (Asmus, 'Rehearsal Notes', p. 341).

108 – 'Seven, eight, nine, wheel' replaced 'Three four five' in both revised texts.

124 – 'except B' added from the French translation.

125 – 'cease' replaced 'silent' in both revised texts.

126 – 'Long' before 'Pause' cut in *Footfalls* (SB) only, and this deletion is made in all post-production editions.

131 – After the first 'Sequel' Beckett added, '(M *begins pacing. After 2 lengths halts facing front at R.*) Sequel.' in *Footfalls* (CI) and '(*Pause. Steps a little slower still. After* *two lengths halts facing front at R. Pause.*) Sequel.' in *Footfalls* (SB). Post-production editions conflate the two revisions by adding '*Begins pacing*' from the *Footfalls* (CI) revisions to the *Footfalls* (SB) version so that the version in *Ends and Odds: Plays and Sketches* (Faber and Faber, London, 1977, p. 36) reads as follows: 'Sequel. (*Pause. Begins pacing. Steps a little slower still. After two lengths halts facing front at R. Pause.*) Sequel.'

The 'Sequel' begins the third part of the play, May's story, and the voice here can be a little more alive. 'One can suppose', noted Beckett, 'that she has written down everything which she has invented up to this, that she will one day find a reader for her story – therefore the address to the reader . . . Words are as food for this poor girl. They are her best friends' (Asmus, 'Rehearsal Notes', p. 339). In the *Footfalls Nb* (*q.v.* p. 293) Beckett contemplated substituting 'hearer' for 'reader' in order to shift the emphasis from page to stage, but he retained 'reader' in production. In the first run-through, Beckett complained that his German actress was using too much colour in her voice: 'Monotone. Without colour, very distant. You are composing. It is not a story, but an improvisation. You are looking for the words, you correct yourself constantly. You are in the church with the girl. The voice is the voice of an epilogue. At the end it can't go any further. It is just at an end' (Asmus, 'Rehearsal Notes', p. 340). The irony, of course, is how precisely orchestrated this improvisation is here.

Part of the reason, Beckett explained, that May's story should parallel the mother's is that 'The daughter only knows the voice of the mother.' For Beckett the 'Not enough' of the mother's story should sound exactly like the 'Not there?' of Mrs W in Amy's story (*vide* the German notebook for *Footfalls*, *Tritte*, p. 333, and Asmus, 'Rehearsal Notes', p. 340). The relationship suggests as well that between Clov and Hamm in *Endgame*. Clov says to Hamm, echoing Caliban in *The Tempest*, 'I use the words you taught me. If they don't mean anything any more, teach me others or let me be silent.' Of Clov one might say as well, 'The son only knows the voice of the father.'

Beckett stressed to Billie Whitelaw that the word 'sequel' should be pronounced so that it suggests the homophone 'seek well'.

135 – 'north' replaced 'south' in both revised texts because it seemed colder to Beckett. 'South door is too warm. North door is colder. You feel cold – the whole time, in the way you hold your body too. Everything is frost and night' (Asmus, 'Rehearsal Notes', p. 339). The French text reads, 'par la porte nord' (p. 13).

136 – The 'His' is capitalized in both revised texts to suggest Christ's arm, but none of the post-production texts makes this change. The change is crucial, at least for readers, to the understanding of this line since Amy is walking along the transept of the church. That is, since churches were designed in the shape of the cross, Amy is walking along what would be the arm of the cross where Christ's arm would hang. This also reinforces the crucifixion imagery of the play. Other girls, according to the Voice of the mother, played *lacrosse*, for example (l. 101). The French text is more explicit on this point, 'le long du bras sauveur' (p. 13).

141 – 'Resumes' replaced 'Begins' in *Footfalls* (CI) only, but the revision appears in all post-production editions.

141 – 'Steps a little slower still' cut in *Footfalls* (SB) and in all post-production editions.

142 – 'Pause' cut in *Footfalls* (CI) only. All post-production editions retain the second 'Pause' which is cut here as in *Footfalls* (CI). The second 'The semblance' was added in both revised texts to parallel the double 'Sequel' above. The 'tangle of tatters' in May's narrative is her semblance which she seeks well. Amy herself is, of course, another semblance.

150 – 'Resumes' replaced 'Begins' in *Footfalls* (CI) only, but the revision appears in all post-production editions.

156 – 'un– . . .' added after 'dreadfully' in both revised texts.

159 – 'raising her head and' added before 'fixing' in both revised texts.

174 – 'now, and for' added before 'evermore' in both revised texts to reflect more closely the closing prayer at Evensong.

175 – 'Resumes' replaced 'Begins' in *Footfalls* (CI) only, but the revision appears in all post-production editions.

176 – 'five' replaced 'three' in *Footfalls* (CI) only.

181 – 'Except B' added from the French translation.

186 – 'ten' replaced 'fifteen' in *Footfalls* (SB) and in all post-production editions.

187 – 'Including B' added from the French translation.

Samuel Beckett's Production Notebooks
for *Footfalls*
at the Royal Court Theatre,
London, May 1976,
and for *Tritte* (*Footfalls*)
at the Schiller-Theater Werkstatt,
Berlin, October 1976

FACSIMILE OF BECKETT'S PRODUCTION NOTEBOOK WITH TRANSCRIPTION

Note on the Royal Court Manuscript

Samuel Beckett's production notes for his 1976 Royal Court Theatre production of *Footfalls* (*RC Nb*) are catalogued along with the first *Spiel* (*Play*) notebook, a red, hard-covered, 90-folio, square-ruled notebook measuring 20.5 × 14.5 cms, on deposit at the University of Reading Samuel Beckett Archive, MS 1976 (see page 5). With the red notebook are three, loose, double notebook sheets measuring 20.5 × 29.6 cms. These contain the notes for Beckett's 1976 Royal Court production of *Footfalls*, written on the recto of the first sheet and on both sides of the second and third sheets.

MS 1976

Footfalls

Sounds of pacing:
1. Footfalls.
2. Trailing wrap.
3. Turns

Hear footfalls ~~before curtain up~~ after echoes of chime 1 before fade up

I

M first discovered nearer R than ~~[illegible]~~ L heading for L.

For "It?" M should halt wherever she happens to be, without turning front and resume pacing only after last "It all." E.g.

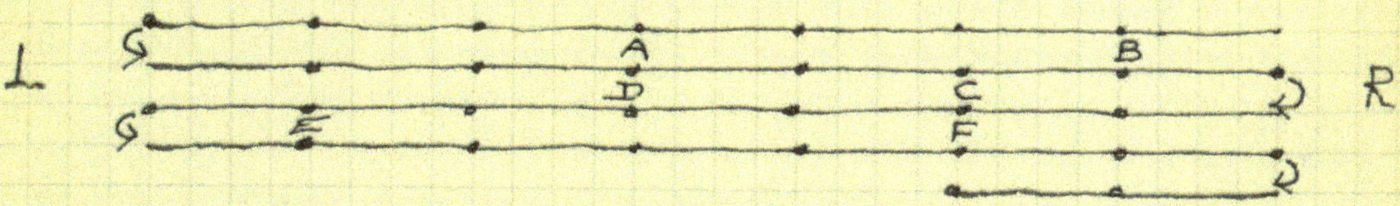

A May.
B "
C Yes mother
D Will you never have done?
E " " " " " ... revolving it all.
F. M halts. It? ... It all. May resumes pacing 5/10".

Try V lying down in I, standing in II.

III

whom } the hearer will remember ?
as }

Footfalls

Sounds of pacing:
1. Footfalls.
2. Trailing wrap.
3. Turns

Hear footfalls [*erasure*] after echoes of chime 1 before fade up

I

M first discovered nearer R than [*erasure*] L heading for L.

For <it> "It?" M should halt wherever she happens to be, without turning front, and resume pacing only after last "It all." E.g.

L[1]

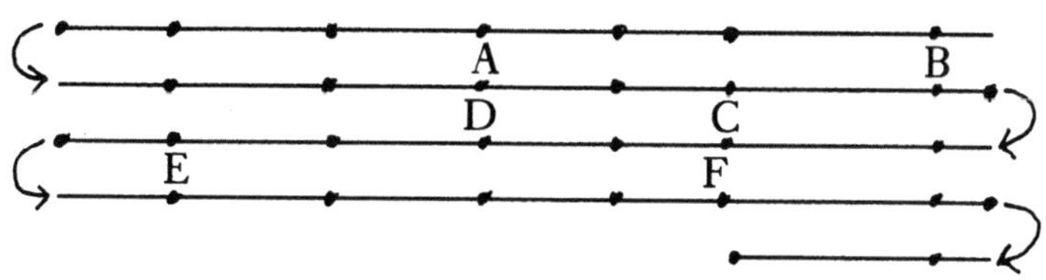

R

A May
B "
C Yes mother
D Will you never have done?
E " " " " " . . . revolving it all.
F M halts. It? . . . It all. May resumes pacing 5″/10″

Try V lying down in I, Standing in II.

III

Whom } the hearer will remember?[2]
as }

MS 1976

III

How avoid end of play audience reaction after 3rd fade-out before last chime, fade-up & final fade-out? By reducing to minimum (in all 3 cases) pause after fade-out. Scarcely dark (and steps silent I + II) when chime preventing reaction. Correct "long" to "brief" in script.

Chime

Record in echo chamber

Steps

9 rather than 7 per length

If even number of steps start with left foot from right, right foot from left.

Turn

No speech with turn.

—

Add 2 lengths after last "too soon" before "What age . . ?"

Better ⎡ or 1 length with halt L for "What age . . ." involving no change in text & steps &c. beyond suppression of 1st length (silent) R → L.

III

How avoid end of play audience reaction after 3rd fade-out before last chime, fade-up & final fade-out? By reducing to minimum (in all 3 cases) pause after fade-out. Scarcely dark (and steps silent I & II) when chime preventing reaction. Correct "long" to "brief" in script.[3]

Chime

Record in echo chamber

Steps

9 rather than 7 per length[4]

If even number of steps start with left foot from right,[5] right foot from left.

Turn

No speech with turn.[6]

Add 2 lengths after last "too soon" before "What age . . . ?"

Better [Or 1 length with halt L for "What age . . ." involving no change in halt & steps [and?] beyond suppression of 1st length (silent)[7]
R → L]

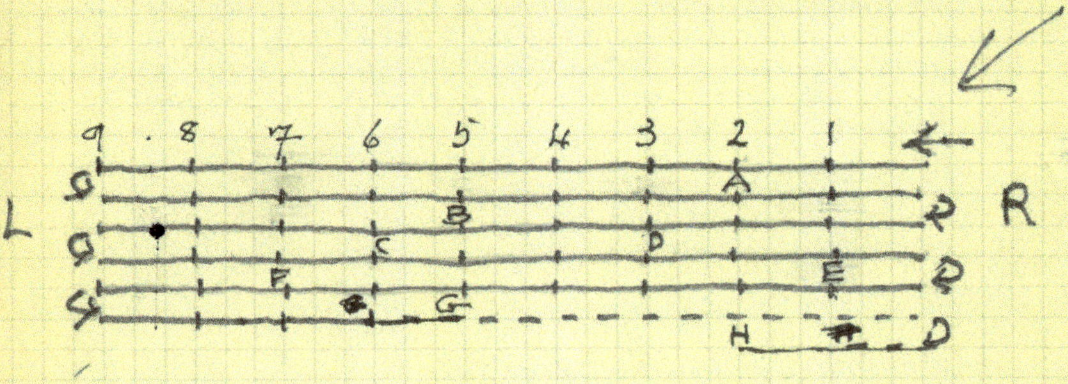

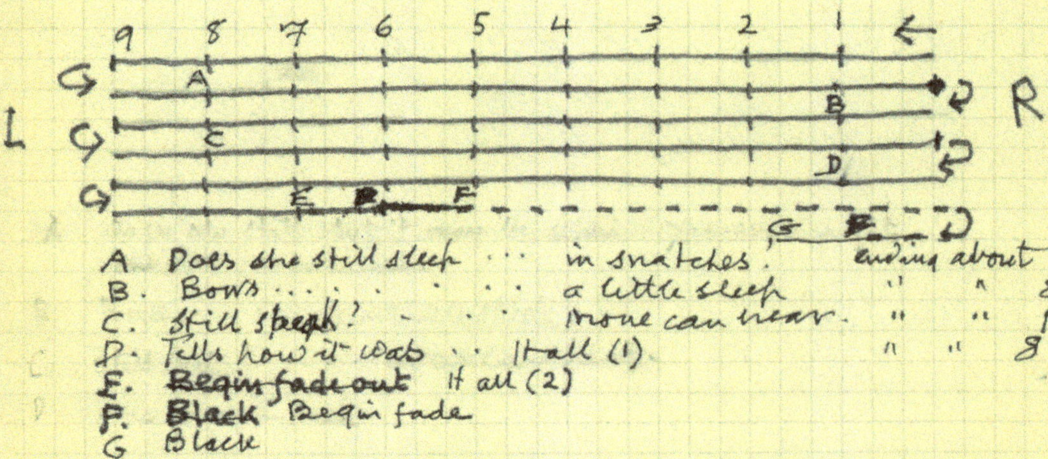

A. Does she still sleep . . . in snatches! ending about 1
B. Bows . . . a little sleep " " 8
C. Still speak? . . . none can hear. " " 1
D. Tells how it was . . It all (1) " " 8
E. ~~Begin fade out~~ It all (2)
F. ~~Black~~ Begin fade
G Black

It 9 steps

End of I

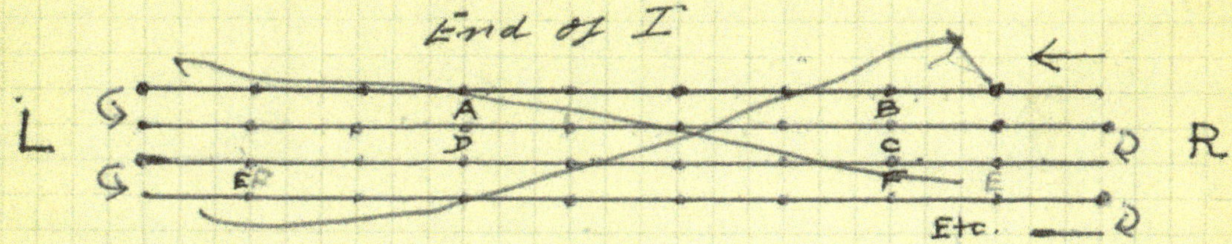

A May.
B "
C Yes mother.
D Will you never have done? (Ending before R)
E " " " " " ... revolving it all.
F. M halts. It? V: It all. In your poor mind. It all.
It all. M resumes pacing.
G. Begin fade out
H. Black

~~End of II~~

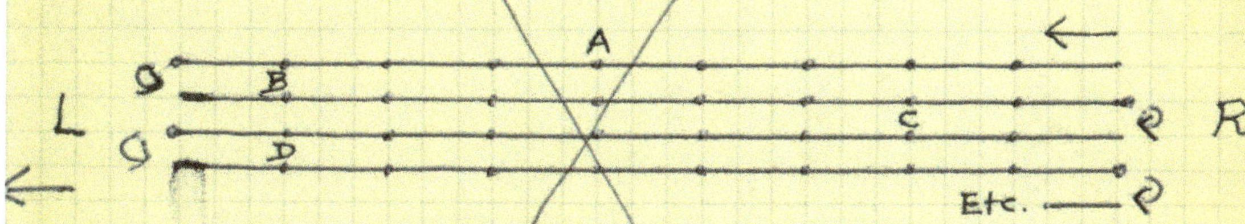

~~A. Does she still sleep etc. (ending before L)~~
~~B Yes, some nights she does etc (" " R)~~
~~C " " " " " " (" " L)~~
~~D Tells how it was etc. (" " R)~~

Revise to leave M near R at fade-out

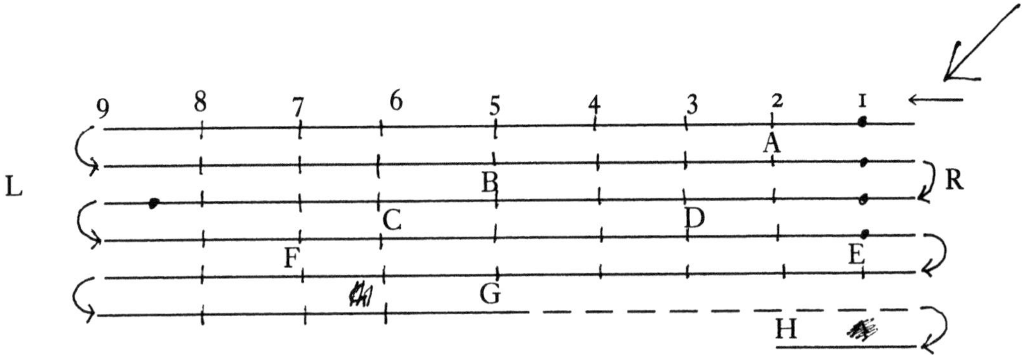

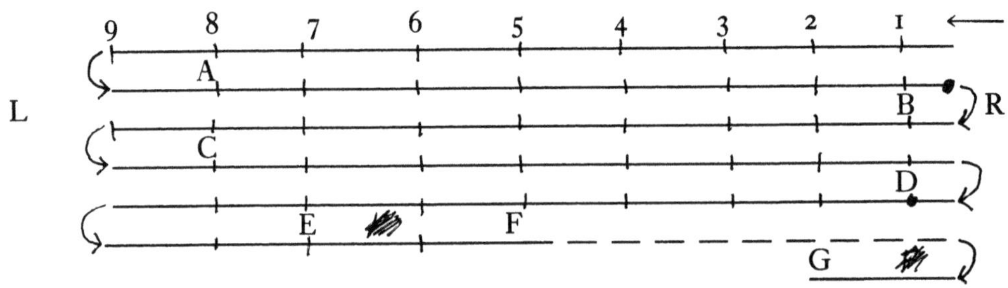

A. Does she still sleep ...... in snatches. ending about 1
B. Bows .... a little sleep. " " 8
C. Still speak? .... none can hear. " " 1
D. Tell how it was .... It all (1) " " 8
E. <Begin fade out> It all (2)
F. <Black> Begin fade
G. Black

If 9 Steps

End of I

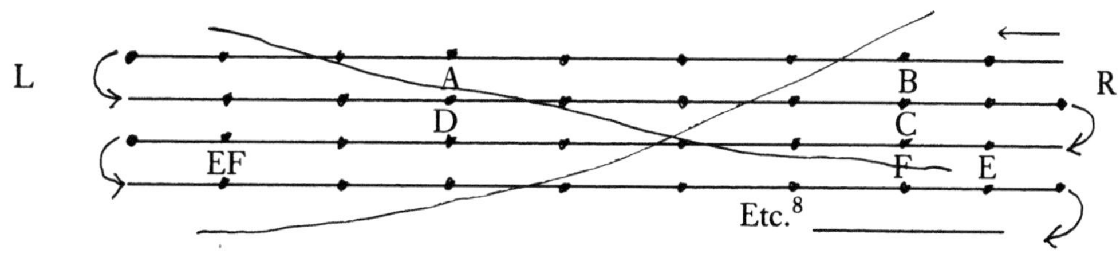

A May.
B ”
C Yes mother.
D Will you never have done? (Ending before R)
E ” ” ” ” ” . . . revolving it all.
F M halts. It? V: It all. In your poor mind. It all.
It all. M resumes pacing.
G. Begin fade out
H. Black

End of II

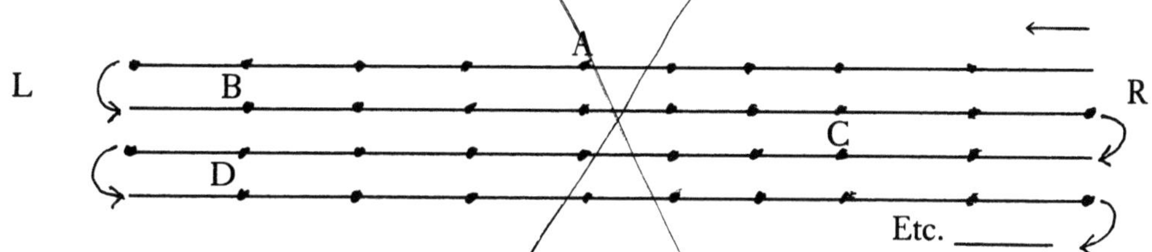

A.	Does she still sleep etc.	(Ending before L)
B	Yes, some nights she does etc	(” ” R)
C	” ” ” ” ” ”	(” ” L)
D	Tells how it was etc.	(” ” R)

Revise to leave M near R at fade-out[9]

MS 1976

Diminuendo

4 chimes (fainter)
" fade-ups (dimmer)
3 pacings (slower, fainter)
" voices (" ")
M's semblance (more tattered) ?

Pacing

I approx. 12 lengths
II " 9 "
III 4 lengths

End of II F.9.

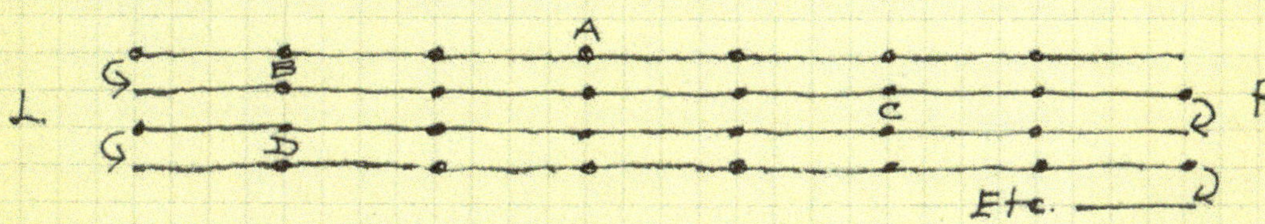

A Does she still sleep etc. Ending before L
B Yes, some nights she does etc. " " R
C Still speak etc. " " L
D Tells how it was etc. " " R

Diminuendo[10]

4 chimes (fainter)
" fade-ups (dimmer)
3 pacings (slower, fainter)
" voices (" ")
M's semblance (more tattered)?

Pacing

I	approx. 12 lengths
II	" 9 "
III	4 lengths

End of II[11] E.g.

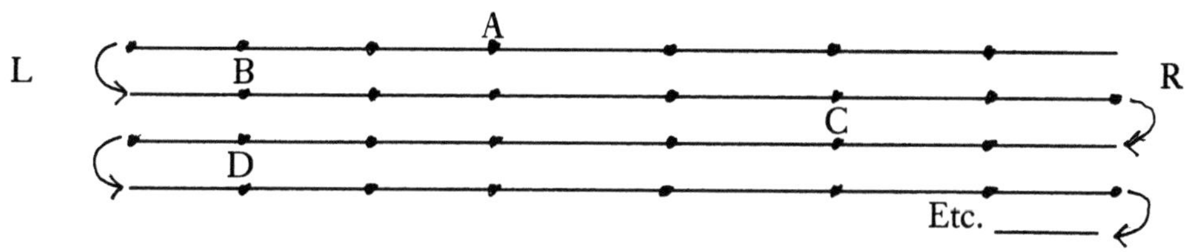

A.	Does she still sleep etc.	Ending before L
B.	Yes, some nights she does etc.	" " R
C	Still speak etc.	" " L
D	Tells how it was etc.	" " R

MS 1976

M's lips sometimes move silently as she walks (or stands).

I = 5'
II " 5'
III " 5'

[*sheet 3v*]

M's lips sometimes move silently as
she walks (or stands)

I = 5′
II " 5′
III " 5′[12]

1 – The 'L' and 'R' here are, of course, audience left and right. While much of the 'action' of the play concerns the obsessional nature of May's pacing, the notebooks suggest Beckett's own equally obsessional attention to that pacing and May's position along her path when she speaks particular lines. This initial diagram suggests that Beckett was still working with the seven-step model. The change to the nine-step model on the following recto suggests that Beckett made the change not in response to the size of any particular stage but to co-ordinate May's dialogue with her positions. In the *German Nb* Beckett began with the nine-step model he developed for the English production, but for part I of the play May's pacing begins at audience left.

2 – This revision is not made in *Footfalls* (SB), p. 12, but it significantly shifts the emphasis from text to performance as Beckett contemplated revising 'reader' to 'hearer'. Beckett retained 'reader', however, since the play's third part constitutes May's narrative, which she hopes will one day be read.

3 – In *Footfalls* (SB), pp. 10, 12, Beckett merely deleted the 'long'. His concern was that the audience might think the play ended if the pause after the third fade out were prolonged. By shortening the length of the two previous blackouts, the penultimate blackout and final fade up on the strip with 'No trace of May' could come more quickly after 'It all'. Beckett did not, however, formally make the change from 'long' to 'brief' in the script. Instead he just cancelled 'long'. In rehearsals for the German production Beckett proposed, according to Walter Asmus, a fuller solution: 'In order to avoid the impression that the piece was over with the second-last fade out, a vertical strip of light should be visible in the background, which would give the impression that the light was falling through the crack of a door. Then it would add a vertical accent to the horizontal light on the strip that would remain lit after each part. At the very end of the play, the empty strip will be faded out first, then, after seven seconds, the vertical strip of light' (Asmus, 'Rehearsal Notes', p. 341).

4 – Beckett's confirmation (to himself) of the new nine-step model.

5 – Again, this is audience right.

6 – This again suggests one of Beckett's most persistent theatrical axioms, speech and action should be separated wherever feasible.

7 – On sheet 2 verso Beckett did indeed cancel the diagrams for parts I and II of *Footfalls* and revise those diagrams to include two more lengths to May's pacing.

One result of the addition was to keep the first length silent as suggested here.
8 – The model Beckett rejected here has May pacing one full length, audience right to audience left, and turning before she speaks. Moreover, in the pattern worked out here the placement of speeches 'E' and 'F' is uncertain. Beckett cancelled this diagram and revised it on the facing side of the double notebook sheet.
9 – This is another example of the sort of conversation with himself that Beckett often conducted in his notebooks. In this case the revised diagram is the one on the facing verso where the blackout, 'G', is indeed near audience right but it occurs after the turn. In the comparable diagram in the *German Nb*, called 'End of II', Beckett placed 'G' at the nearest point to audience right before the turn.
10 – Beckett outlined here the parallel sets of diminuendo. Each of the four soundings of the chimes is fainter than its predecessor. Each of the four fade-ups is fainter than its predecessor. The pacing is progressively slower and the voices progressively fainter in each of the three speaking scenes. And in M's 'semblance' she appears 'more tattered'.
11 – Although not cancelled here, this is the seven-step model of May's pacing that Beckett rejected. The placement of this seven-step diagram suggests that the loose pages may have been shuffled.
12 – This chart presumably outlines the symmetrical running time of each of the play's three speaking sections, five minutes each.

FACSIMILE OF BECKETT'S PRODUCTION NOTEBOOK WITH TRANSCRIPTION AND TRANSLATION

Note on the Schiller Manuscript

Samuel Beckett's production notes for his 1976 Schiller-Theater Werkstatt production of *Tritte* (*Footfalls*) are contained in the first *Spiel* (*Play*) notebook, a red, hard-covered, 90-folio, square-ruled notebook measuring 20.5 × 14.5 cms, on deposit at the University of Reading Samuel Beckett Archive, MS 1976. Across the front cover Beckett wrote 'DAMALS' (*That Time*) and beneath it 'SPIEL' (*Play*); on the back cover, inverted, Beckett wrote 'TRITTE'. For a full description of this notebook, see page 5. The *Tritte* notes, counting from the back of the inverted notebook, the way they were written, begin on the recto of folio 1 and continue to the recto of folio 9; the figures in square brackets at the top of each page of transcription accord with this foliation. (Foliating from the front of the notebook, the *Tritte* notes occupy folios 82 verso to 90 verso.)

MS 1976

End of I

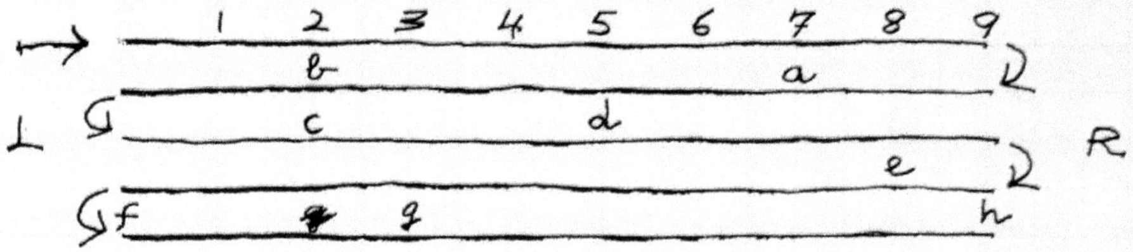

a May
b May
c Ja, Mutter.
d Wirst du nie aufhören? (Ending about 8.)
e Wirst du nie aufhören, es alles hin- u. herzuwälzen?
(Ending about 1.)
f (M halts facing front.) M: Es? Mother: Es alles.
In deinem armen Kopf. Es alles. Es ... alles.
(M resumes pacing.)
g. Begin fade.
h. Black. Stefs cease.

[*Inside back cover*]

End of I

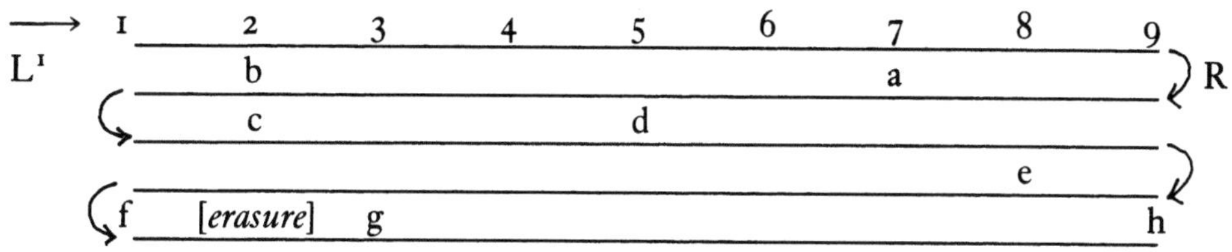

a May

b May

c Ja, Mutter. [Yes, Mother]

d Wirst du nie aufhören? [Will you never have done?] (Ending about 8.)

e Wirst du nie aufhören, es alles hin – u. [und] herzuwälzen? [Will you never have done revolving it all.] [*erasure*] (Ending about 1.)

f (M halts facing front.) [*erasure*] M: Es? Mother: Es alles.
In deinem armen Kopf. Es alles. Es . . . alles. [It? V: It all. In your poor mind. It all. It all.]

[*erasure*] (M resumes pacing.)

g. Begin fade.

h. Black. Steps cease.

End of II

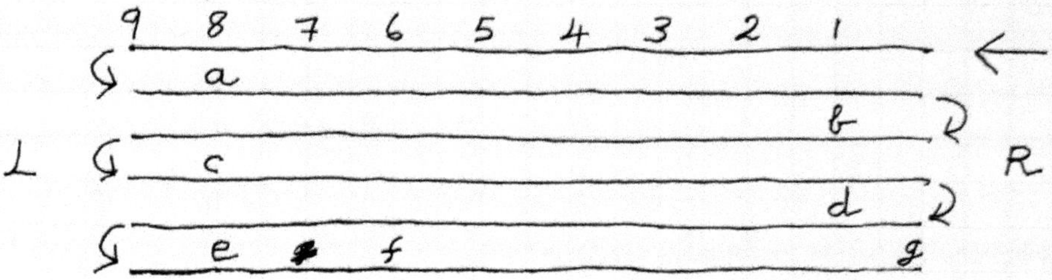

a Ob sie noch schläft, mag man fragen. Ja, manchmal nachts schläft sie, ~~ab u. zu~~ kein u. wieder. (Ending about 1.)

Kein u. wieder / b /Neigt ihren armen Kopf zur Wand u. macht ein Schläfchen. (Ending about 8.)

c Noch spricht? Ja, manchmal nachts spricht sie, wenn sie meint, kein Mensch höre. (Ending about 1.)

d. Erzählt wie es war. Versucht zu erzählen wie es war. Es alles. (Ending about 8.)

e Es alles.

f. Begin fade.

g. Black. Steps cease.

[*fol. 1v*]

[*fol. 2r*]

End of II

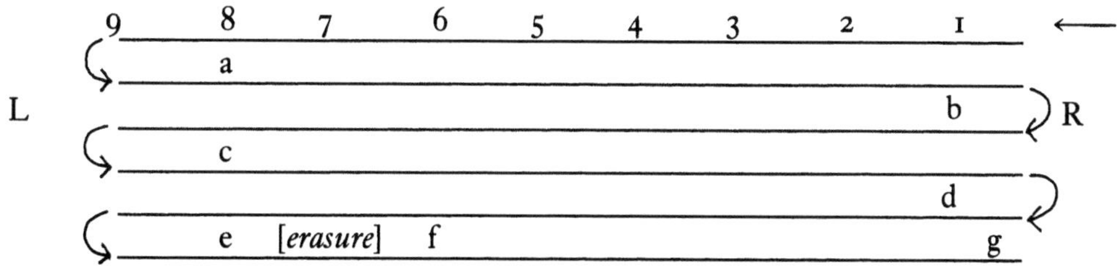

a Ob sie noch schläft mag man fragen. Ja, manchmal nachts schläft sie, [*erasure*] {hin u. [und] wieder]}. (Ending about 1.)
[Does she still sleep, it may be asked? Yes, some nights she does, in snatches . . .]

b {Hin u. [und] wieder}[2] Neigt ihren armen Kopf zur Wand u. [und] macht[3] ein Schläfchen.
(Ending about 8.)
[bows her poor head against the wall and snatches a little sleep.]

c Noch spricht? Ja, manchmal nachts spricht sie, wenn sie meint, kein Mensch höre. (Ending about 1.)
[Still speak? Yes, some nights she does, when she fancies none can hear.]

d. Erzählt[,] wie es war. Versucht zu erzählen[,] wie es war. Es alles. (Ending about 8.)
[Tells how it was. Tries to tell how it was. It all.]

e. Es alles.
[It all.]

f. Begin fade.

g. Black. Steps cease.

Pacing

I

1. 4 lengths +
2. 4 " +
3. 1 " +
4. 5 " = 14 lengths = 126 steps

II

1. 4 " +
2. 6 " = 10 / −4 " = 90 / −36 "

III

1. 2 " +
2. 2 " +
3. 1 " +
4. 1 " = 6 / −4 / **30** " = 54 / −36 / **270** "

[*fol. 2v*]

[*fol. 3r*]

Pacing[4]

I

1.	4	lengths	+					
2.	4	”	+					
3.	1	”	+					
4.	5	”						
				=	14	lengths	= 126	steps

II

1.	4	”	+					
2.	6	”		=	10	”	= 90	”
					−4		−36	

III

1.	2	”	+					
2.	2	”	+					
3.	1	”	+					
4.	1	”		=	6	”	= 54	”
					−4		−36	
					30		270	

M mutters silently, on + off, pacing + standing.

Where?

Pacing

I 1 Lengths 2 + 3
" 2 " " "

II 1 " " "
" 2 " 4 + 5

III 2 " 1 2nd half
" 2 1st "

Standing

II 1 { From "Sie war nicht aus . . ." to ". . . dem selben wo die — ~~wann begann dies~~?"
and a few lip movements during story to indicate unhearing.

2 { From "bis eines Nachts" ~~[illegible]~~ to "May: Nicht genug" ~~[illegible]~~

[*fol. 3v*]

[fol. 4r]

M mutters silently, on & off, pacing & standing

Where?

Pacing

I1	Lengths	2	&	3
" 2	"	"		"
II1	"	"		"
" 2	"	4	&	5
III2	"	1	2nd half	
	"	2	1st	"

Standing

II 1 From "Sie war nicht aus . . ." [She has not been out] to "... <wann begann dies>?" {dem selben, wo sie –} [The same where she] and a few lip movements during story to indicate unhearing.

2 From [*erasure*] {"bis eines Nachts"} [Till one night] to "[*erasure*]" {May: Nicht genug} [May: Not enough]

Or III M's own voice for Frau W, assumed for Amy as V's for May equating May with Amy ←

Voices distinguished in 2 related dialogs:

II. V's own voice for mother, assumed for May

— III. M's " " " daughter, " " Frau W.

Same style for both relations, e.g.

"The mother:" (II) = "Frau W:" (III)

"May:" (II) = "Amy:" (III)

"Was meinst du damit, nicht genug... etc" = "Was meinst du damit, gelinde gesagt ... etc"

[*fol. 4v*]

or III M's own voice for Frau W, assumed for Amy ←
as V's for May equating May with Amy

Voices distinguished in 2 related dialogues:
II V's own voice for mother, assumed for May
III M's " " " daughter, " " Frau W.

Same style for both relations, e.g.
"The mother:" (II) = "Frau W:" (III)
"May: (II) = "Amy:" (III)
"Was meinst du damit, = "Was meinst du damit,
["What do you mean, (May)] = ["What do you mean, (Amy)]
nicht genug . . etc" = gelinde gesagt . . . etc."
[not enough . ."] = [to put it mildly"]

V I Localised ~~[illegible]~~ loudspeaker (one position backstage)
II Delocalised " (one or two of these used for *That Time*)

[*fol. 5v*]

Loudspeaker

V	I Localized [*erasure*]	(her position backstage)
	II Delocalized "	(one or two of those used for <u>That Time</u>)

Light

I
1. With end of echoes 1 fade up [1] incl. blur if used approx. 7"
2. With 3rd step → R after last <u>alles</u> begin fade out [1] less blur completed with M's arrival at R i.e. approx 7".

II
3. With end of echoes 2 fade up [2] to slightly less approx. 7".
4. With last <u>alles</u> i.e. 3rd step → R begin fade out [2] less blur completed with M's arrival at R i.e. approx. 7".

III
5. With end of echoes 3 fade up [3] to slightly less still approx. 7"
6. after last <u>alles</u> hold 7" before fade out [3] less blur approx. 7".

IV
7. With end of echoes 4 fade up [4] to slightly less still approx. 7". Hold approx. 7" before final fade out [4] incl. blur approx. 7"

[*fol. 6v*]

Light[5]

I

1. With end of echoes 1 fade up {1} incl. blur if need approx. 7″

2. With 3rd step ⟶ R after last alles begin fade out {1} less blur completed with M's arrival at R i.e. approx. 7″.

II

3. With end of echoes 2 fade up {2} to slightly less approx. 7″.

4. With last alles i.e. 3rd step ⟶ R begin fade out {2} less blur completed with M's arrival at R i.e. approx. 7″.

III

5. With end of echoes 3 fade up {3} to slightly less still approx. 7″

6. After last alles hold 7″ before fade out {3} less blur approx. 7″.

IV

7. With end of echoes 4 fade up {4} to slightly less still approx. 7″. Hold approx. 7″ before final fade out {4} incl. blur approx. 7″

Consider bell immediately fade out completed removing need for blur.

<u>Bell</u>

House lights down.
Curtain up.
7" dark.
<u>Bell 1</u>. amplify echoes. 7".
Fade out 1
7" dark
<u>Bell 2</u>. [amplify ^fainter echoes. 7". [slightly fainter.
Fade out 2
7" dark.
<u>Bell 3</u> slightly fainter still. amplify ^still fainter echoes. 7"
Fade out 3
7" dark
<u>Bell 4</u> slightly fainter still. amplify ^still fainter echoes. 7"
Fade out 4

[*fol. 7v*]

Consider bell immediately fade out completed removing need for blur.[6]

Bell[7]

House lights down.
Curtain up.
7″ dark.
Bell 1. Amplifying echoes. 7″.
Fade out 1
7″ dark
Bell 2. {slightly fainter.} Amplify {fainter} echoes. 7″.
Fade out 2
7″ dark.
Bell 3 slightly fainter still. Amplify {still fainter} echoes. 7″
Fade out 3
7″ dark
Bell 4 slightly fainter still. Amplify {still fainter} echoes. 7″
Fade out 4

Immediately after Echoes 1 May's pacing
audible in dark say from near L → R.
Turns at R about halfway through FV
and is about ⅓ of way to L when FV completed.
i.e. between Echoes <u>1</u> & FV <u>1</u>
a few seconds of dark, whereas all
other cases FV hard on end of echoes.

Immediately after Echoes 1 May's pacing
audible in dark say [*erasure*] {from near L ⟶} R.
Turns at R about halfway through FU [fade up]
and is about 1/3 of way to L when FU completed.
i.e. [*erasure*] between Echo 1 & FU 1
a few seconds of dark, whereas all
other cases FU hard on end of echoes.

1 – For the German production Beckett began immediately with the nine-step model that he developed for the English production, but in this drawing of the play's first part, May begins her pacing at audience left. Compare this with the drawing for the English production where May begins from audience right.
2 – Beckett indicated the insertion here, but he also revised the previous line to include it there. It is doubtful that he intended the repetition, but the insertion is not cancelled.
3 – Earlier German texts have 'hält' for 'macht'.
4 – Beckett's preoccupation with structure and mathematical precision are again evident here as he charted the precise shape of the diminuendo in May's pacing. In the first section Beckett calculated that May would pace her strip of light 14 times with 9 steps each time for a total of 126 steps. For the second part she would pace 4 fewer times and so take 36 fewer steps. In the third section she would again pace 4 fewer times and also take 36 fewer steps than she did in section II. This pattern appears to be more precise and symmetrical than the one outlined in the *RC Nb* where Beckett noted under the category of '*Pacing*': approximately 12 lengths for section I, 9 for section II, and four for section III.
5 – Like the following section on 'Bell', Beckett here outlined symmetrically the lighting during the play and detailed the diminuendo in the lighting.
6 – Beckett seemed here concerned with shortening the period between scenes.
7 – See note 5 above.

PART V

That Time

Samuel Beckett's Production Notebooks
for *That Time*
at the Royal Court Theatre,
London, May 1976,
and for *Damals* (*That Time*)
at the Schiller-Theater Werkstatt,
Berlin, October 1976

FACSIMILE OF BECKETT'S PRODUCTION NOTES WITH TRANSCRIPTION

Note on the Royal Court Manuscript

The Royal Court production of *That Time* that opened on 20 May 1976 was directed by Donald McWhinnie.[1] Beckett's notes (*RC ms*) for Donald McWhinnie's production of *That Time* are contained on two sheets of A4 typing paper at the University of Reading Samuel Beckett Archive, MS 1639.

43

MS 1639

Reading University Library

smaller in the [illegible] that [illegible] more, H?

That Time

To the direction visual component [illegible] for [illegible] out of face as [illegible] with aural, answer: [illegible] it

p. 9 Opening: establish face in full light, eyes open & closed. after [illegible] seconds eyes close (all on from here) Start fade to half [illegible] (when we that). Next reached with end of speech light change

p. 11 Speech B to opening silence start fade up (at [illegible]) to opening reached (all [illegible]) (the shroud). Next light with end of speech to half full (another [illegible] change after eyes close) but the [illegible] shortly after "that time" fade down (one "[illegible]" reached with end of speech

p. 12 Next light change

p. 14 speech A preceding silence start fade up (all full intensity reached with end of speech ("[illegible]") to "[illegible] was come") fade change ("[illegible] with the ghosts") shortly after eyes close (one intensity reached at end down to half full ("all vanished")). Next light change

p. 14 of speech (all "only get back") to ("never come back")

p. 16 last speech A start fade up full reached with end of speech
Next light change
Final fade out.

p. 16

1639

Reading University Library

p. 2

~~ACB~~
~~ABC~~

ACBACBACBACB

ACBCABCABCAB
~~ABC~~
ACBACBCABCAB

ABCABCABCACB
CABCABCABCBA
BCABCABCABAC

ACBCABACBCA

ACBACBACBACB
CBACBACBABCA
BACBACBACBAC

~~when was that~~

A1 that time .. when was that
1 C1 when you went .. when was that
2 B1 on the stone .. no sound
3 A2 straight off .. someone's folly
4 C2 was yr. mother .. dying away
5 B2 all still .. that scene
6 A3 Foley was it .. picture book
7 C3 till you lifted .. at yr. elbow
8 B3 on the stone .. long white hair
9 A4 or talking .. looking for you
11 C4 never the same .. never the same after that
10 B4 or on the window .. the shroud

13 C5 never the same .. another time
B5 muttering that time .. see it no more
14 A5 that time .. began to dawn
15 C6 when you began .. closing time
16 B6 no sight .. for the vows
17 A6 no setting .. so what next
18 C7 the rain .. gave up whoever it was
19 B7 stock still .. whoever it might be
20 A7 gave it up .. lay on the other side
21 C8 always winter .. another time
23 B8 stock still .. no sight or sound
22 A8 huddled on the step .. where none ever came

24 B9 or alone .. all vanished
25 A9 none ever came .. none ever came
26 C9 always winter .. drowsing away
27 B 10 or that time alone .. soon after long after
28 A 10 eleven or twelve .. forgetting it all
29 C 10 perhaps fear .. another place another time
30 B 11 the slider .. time came in the end
31 A 11 making it all up .. till that time came
32 C 11 in the library .. not a sound
33 B 12 that time .. little or nothing
34 A 12 back down to the wharf .. never come back
35 C 12 only the old breath .. gone in no time
36

[*1*]

43 [*erasure*]

That Time[2]

To the objection visual component too small,
[*erasure*] out of all proportion
with aural, answer: make it {smaller, on the principle that less
is more.} [*erasure*][3]

+

p. 9[4] opening: establish face in <strong> {full} light, eyes
open & closed. <A few seconds> {shortly?} after eyes close (cue on from there)
Start [*erasure*] fade to half full <opening intensity>
reached with end of speech (when was that). Next
light change

p. 11 Speech B [*erasure*] preceding silence start fade up
(cue <loved them>) {to believe} to <opening intensity> {full} reached
with end of speech (the shroud). Next light
change

p. 12 {Shortly after eyes close}[5] fade down (cue <"that time">
{but the one}) to half <opening intensity>
{full} reached with end of speech (another time).
Next light change.

p. 14 Speech A preceding silence start fade up (cue
<"where you were"> {not knowing}) to <opening> {full} intensity reached
with
end of speech ("none ever came"). Next light
change.

p. 14 Shortly after eyes close (cue "with the ghosts") fade
down to half full intensity reached with end
of speech ("all vanished"). Next light change.

p. 16 Last speech A start fade up (cue "only get back") to
full reached with end of speech ("never come back")
Next light change.

p. 16 Final fade out.

[2]

<ACB>
<ABC>   ACBACBACBACB

ACBCABCABCAB
<ABC>
ACBACBCABCAB[6]

ABCABCABCACB
CABCABCABCBA
BCABCABCABAC[7]

ACBCABACBCA

                    C A
√√√√√√√√√ √√ √
A C B A C B A C B <A C>B
C B A C B A C B A <C B>B C A
B A C B A C B A C B A C[8]

<when was that>

1 A1 that time . . when was that
2 C1 when you went . . when was that
3 B1 on the stone . . no sound
4 A2 straight off . . someone's folly
5 C2 was yr. [your] mother . . dying away
6 B2 all still . . that scene
7 A3 Foley was it . . picture book
8 C3 til [*recte* till] you lifted . . at yr. [your] elbow
9 B3 on the stone . . long white hair
11 <10> A4 or talking . . looking for you[9]
10 <11> C4 never the same . . never the same after that
<11 12> B4 or by the window . . its shroud

---

13 C5 never the same . . another time
14 B5 muttering that time . . see it no more
15 A5 that time . . began to dawn
16 C6 when you began[10] . . closing time[11]
17 B6 no sight . . for the vows
18 A6 no getting . . so what next
19 C <6>7 the rain . . gave up where it was
20 B7 stock still . . wherever it might be

Transcription continues on p. 363.

21 A7 gave it up . . by on the other side
23 ⟵ C8 always winter . . another time
22 ⟵ B8 stock still . . no sight or sound[12]
24 A8 huddled on the step[13] . . where none ever came

---

25 B9 or alone . . all vanished
26 A9 none ever came . . none ever came
27 C9 always winter . . drowsing away
28 B10 or that time alone . . soon after long after
29 A10 eleven or twelve . . forgetting it all
30 C10 perhaps fear . . another place another time
31 B11 the glider . . time came in the end
32 A11 making it all up . . till that time came
33 C11 in the Library . . not a sound
34 B12 that time . . little or nothing
35 A12 back down to the wharf . . never come back
36 C12 only the old breath[14] . . gone in no time

1 – This production, coupled with *Footfalls*, was part of the Royal Court Theatre's seventieth birthday celebration for Samuel Beckett. Although Beckett himself only directed Billie Whitelaw in *Footfalls*, he prepared these notes for McWhinnie.
2 – This sheet of notes documents Beckett's suggestions for lighting changes. The principle is essentially that the face is established in full light during the pauses, and the lighting fades to half full during the voices, or essentially as Listener's eyes close. Beckett detailed the cues for the fades up and down. The final speech of voice C, for instance, is heard in full light, the fade up having begun with 'only get back' in the preceding speech by voice A, and full intensity reached with A's 'never come back' (see the folio headed '*Light*' in the *German Nb*).
3 – This adaptation of the famous aesthetic dictum of German-born, American architect Mies van der Rohe is as succinct and direct a statement of Beckett's late minimalist aesthetics as we have.
4 – Page numbers are keyed to *That Time* (Faber and Faber, London, 1976).
5 – In the Faber edition of *That Time* the '*eyes close*' in C's last speech referred to here is actually on page 11.
6 – This outline of the play's first twelve sections suggests an alternative to the pattern of speeches in the first third of the play, that is, the twelve segments that precede the first silence. The final line in this outline is the pattern of the first section of *That Time* as it appears in the (corrected) outlines below and in the published Faber text.
7 – This appears to be a total rewrite of the pattern of paragraphs for *That Time.*
8 – This pattern represents the Faber texts as printed and incorporates the two corrections in the fuller outline below. The check marks above this outline suggest that Beckett double-checked it.
9 – This is not a revision but a correction to conform with the Faber text as printed. The phrase 'never the same' is the tenth 'episode' in the Faber text and so follows the 'on the stone' paragraph and precedes the 'or talking' paragraph, p. 11.
10 – 'when you started' in the Faber text, p. 12.
11 – The phrase is hyphenated in the Faber text, 'closing-time', p. 12.
12 – This is not a revision but a correction to conform with the Faber text as printed. The second 'stock still' paragraph is the twenty-second 'episode' in the

Faber text and so follows the 'gave it up' paragraph and precedes the 'always winter' paragraph, p. 13.

13 – 'huddled on the doorstep' in the Faber text, p. 14.

14 – The Faber text for this final paragraph actually begins 'not a sound only the old breath', p. 16.

FACSIMILE OF BECKETT'S PRODUCTION NOTEBOOK
WITH TRANSCRIPTION AND TRANSLATION

Note on the Schiller Manuscript

Samuel Beckett's production notes for his 1976 Schiller-Theater production of *Damals* (*That Time*) are contained in the same notebook Beckett used for *Spiel* (*Play*), a red, hard-covered, 90-folio, square-ruled notebook measuring 20.5 × 14.5 cms, on deposit at the University of Reading Samuel Beckett Archive, MS 1976. Across the front cover Beckett wrote 'DAMALS' and beneath it 'SPIEL'; on the back cover, overturned, Beckett wrote 'TRITTE' (*Footfalls*). For a full description of this notebook, see page 5. The notes for Beckett's 1976 Schiller-Theater *Damals* begin on the recto of folio 1 and continue to the recto of folio 6.

MS 1976

Before silences after B4, A8, C12 speech should falter (slower, fainter) beginning at

B4: bis nur eines von diesen Dingen...

A8: oder wann du warst...

C12: nur was war es was er sagte...

Conversely after silences faltering return to normal débit (C5, B9) ?

On approach to silence bring light up. as memories resume bring it down. i.e. opening & end (before fade out) in maximum light.

[*Inside front cover*]

Before silences after B4, A8, C12 speech should falter (slower, fainter) beginning at[1]

B4: bis nur eines von diesen Dingen . . .
[just one of those things]

A8: oder wann du warst . . .
[or when you were]

C12: nur was war es was er sagte . . .
[only what was it it said]

Conversely after silences faltering return to normal débit [i.e., flow or output] (C5, B9)[2] ?

On approach to silence bring light up.
As memories resume bring it down.[3]
i.e. opening & end (before fade out)
in maximum light.

~~or earlier before max. reached~~ ←

Listener's reactions

1. Eyes: open as soon as ~~light to fade~~ FU begins, i.e. from outset of silence (earlier than in text) & remain till with failing light & resumption of which they close again

2. Breath: up with growing light, audible throughout silence & open eyes, down to inaudible with failing light for resumption.

3. Perhaps very slight restlessness coming up to silence (B4, A8, C12)?

4. If hand allowed in image, holding sheet at neck or collar of shirt, it should tighten hold for silence, relax for listening.

—

In final 10" max. light 5" open eyes alone, then 5" open eyes & smile contin'd. during fade out.

—

Speech during first fade up to max??

[*fol. 1v*]

<or earlier before max. reached> ←

[*fol. 2r*]

Listener's reactions

— 1. Eyes: open as soon as <light to full> {FU [fade up] begins}, i.e. from outset of silence (earlier than in text)[4] & remain till with failing light & resuming speech they close again

2. Breath: up with growing light, audible throughout silence & open eyes, down to inaudible with failing light for resumption.

3. Perhaps very slight restlessness coming up to silence (B4, A8, C12)?

4. If hand allowed in image, holding sheet at neck or collar of shirt, it should tighten hold for silence, relax for listening.[5]

—

In final 10″ max. light 5″ [*erasure*] open eyes alone, then 5″ open eyes & smile [*erasure*] contind. during fade out.[6]

Speech [*erasure*] during first fade up to max??

—

1 1 1 | 2 2 2 | 3 3 3 | 4 4 4 | 5 5 5 | 6 6 6 || 7 7 7 | 8 8 8 | 9 9 9 | 10 10 10 | 11 11 11 | 12 12 12

A C B | A C B | A C B | C A B | C B A | C B A || C B A | B C A | B A C | B A C | B A C | B A C

S S S S

A1 damals
C1 als du
B1 auf dem
A2 gleich runter
C2 war deine
B2 alles still
A3 Tuchy
C3 bis du den
B3 auf dem
C4 nie mehr
A4 oder zu dir
B4 oder am Fenster

C5 nie mehr
B5 murmelnd
A5 damals
C6 als du anfingst
B6 nie das Gesicht
A6 kein Hinkommen
C7 der Regen
B7 Stockstill
A7 gabst es auf

S

wann war das
wann war das
kein Laut
jemandes Tusculum
daheimschwindend
diese Szene
Bilderbuch
Ellbogen
geboren
danach
suchend
Grabtuch

S

ein andermal
~~zu dämmern begann~~ sehen konntest
zu dämmern begann
Schliessung
Gelöbnisse gewesen
was dann
auch immer es war
auch immer es sein mochte
andere Seite

B8 Stockstill
C8 immer Winter
A8 hockend

B9 oder allein
A9 nie jemand hinkam
C9 immer Winter
B10 oder damals allein
A10 elf oder zwölf
C10 vielleicht Angst
B11 das Segelflugzeug
A11 es alles erfindend
C11 die Bücherei
B12 damals am Ende
A12 zurück runter
C12 kein Laut

Kein Laut
ein andermal
nie jemand hinkam — S

alles verschwand
nie jemand hinkam
vorm Hindösen
lange danach
es alles vergessend
ein andermal
am Ende
bis damals kam
Kein Laut
oder kaum
nie wieder zurück
auf einmal — S

[*fol. 2v*]

					[*erasure*]						
1 1 1	2 2 2	3 3 3	4 4 4	5 5 5	6 6 6	7 7 7	8 8 8	9 9 9	10 10 10	11 11 11	12 12 12
ACB|	ACB|	ACB|	CAB|	CBA|	CBA|	|CBA|	BCA|	BAC|	B A C|	B A C|	B A C
S [silence]			S				S				S
						________	________	________	S		

A1 damals [that time]	wann war das [when was that]
C1 als du [when you]	wann war das [when was that]
B1 auf dem [on the]	kein Laut [no sound]
A2 gleich runter [straight off]	jemandes Tusculum [someone's folly]
C2 war deine [was your]	dahinschwindend [dying away]
B2 alles still [all still]	diese Szene [that scene]
A3 Tuohy[7] [Foley]	Bilderbuch [picturebook]
C3 bis du den [till you hoisted]	Ellbogen [elbow]
B3 auf dem [on the]	geboren [white hair]
C4 nie mehr [never the same]	danach [after that]
A4 oder zu dir [or talking to]	suchend [looking for you]
B4 oder am Fenster [or by the window]	Grabtuch [shroud] S
C5 nie mehr [never the same]	ein andermal [another time]
B5 murmelnd [muttering]	[*erasure*] sehen konntest [see it no more]
A5 damals [that time]	zu dämmern begann [began to dawn]
C6 als du anfingst [when you started]	Schliessung [closing time]
B6 nie das Gesicht[8] [no sight of the face]	Gelöbnisse gewesen [wasn't for the vows]
A6 kein Hinkommen [no getting out of it]	Was dann [what next]
C7 der Regen [the rain]	auch immer es war [whoever it was]
B7 Stockstill[9] [stock still]	auch immer es sein mochte [wherever it might be]
A7 gabst es auf [give it up]	andere Seite [on the other side]

B8 Stockstill[10] [stock still]	kein Laut [no sight or sound]	
C8 immer Winter [always winter]	ein andermal [another time]	
A8 hockend [huddled]	nie jemand hinkam[12] [none ever came]	S
B9 oder allein [or alone]	alles verschwand [all vanished]	
A9 nie jemand hinkam [none ever came]	nie jemand hinkam[13] [none ever came]	
C9 immer Winter [always winter]	voran [d]ahindösen [drowsing away]	
B10 oder damals allein [or that time alone]	lange danach [long after]	
A10 elf oder zwölf [eleven or twelve]	es alles vergessend[14] [forgetting it all]	
C10 vielleicht Angst [perhaps fear]	ein andermal [another time]	
B11 das Segelflugzeug [the glider]	am Ende [in the end]	
A11 es alles erfindend [making it all up]	bis damals kam [that time came]	
C11 die Bücherei [the Library]	kein Laut [not a sound]	
B12 damals am Ende [that time in the end]	oder kaum [or nothing]	
A12 zurück runter [back down]	nie wieder zurück[15] [never come back]	
C12 kein[11] Laut [not a sound]	auf einmal [in no time]	S

A1 Leading from S0 – damals – (damals) – als du rüberfurst – das letzte Mal –

B4 " to S1 um die Leere – nicht hereinströmen – zu lassen – über dich – das Grabtuch.

C5 " from " nie mehr – (nie mehr) – derselbe – aber derselbe – wie was –

A8 " to S2 damals – (damals) – auf dem Stein – das Kind auf dem Stein – wo nie jemand – hinkam.

B9 " from " oder allein – (allein) – in den gleichen – den gleichen – Szenen –

C12 " to S3 gekommen – u. gegangen – niemand – (gekommen – u. gegangen – auf einmal – gegangen. auf · ein · mal.

[*fol. 3v*]

A1 Leading from S0[16]	– damals – (damals) – als du rüber- furst [*recte* fuhrst] – das letzte Mal [that time you went back that last time]
B4 " to S1	um die Leere – nicht hereinströmen – zu lassen – über dich[17] – das Grabtuch – [to keep the void from pouring in on top of you the shroud]
C5 " from "	nie mehr – (nie mehr) – derselbe – aber derselbe – wie was – [never the same but the same as what]
A8 " to S2	damals – (damals) – auf dem Stein – das Kind auf dem Stein – wo nie jemand – hinkam.[18] [that time on the stone the child on the stone where none ever came]
B9 " from "	oder allein – (allein) – in den gleichen – don [*recte* den] gleichen – Szenen – [or alone in the same the same scenes]
C12 " to S3	gekommen – u. [und] gegangen – {niemand}[19] – gekom- men – u. [und] gegangen – auf einmal – gegangen. auf . ein . mal. [come and gone no one come and gone in no time gone in no time]

Or – Simpler

I

1. Curtain
2. 5" dark.
3. Fade up 10" to max. Eyes open as soon as FU begins
4. Hold max. 10". Eyes open.
5. Fade down 10" to min. Eyes open.
6. Min. reached, speech resumes, eyes close.

Same throughout

End I. Grabtuch. FU begins
~~Beginning~~
" II Nie jemand hinkam FU begins
" III gegangen " "

Beginning II. FU ends. Nicht mehr derselbe
" III " " auf in den gleichen

Light

10" approx.

1. Fade up to max. on face eyes open. Hold 10".

2. With damals (A1) begin fade down to min. reached with wann war das + closing of eyes i.e. approx. 10"

3. With um die Leere! (B4) begin fade up to max. reached with Grabtuch + opening of eyes i.e. approx. 10" Hold 10".

4. With nie mehr (C5) begin fade down to min. reached with na komm + closing of eyes i.e. approx. 10".

5. With der Ort (A8) begin fade up to max. reached with hinkam + opening of eyes i.e. approx. 10". Hold 10".

6. With oder in den gleichen (B9) begin fade down to min. reached with draussaufzuhalten + closing of eyes, i.e. approx. 10".

7. With so etwas (C12) begin fade up to max. reached with last auf einmal + opening of eyes i.e. approx. 10". Hold 10".

8 Fade out 10" approx.

[*fol. 4v*]

Or – Simpler[20]

I

1. Curtain
2. 5″ dark
3. Fade up 10″ to max. Eyes open as soon as FU [fade up] begins
4. Hold max. 10″. Eyes open.
5. Fade down 10″ to min. Eyes open.
6. Min. reached, speech resumes, eyes close.

Same throughout

[*erasure*]

End I. Grabtuch [shroud]. FU begins
[*erasure*]
 ” II Nie jemand hinkam [none ever came] FU begins
 ” III gegangen [gone] ” ”

Beginning II. FO [fade out] ends. Nie {mehr} derselbe [never the same]
 ” III ” ” Auf in den gleichen [in the same]

Light[21]

10″ approx.

1. Fade up to max. on face eyes open. Hold 10″.
2. With damals [that time] (A1) begin fade down to min. reached with wann war das [when was that] – closing of eyes i.e. approx. 10″
3. With um die Leere [the void] 1 (B4) begin fade up to max. reached with Grabtuch [shroud] & opening of eyes i.e. approx. 10″ Hold 10″.
4. With nie mehr [never the same] (C5) begin fade down to min. reached with na komm [come on now] & closing of eyes i.e. approx 10″.
5. With der Ort [the place] (A8) begin fade up to max. reached with hinkam [ever came] & opening of eyes i.e. approx. 10″. Hold 10″.
6. With oder [allein] in den gleichen [or alone in the same] (B9) begin fade down to min. reached with draussen zu halten [on the stone][22] & closing of eyes, i.e. approx. 10″.
7. With so etwas [something like that] (C12) begin fade up to max. reached with last auf einmal [in no time] & opening of eyes i.e. approx. 10″. Hold 10″.
8. Fade out 10″ approx.

B

Alles war nun stille. Wir sprachen kein Wort, wir berührten uns nicht, wir sahen uns nicht an . . .

Hölderlin
Hyperion-Fragment

B

Alles war nun stille. Wir sprachen kein Wort,
wir berührten uns nicht, wir sahen uns nicht an . . .[23]

Hölderlin
Hyperion-Fragment

[Everything was now quiet. We didn't speak a word, we didn't touch, we didn't look at each other . . . (ed. trans.)]

1 – The pattern of aural diminuendo that Beckett outlined here roughly corresponds but runs counter to the lighting patterns. The voice of B4 begins faltering at 'just one of those things', while the light begins its fade *up* six words later at the first mention of 'the void'. With the mention of the last word of this speech, 'shroud', voice is at its weakest; lighting is at full. Eyes open 3 seconds into the 10-second silence.

2 – That is, immediately after the 10-second silences.

3 – This is the pattern that Beckett established in his notes to Donald McWhinnie for the Royal Court Theatre production (q.v.).

4 – Here the opening of the eyes is keyed to the fade up of light much more systematically than it was in Beckett's notes for Donald McWhinnie's Royal Court production in May, some five months earlier (q.v.).

5 – Beckett here suggests something of the experiment in perspective that *That Time* represents. If Listener's hand can be seen at full light increasingly clutching a sheet around his neck during the silences, then our perspective may be that of watching him from above as if he were in bed.

6 – The enigmatic smile at the end of the play may have less to do with the content of the voices (or memories), which invariably feature failures, than their formal arrangement, the pattern of their presentation. See the outline of that pattern on folio 3 recto. The pattern of presentations is regular for the first set of three triplets, ACB. The regularity, although in a different pattern, is restored in the final set of triplets, BAC, and hence the smile. If, on the other hand, we consider the pattern of twelve sets of triplets to be divided by four, then the first two quadruplets are irregular and the final a regular pattern of four consecutive BAC triplets. And so, although the memories themselves may be discomfiting to listener, their formal presentation brings a smile (see Gontarski, 1985, pp. 150–61).

7 – The bilingual German edition of *Damals/That Time* (Suhrkamp, Frankfurt am Main, 1976), p. 21, retains the English 'Foley', which Beckett revised to 'Tuohy' in *TT* (SB).

8 – The bilingual 1976 Suhrkamp edition of *Damals/That Time*, p. 41, prints 'weder das Gesicht', which Beckett revised to 'nie das Gesicht'.

9 – The bilingual 1976 Suhrkamp edition of *Damals/That Time* has 'regungslos', p. 47, which Beckett revised to 'ganz still' not 'Stockstill' in *TT* (SB).

10 – Again, the bilingual 1976 Suhrkamp edition of *Damals/That Time* has 'regungslos', p. 47, which Beckett revised to 'ganz still' not 'Stockstill' in *TT* (SB).
11 – The bilingual 1976 Suhrkamp edition of *Damals/That Time*, p. 79, prints 'keinerlei Laut', which Beckett revised to 'kein Laut' to echo the end of B1.
12 – The bilingual 1976 Suhrkamp edition of *Damals/That Time*, p. 55, has 'niemand je hinkam', which Beckett revised to 'nie jemand hinkam'.
13 – Again, the bilingual 1976 Suhrkamp edition of *Damals/That Time*, p. 55, has 'niemand je hinkam', which Beckett revised to 'nie jemand hinkam'.
14 – The bilingual 1976 Suhrkamp edition of *Damals/That Time*, p. 65, has 'das alles vergessend', which Beckett revised to 'es alles vergessend'.
15 – The bilingual 1976 Suhrkamp edition of *Damals/That Time*, p. 77, has 'nie mehr dahin zurück', which Beckett revised to 'nie wieder zurück'.
16 – This silence zero (So) was Beckett's designation of the opening silence. The other three silences are then numbered consecutively.
17 – The bilingual 1976 Suhrkamp edition of *Damals/That Time*, p. 31, has 'über dir das', which Beckett revised to 'über dich das'.
18 – As above (notes 12 and 13) the bilingual 1976 Suhrkamp edition of *Damals/That Time*, p. 55, has 'niemand je hinkam', which Beckett revised to 'nie jemand hinkam'.
19 – The bilingual 1976 Suhrkamp edition of *Damals/That Time*, p. 79, has 'kein einziger', which Beckett revised to 'niemand'.
20 – What Beckett suggested as a lighting simplification here, 'Or – Simpler', is basically an outline of lighting during the now extended silences.
21 – The pattern of lighting changes here follows fairly closely those Beckett outlined for Donald McWhinnie's Royal Court production; each outline is in eight scenes. But the fades were shorter in Beckett's own production, and they were keyed more closely to the opening and shutting of Listener's eyes. In A's first speech, for instance, the fade down for Beckett's own production began immediately with A's first words and was completed as the eyes close. In the English production, Beckett suggested that the fade down begin with 'there', the fifteenth word in the opening speech, and end with the completion of A's first speech, 'when was that', well after the eyes had closed. Compare the 10-second pattern in the lighting of *Damals* (*That Time*) with the 7-second pattern Beckett outlined for lighting *Tritte* (*Footfalls*), which was, of course, on the same programme.
22 – This is, of course, the equivalent place in the English text. *Passim.*
23 – The *Fragment von Hyperion (Fragment of Hyperion)* contains much of

Hölderlin's transcendental Romanticism, his concept of 'All-Unity' and faith in divine beneficence: 'Alles ist gut.' This quotation suggests a literary source for B's romantic (and Romantic) posturing: B1, 'vowing every now and then you loved each other just a murmur not touching or anything of that nature . . . no looks just there together.' The scene may also suggest Christ's *noli me tangere.*

CUTS AND CHANGES TO THE SCHILLER-THEATER PRODUCTION TEXT

Page references are to the bilingual edition Beckett used to prepare for the Schiller-Theater Werkstatt production in October of 1976, *TT* (SB).

Page 9

'*geschlossen*' revised to '*schliessen sich*'.

'Tag die Elf nahmst . . .' revised to 'Tag nahmst die Elf . . .'.

'Trambahn mehr nur die alten Schienen . . .' revised to 'Trambahn mehr da nur die alten Schienen . . .'.

Page 11

'immer Winter wars immer Regenwetter damals in der Gemäldegalerie . . .' revised to 'immer Winter damals immer Regen damals in der Porträtgalerie . . .'.

'reinschlichst als niemand hinguckte . . .' revised to 'reinschlichst wenn niemand hinguckte . . .'.

Page 17

'und allenfalls der Wärter herumdröselnd . . .' revised to 'und allenfalls ein Wärter herumdröselnd . . .'.

The final word, 'verschwindend', revised to 'dahinschwindend'.

Page 19

'und du auch still auf dem Stein wie betäubt kein Laut nicht ein Wort . . .' revised to 'und ihr auch still auf dem Stein wie betäubt kein Laut kein einziges Wort . . .'.

Page 21

'Tuohy' replaced 'Foley' twice in the first line.

'nein sie war bei dir damals immer noch bei dir damals . . .' revised to 'nein sie war mit dir damals immer noch mit dir damals . . .'.

Page 23

'ein Ölgemälde . . .' revised to 'ein riesiges Ölgemälde . . .'.

'seinerzeit eine Berühmtheit . . .' revised to 'seinerzeit irgend eine Berühmtheit . . .'.

'oder ein Kind . . .' revised to 'oder gar ein Kind . . .'.

'irgendein Prinz . . .' revised to 'irgendein junger Prinz . . .'.

Page 25

'ausser dem Weizen der gelb wurde und dem blauen Himmel . . .' revised to 'nur der Weizen der gelb wurde und der blaue Himmel . . .'.

'Oder beim alten Chinesen . . .' revised to 'oder bei jenem Chinesen . . .'.

Page 27

'murmelnd' revised to 'flüsternd'.

Page 28

Second 'or' deleted in 'there was childhood for you ten or eleven or a stone . . .'.

Page 29

'das war mir eine Kindheit' revised to 'das war dir eine Kindheit . . .'.

'sie erfindend bald eine Stimme . . .' revised to 'es alles erfindend bald eine Stimme . . .'.

'in der Finsternis oder bei Mondschein und sie alle draussen auf den Strassen um nach dir zu suchen . . .' revised to 'im Finstern oder Mondschein und sie alle draussen auf den Strassen nach dir suchen . . .'.

Page 31

'oder am Fenster im Dunkeln auf die Eule horchend nicht der geringste

Gedanke in deinem Kopf . . .' revised to 'oder am Fenster im Finstern auf die Eule horchend keinen Gedanken in deinem Kopf . . .'.

'du je einem sagtest du liebtest ihn oder einer dir bis nur eines von diesen Dingen . . .' revised to 'du je jemandem sagtest du liebtest ihn oder jemand dir bis nur noch eines von diesen Dingen . . .'.

'eine andere von den alten Geschichten . . .' revised to 'noch eines von den alten Märchen . . .'.

'über dir das Grabtuch . . .' revised to 'über dich das Grabtuch . . .'.

'(*Nach 3″ Augen geöffnet*)' revised to '(*Nach 3″ Augen öffnen sich*)'.

Page 33

'ich zu dir selbst . . .' revised to 'ich zu dir selber . . .'.

'(*Augen geschlossen*)' revised to '(*Augen schliessen sich*)'.

'ich zu sagen in deinem Leben' revised to 'ich zu dir selber zu sagen in deinem Leben'.

'Wurm im Schlamm . . .' revised to 'Wurm im Schleim . . .'.

'und dich abrieben und dich aufrichteten nie mehr einen danach nie mehr zurückgeblickt danach war es damals oder war es ein andermal' revised to 'und dich abwischten und dich gerade streckten nie mehr einen danach nie mehr zurückgeblickt danach war das damals oder war das ein andermal'.

Page 34

'See it not more' revised to 'see it no more'.

Page 35

'Ratte aussah kam auf dich zu von hinten und trieb dann weiter bis du es nicht mehr sehen konntest' revised to 'Ratte aussah kam auf euch zu von hinten und trieb dann weiter bis ihr es nicht mehr sehen konntet'.

Page 38

'not knowing who were from Adam . . .' revised to 'not knowing who you were from Adam . . .'.

Page 39

'in wessen Schädel du versetzt warst wegen . . .' revised to 'in wessen Schädel du gesperrt warst wegen . . .'.

Page 41

'weder das Gesicht . . .' revised to 'nie das Gesicht . . .'.

'nur was Verschwommenes am Rande des Blickfelds' revised to 'nur Verschwommenes am Rande der Blickfelder'.

Page 47

'regungslos' revised to 'ganz still' three times.

'warst du' revised to 'wart ihr'.

Page 49

'gab es auf gab auf und setzte mich hin auf die Stufen . . .' revised to 'gabst es auf gabst auf und setztest dich hin auf die Stufen . . .'.

'also gab . . .' revised to 'also gabst . . .'.

'und hingesetzt' revised to 'und setztest dich hin . . .'.

'und weg verdammt weg von dort . . .' revised to 'und los verdammt raus da . . .'.

Page 50

'All still all sides where it might be . . .' revised to 'All still all sides wherever it might be . . .'.

'Reed . . .' revised to 'Reeds . . .'.

Page 51

'regungslos' again revised to 'ganz still'.

'der Sonne dann ihr Sinken und Verschwinden ohne uns . . .' revised to 'der Sonne bis ihr Versinkt und Verschwindet ohne euch . . .'.

'ringsherum . . .' revised to 'ringsum . . .'.

'alles regungslos überall wie immer es sein . . .' revised to 'alles Still überall wie auch immer es sein . . .'.

'Wäldchen hinten oder die Ähren oder das Gras . . .' revised to 'Wäldchen dahinter oder die Ähren oder das Sandgras . . . '.

Page 52

Space added between 'free' and 'culture'.

Page 53

'immer Winter wars immer Regenwetter immer irgendwo reinschleichen wenn keiner hinguckte rein von der Strasse weg aus Kälte . . .' revised to 'immer Winter damals immer Regen immer irgendwo reinschleichen wenn niemand hinguckte von der Strasse rein aus Kälte . . .'.

Page 55

'niemand je hinkam' revised to 'nie jemand hinkam'.

'(*Nach 3″ Augen geöffnet*)' revised to '(*Nach 3″ Augen öffnen sich.*)'.

Page 57

'auf dem Stein' added after, 'zu halten'.

'(*Augen geschlossen*)' revised to '(*Augen schliessen sich*)'.

'und Blau oder dem Treidelpfad . . .' revised to 'und Blau oder der Treidelpfad allein auf dem Treidelpfad . . .'.

'Sonnenuntergang bis man es nicht mehr sehen konnte . . .' revised to 'Sonnenuntergang bis du es nicht mehr sehen konntest . . .'.

'Sonne bis sie untergegangen war . . .' revised to 'Sonne bis sie unterging . . .'.

Page 59

'und sie alle auf den Strassen . . .' revised to 'und sie alle draussen auf den Strassen . . .'.

'oder mehr teilend so zu sich selber sprechend so zusammen da wo niemand je hinkam . . .' revised to 'oder mehr teilend zu sich selber sprechend um so mit sich selber zusammen zu sein da wo nie jemand hinkam . . .'.

Page 61

'immer Winter wars endloser Winter . . .' revised to 'immer Winter endloser Winter . . .'.

'das alte Jahr nie enden als ob die Zeit nicht weitergehen könnte . . .' revised to 'das alte Jahr nie enden die Zeit nicht weitergehen . . .'.

'rein weg von der Strasse als niemand hinguckte raus aus Kälte . . .' revised to 'von der Strasse rein wenn niemand hinguckte aus Kälte . . .'.

'an ihren Ketten hingesetzt auf den ersten freien Platz . . .' revised to 'an ihren Ketten setztest dich hin auf den ersten freien Platz . . .'.

Page 63

'wo auch immer es sei gewesen sein mag die gleiche alte Szene vorher wie damals damals wie später mit der Ratte . . .' revised to 'wo auch immer es sein mochte gewesen sein mochte die gleiche alte Szene davor wie damals damals wie danach mit der Ratte . . .'.

'als das Segelflugzeug vorbeiglitt damals als du rüberfuhrst bald danach lange danach . . .' revised to 'als das Segelflugzeug vorüberglitt damals als du zurückkehrtest bald danach lange danach . . .'.

Page 65

'Dunkel' revised to 'Finstern'.

'das war mir eine Kindheit . . .' revised to 'das war dir eine Kindheit . . .'.

'der fahlen Sonne dich selber wieder dabei hörtest . . .' revised to 'der fahlen Sonne dich wieder dabei hörtest . . .'.

'um das Ärgernis zu begaffen da hockend . . .' revised to 'um das Ärgernis anzugaffen da hockend . . .'.

'der fahlen Sonne das alles vergessend' revised to 'der fahlen Sonne es alles vergessend'.

Page 67

'da wirklich keine Befugnis . . .' revised to 'da offenbar keine Befugnis . . .'.

'dies eine Mal auf deine elenden Mitmenschen Gott dankend dies eine Mal so schlecht oder wer weiss was du warst . . .' revised to 'dies eine Mal auf deine Mitunmenschen Gott dankend dies eine Mal so elend du auch warst . . .'.

Page 69

'das Segelflugzeug das vorbeiglitt nie die geringste Veränderung . . .' revised to 'das Segelflugzeug das vorüberglitt nie die geringste Veränderung . . .'.

'sich je ausser ihr mit dir da . . .' revised to 'sich je nur sie mit dir da . . .'.

'dass du sogar du sowas erfunden hast bis die Zeit kam am Ende' revised to 'dass du selbst du je sowas erfandest bis damals am Ende'.

Page 71

'all das erfindend auf der Türstufe aus dem Stegreif dich selber wieder ganz erfindend zum millionsten Mal das alles vergessend . . .' revised to 'es alles erfindend da auf der Türstufe nach und nach dich wieder erfindend zum millionsten Mal es alles vergessend . . .'.

'Foley's' revised to 'Tuohy's'.

Page 73

'die Bücherei das war was anderes ein anderer Ort . . .' revised to 'die Bücherei noch so einer ein anderer Ort . . .'.

'von der Strasse weg aus Kälte und Regen als niemand hinguckte was war es damals du warst nie mehr derselbe danach nie wieder danach etwas mit Staub . . .' revised to 'von der Strasse rein aus Kälte und Regen wenn niemand hinguckte was war es damals wonach du nie mehr derselbe warst nie wieder warst etwas mit Staub . . .'.

'mit einer Schar alter Leute . . .' revised first to 'Mit einer Schar Tapergreise . . .', then to 'Mit einer Schar alter Wracks . . .'.

Page 75

'und nicht konntest am Fenster . . .' revised to 'Und nicht konntest da am Fenster . . .'.

'und die Eule weggeflogen war' revised to 'und die Eule weggeflogen'.

'und kein anderer Laut . . .' revised to 'und kein Laut mehr . . .'.

'keine Worte mehr übrig um es draussen zu halten da gab es auf gab auf da bei dem Fenster im Finstern oder Mondschein gab endgültig auf und liess es herein und gar nicht so schlimm ein grosses Grabtuch . . .' revised to 'keine Worte mehr um es draussen zu halten also gabst es auf gabst auf da am Fenster im Finstern oder Mondschein gabst endgültig auf und liessest es herein und gar nicht schlimmer als vorher ein grosses Grabtuch . . .'.

'und gar nicht so schlimm oder kaum gar nicht oder kaum' revised to 'und gar nicht schlimmer als vorher oder kaum gar nicht oder kaum'.

Page 77

'und weit weg von dort verdammt raus da und nie mehr dahin zurück . . .' revised to 'und los verdammt raus da und nie wieder zurück . . .'.

'damals weit weg verdammt raus aus alledem und nie mehr dahin zurück . . .' revised to 'damals los verdammt raus aus alledem und nie wieder zurück . . .'.

Page 79

'keinerlei Laut . . .' revised to 'kein Laut . . .'.

'und gegangen kein einziger gekommen . . .' revised to 'und gegangen niemand gekommen . . .'.

'(*Nach 3″ Augen geöffnet*)' revised to '(*Nach 3″ Augen öffnen sich.*)'.

PART VI

What Where

Revised Text

TYPOGRAPHICAL NOTE

Text between square brackets [ ] has been added to the original English text.
Text between pointed brackets {} has been revised.
A pair of angle brackets <> indicates that a section of text has been cut from the original English text.
All changes indicated by the above brackets are explained in the Textual Notes.

PUBLISHER'S NOTE

The publisher has taken this opportunity to make a number of minor adjustments to the layout and typographical style adopted for earlier editions of *What Where.*

BAM
BEM
BIM
BOM
VOICE OF BAM (V)

Note

[Black ground unbroken.] 7
Players as alike as possible. {Only oval faces. Hair, etc. eliminated by make-up and 8
invisible black material.} 9
{V = *mirror reflection of* BAM*'s face, slightly distorted, faintly lit, enough to distinguish* 10
closed eyes and lips in speech. Four–five times the size of P *[playing area] faces. Eyes closed* 11
throughout. Motionless until head bowed before final fade out.} 12
<> 13

General dark.
Light on V.
Pause.

V: [This is BAM.] 17
We are the last five. 18
In the present as were we still.
It is spring.
Time passes.
<> 22
I switch on.
(<> 24
Light on <> BAM *alone at 3 head haught.* 25
Pause.)
Good.
I am alone.

It is spring.
Time passes.
First without words.
In the end Bom appears.
Reappears.
34 (BOM *enters at <> 1 head bowed.*
Pause.
BIM *enters at <> 2 head haught.*
Pause.
BIM *exits <> followed by* BOM.
Pause.
BIM *enters at <> 2 head bowed.*
Pause.
BEM *enters at <> 1 head haught.*
Pause.
BEM *exits <> followed by* BIM.
Pause.
BEM *enters at <> 1 head bowed.*
Pause.
BAM *exits <> followed by* BEM.
Pause.
BAM *enters at <> 3 head bowed.*
51 *Pause.*
52 <>
53 *Light on <>* BAM *alone at 3 head haught.*
Pause.)
55 Good.
I am alone.
It is spring.
Time passes.
Now with words.
In the end Bom appears.
61 Reappears.
62 (BOM *enters at <> 1 head bowed.*)
63 <>

BAM: Well?
BOM: (*Head bowed throughout*) Nothing.
BAM: He didn't say it?

<> 67

BOM: No.

[BAM: He didn't say what?

BOM: No.

BAM: He didn't say where?

BOM: No.]

BAM: You gave him the works?

BOM: Yes.

BAM: And he didn't say it?

BOM: No.

BAM: He wept?

BOM: Yes.

BAM: Screamed?

BOM: Yes.

BAM: Begged for mercy?

BOM: Yes.

BAM: But didn't say it?

BOM: No.

BAM: Then why stop?

BOM: He passed out.

BAM: And you didn't revive him?

BOM: I tried.

BAM: Well?

BOM: I couldn't.

(*Pause.*)

BAM: It's a lie. (*Pause.*) He said it to you. (*Pause.*) Confess he said it to you. (*Pause.*) You'll be given the works until you confess.

V: Good.

In the end Bim appears.

(BIM *enters at* <>*2 head haught.*) 96

BAM: (*To* BIM) Are you free?

BIM: Yes.

BAM: Take him away and give him the works until he confesses.

BIM: What must he confess?

BAM: That he said {what}. 101

BIM: Is that all?

[BAM: And where.

BIM: Is that all?]

BAM: Yes.

106 <>

BIM: Then stop?

BAM: Yes.

BIM: Good. (*To* BOM) Come.

110 (BIM *exits* <> *followed by* BOM.)

V: Good.

I am alone.
It is summer.
Time passes.
In the end Bim appears.
Reappears.

117 (BIM *enters at* <> *2 head bowed.*)

BAM: Well?

BIM: (*Head bowed throughout*) Nothing.

BAM: He didn't say it?

BIM: No.

[BAM: He didn't say what?

BIM: No.

BAM: He didn't say where?

BIM: No.]

BAM: You gave him the works?

BIM: Yes.

BAM: And he didn't say it?

BIM: No.

130 <>

BAM: He wept?

BIM: Yes.

BAM: Screamed?

BIM: Yes.

BAM: Begged for mercy?

BIM: Yes.

137 BAM: But didn't say {it}?

BIM: No.

BAM: Then why stop?

BIM: He passed out.

BAM: And you didn't revive him?

BIM: I tried.

BAM: Well?

BIM: I couldn't.

(*Pause.*)

BAM: It's a lie. (*Pause.*) He said {it} to you. (*Pause.*) Confess he said {it} to you. (*Pause.*) You'll be given the works until you confess.

V: Good.

In the end Bem appears.

(BEM *enters at* <> *1 head haught.*)

BAM: (*To* BEM) Are you free?

BEM: Yes.

BAM: Take him away and give him the works until he confesses.

BEM: What must he confess?

BAM: That he said {what}.

BEM: Is that all?

[BAM: And where.

BEM: Is that all?]

BAM: Yes.

<>

BEM: Good. (*To* BIM) Come.

(BEM *exits* <> *followed by* BIM.)

V: Good.

I am alone.

It is autumn.

Time passes.

In the end Bem appears.

Reappears.

(BEM *enters at* <> *1 head bowed.*)

BAM: Well?

BEM: (*Head bowed throughout*) Nothing.

BAM: He didn't say {it}?

BEM: No.

V: So on.

BAM: It's a lie. (*Pause.*) He said {it} to you. (*Pause.*) Confess he said {it} to you. (*Pause.*) You'll be given the works until you confess.

BEM: What must I confess?

BAM: That he said {what}.

BEM: Is that all?

BAM: And where.

BEM: Is that all?
BAM: Yes.
BEM: Then stop?
BAM: Yes. Come.
(BAM *exits* <> *followed by* BEM.)
V: Good.
It is winter.
Time passes.
In the end I appear.
Reappear.
(BAM *enters at* <> *3 head bowed.*)
Good.
I am alone.
In the present as were I still.
It is winter.
Without journey.
Time passes.
That is all.
Make sense who may.
I switch off.
(*Light off* {BAM}.
Pause.
Light off V.)

7–12 – Although Beckett revised the dialogue for *What Where* three times in three different languages for three separate productions, the only revision of the visual image is that in the *Stuttgart Nb*, which Beckett prepared *before* and modified during rehearsals for the German television adaptation of his stage play, which was aired by Süddeutscher Rundfunk on 13 April 1986, Samuel Beckett's eightieth birthday. Subsequently, Beckett prepared a revised French text for Pierre Chabert and a revised English text for S. E. Gontarski (see Bibliography: Primary Sources for production details).

Beckett's original numbering of character positions was retained in the revised text but it now corresponds to the revised diagram.

10 – 'V = *mirror reflection of* BAM'*s face*', an enlarged and distorted death mask, has replaced the suspended 'small megaphone at head level' of the original publication. As Beckett noted in the *Stuttgart Nb*, 'Loudspeaker out'.

13 – '*Playing area* (P) *rectangle 3m × 2m, dimly lit, surrounded by shadow, stage right as seen from house. Downstage left, dimly lit, surrounded by shadow,* V' cut. All references to P (line 25 below and throughout) cut as well by Beckett except for the final one (line 201), which he neglected to revise and which has been replaced with '{BAM}' by the editor. The excision also eliminates the confusing stage direction, 'stage right as seen from the house'. As the original diagram clearly indicates, the lit playing area was stage left (or audience right).

In place of the lit playing area, a stage within a stage which Beckett has called the 'field of memory', all three productions of the revised script used '*Black ground unbroken*' (line 7) against which faces appear and disappear. In the video productions the TV screen itself became the 'field of memory'.

17 – In the *Stuttgart Nb* Beckett wrote, 'Name Bam never spoken. Perhaps open with "Ich bin (heisse) Bam."' All three productions of the revised text, German, French and English, include some version of that opening line.

18 – 'We are the last five.' With only four characters listed, the fifth may be the separate, remembering consciousness, the 'Voice of BAM', the voice, as it were, 'from beyond the grave', according to Beckett. Since Beckett also associated Rimbaud's sonnet 'Voyelles' with the play, the fifth character might be the already dispatched figure whose name might contain the missing fifth vowel. Bom does not appear, we may recall, but 'Reappears'; having already failed to elicit the required information from another (Bum?), he enters '*head bowed*'.

22 – 'First without words' cut in all three productions. With the cut of the false start below (line 24), this introduction of the mime followed too closely its repetition below.

24 – The false start has been cut as follows:

> (*Light on* P.
> BAM *at 3 head haught.* BOM *at 1 head bowed.*
> *Pause.*)
> V: Not good.
> I switch off.
> (*Light off* P.)
> I start again.
> We are the last five.
> It is spring.
> Time passes.
> First without words.
> I switch on.

Beckett's comment in the *Stuttgart Nb* on this revision was 'Simplify [?]. Stimme should not intervene in "action".'

25 – 'P' [i.e., Playing Area] cut, and two sentences conflated.

34 – Compass points, which were used in the original to describe the location of characters around three sides of the rectangular playing area, and the subsequent 'halts at' before the place number have been cut throughout. Pierre Chabert's directorial note suggests that at least the idea of the north remains: 'Il n'y a plus que le Nord' *QO* (PC).

This mime (lines 34–51), the initial enactment of the play's pattern of appearance and disappearance, was cut in the French text and performance, *QO* (PC), and initially in the English text, *WW* (SEG). Subsequently, Beckett felt that he overcut the French text and so restored the mime for the American première. The revised text follows Beckett's restoration of the mime.

52 – The following false start was cut:

> V: Good.
> I switch off.
> (*Light off* P.)
> I start again.
> We are the last five.
> It is spring.
> Time passes.
> I switch on.

53 – 'P' cut.

55–61 – Originally cut in *WW* (SEG) but subsequently restored by Beckett.

62 – 'N, *halts at*' cut.

63 – The following false start is cut:

BAM: Well?
BOM: (*Head bowed throughout*) Nothing.
BAM: He didn't say anything?
BOM: No.
BAM: You gave him the works?
BOM: Yes.
BAM: And he didn't say anything?
BOM: No.
BAM: He wept?
BOM: Yes.
BAM: Screamed?
BOM: Yes.
BAM: Begged for mercy?
BOM: Yes.
BAM: But didn't say anything?
BOM: No.
V: Not good.
I start again.

67 – 'V: Good' cut.

96 – 'E, *halts at*' cut.

101 – 'That he said it to him' revised to 'That he said what'.

106 – Another false start cut as follows:

V: Not good.
I start again.
BAM: Take him away and give him the works until he confesses.
BIM: What must he confess?
BAM: That he said it to him.
BIM: Is that all?
BAM: And what.
V: Good.
BIM: Is that all?
BAM: Yes.

110 – '*at* E' cut.

117 – 'E, *halts at*' cut.

130 – Another false start cut as follows:

V: Not good.
I start again.
BAM: Well?
BIM: Nothing.
BAM: He didn't say where?
V: Good.
BIM: Where?
V: Ah!
BAM: Where.
BIM: No.
BAM: You gave him the works?
BIM: Yes.
BAM: And he didn't say where?
BIM: No.

137 – 'But didn't say where?' revised to 'But didn't say it?'
146 – 'He said where to you' revised to 'He said it to you'.
146 – 'Confess he said where to you' revised to 'Confess he said it to you'.
150 – 'N, *halts at*' cut.
155 – 'That he said where to him' revised to 'That he said what'.
160 – Another false start cut as follows:

V: Not good.
I start again.
BAM: Take him away and give him the works until he confesses.
BEM: What must he confess?
BAM: That he said where to him.
BEM: Is that all?
BAM: And where.
V: Good.
BEM: Is that all?
BAM: Yes.
BEM: Then stop?
BAM: Yes.

This excised portion contained, moreover, a critical crux with the repetition of 'where'. Of the confession Bam says, 'That he said where to him.' Bem responds, 'Is that all?' Bam replies, 'And where.' When I suggested to Beckett that this repetition might be a misprint, his response was that it definitely was not. The point was that Bam wanted to know both 'That he said where to him' and 'where' that information (the saying of the where) was conveyed to Bem.

162 – '*at* N' cut.

169 – 'N, *halts at*' cut.

172 – 'He didn't say where?' revised to 'He didn't say it?'

175 – 'He said where to you' revised to 'He said it to you'.

175 – 'Confess he said where to you' revised to 'Confess he said it to you'.

178 – 'That he said where to you' revised to 'That he said what'.

185 – '*at* W' cut.

191 – 'N, *halts at*' cut.

201 – 'P' revised to 'BAM' by editor.

Samuel Beckett's Production Notebook for *Was Wo* (*What Where*) at the Studios of Süddeutscher Rundfunk, Stuttgart, June 1985

FACSIMILE OF BECKETT'S PRODUCTION NOTEBOOK WITH TRANSCRIPTION AND TRANSLATION

Note on the Manuscript

Samuel Beckett's production notes for his 1985 television adaptation of *What Where* (*Stuttgart Nb*) for Süddeutscher Rundfunk, Stuttgart, are contained on six unpaginated, square-ruled folios torn from a spiral notebook, 8 × 14 cms. They are catalogued by the Samuel Beckett Archive at the University of Reading as MS 3097. The notes were made primarily on the recto of each folio, except for the verso of folio 1, which contains an emendation to the recto of folio 2, and the verso of folio 3 which contains the cast list.

MS 3097

Was Wo May 85

TV

Project

Bodies & movement eliminated.
Faces only.
Each face strongly lit
As alike as possible.
Differentiated by colour.
BAm – black
BEm – white
BIm – Red
BOm – Blue
(cf Rimbaud's sonnet)
colour in headdress
(Toque, Fez, tarboosh, Kappe, Mönchkappe – turban, cowl, hood)

Retain "bowed" & "haught"

Exits (simul. or sequent) expressed by fade-outs.
Entrances by fade-ups
Reinforced by sound
of steps ~~app~~ receding –
approaching

LIBRARY UNIVERSITY OF READING

Was Wo May 85
TV
Project

Bodies & movement eliminated
Faces only.
Full face throughout
As alike as possible.
Differentiated by colour.[1]
BAm – black
BEm – White
BIm – Red
BOm – Blue
(cf Rimbaud's Sonnet)[2]
Colour in headdress
(Toque, Fez, tarboosh,
Kappe [cap or hood], Mönchkappe [monk's hood]
turban, cowl, hood)
–
Retain 'bowed' & 'haught'[3]
Exits (simul. or sequent [i.e., simultaneous or sequential])[4]
expressed by fade-outs.
Entrances by fade ups
Reinforced by sound
of steps [*erasure*] receding –
approaching[5]

Dim light.
Face blurred.

Production
Stuttgart June 18 – 28

—

Process of elimination

—

Colour eliminated.
Lit PA eliminated. Black ground introduced.
Drum eliminated. No sound reinforcement of fades.

—

S (Stimme) = mirror reflection of Bam's face, slightly distorted, faintly lit, enough to distinguish closed eyes & lips in speech. 4–5 times size of PA faces. Eyes closed throughout. Motion: just his head bowed before final fade-out.

No visible head-dress. Hair etc eliminated by make up & invisible black material. Only oval of face to be lit

[*fol. 1v*]

Dim light. ⟵
Faces blurred.

Production[6]
Stuttgart June 18–28 [1985]

–

Process of elimination[7]

–

Colour eliminated.
Lit PA. [playing area] eliminated. Black
ground unbroken.[8]
Drum eliminated. No
sound reinforcement of fades.

–

S (Stimme [Voice]) = mirror
reflection of Bam's face,
slightly distorted, faintly
lit, enough to distinguish
closed eyes & lips in speech.[9]
4–5 times size of PA [playing area] faces
Eyes closed throughout. Motion-
less till head bowed before
final fade-out[10]

[Sketch]

No visible headdress
Hair etc. eliminated by
make up & invisible
black material. Only oval of
face to be seen

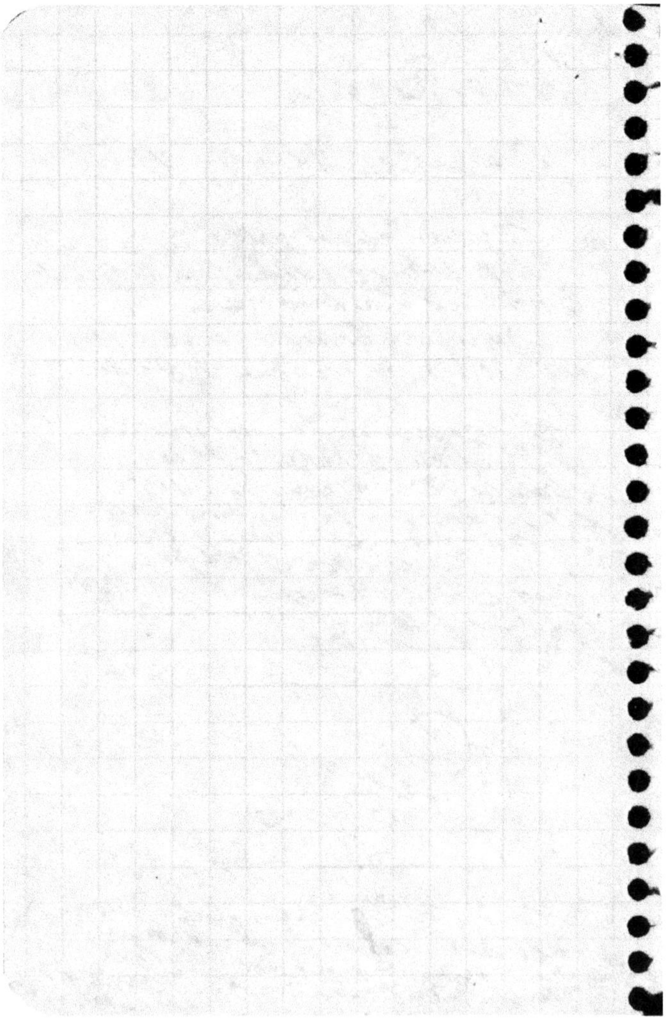

S's voice prerecorded.
Bam's, but changed
(entfernt)

<u>Colour sequence</u>

1. Black
2. Black Blue
3. Black Blue Red.
4. Black
5. Black Red.
6. Black Red White
7. Black
8. Black White

—

9. Black

-

Bam – Bom dialogue model for following. Sim. Bam – Bim with Bom for Bam – Bem with Bim. Same rhythm – tone (-lessness)

-

S voice recognizable as Bam's but changed (entfernt). Same flat tone.

-

Name <u>Bam</u> never spoken. Perhaps open with <u>Ich bin (heisse) Bam</u>.

-

<u>Was – wo</u> der Akzent wird von "was" auf "wo" versetzt

-

[*fol. 2v*]

S's voice prerecorded.
Bam's, but changed
(entfernt [removed, distant])

colour sequence

1. Black
2. Black Blue
3. Black Blue Red.
4. Black
5. Black Red.
6. Black Red White
7. Black
8. Black White

–

9. Black

–

Bam – Bom dialogue model for
following. [*erasure*] Sim. [Similarly] Bam – Bim
with Bom for Bam – Bem with Bim.
Same rhythm & tone (-lessness)

S voice recognizable as Bam's
but changed (entfernt [distant]). Same
flat tone.

–

Name Bam never spoken. Perhaps
open with Ich bin (heisse) Bam. [This is Bam.][11]

–

Was – Wo Der Akzent wird von "was"
auf 'wo' versetzt

[The accent will be transferred from 'what' to 'where']

Bam - Friedhelm Becker
Bom - Edwin Dorner
Bim - Walter Langwitz
Bem - Alfred Querbach

} Karlsruhe

A alone before – Spring
" " after O - I – Summer
" " " I - E – autumn
" " after – Winter

—

Dialog BAM-BOM } Muster
" BAM-BIM

—

A
A O
A O I
A
A I
A I E
A
A E
Ā

—

[*fol. 3v*]

Bam – Friedhelm Becker	}	Karlsruhe
Bom – Edwin Dorner		
Bim – Walter Langwitz		
Bem – Alfred Querbach[12]		

A [Bam] alone before – Spring
" " after O [Bom] & I [Bim] – Summer
" " " I [Bim] & E [Bem] – Autumn
" " after – Winter[13]

–

Dialog BAM – BOM
" BAM – BIM } Muster [i.e., sample or pattern]

A
A O
A O I
A
A I
A I E
A
A E
–
A

—

Each player his separate camera

–

S recorded separately.
slow playback.

–

Bam's voice in dialogue
with some colour. S
colourless

–

Time: 12 – 13 minutes

–

[*fol. 4v*]

Each player his separate camera

—

S [Stimme (voice)] recorded separately.
then playback.

—

Bam's voice in dialogue
with some colour. S [Stimme]
colourless

—

Time: 12–13 minutes

—

Steps = drumbeats. Each its pitch, descending to Bam lowest

—

If pads too short start beats before

—

Simplify text. Stimme should not intervene in "action".

Hauptproblem S. (Stimme). Loudspeaker out. Perhaps best Bam's face as in action but modified (entfernt). Different light from PA (playing area), different size. For PA "the light of other days".

—

PA lit throughout so as to be present empty when Bam – Bem go

—

No further need of shadow surrounding PA. 3/4 of screen (PA) dimly lit. Remainder in dark except for S ~~[illegible]~~ spot lit throughout

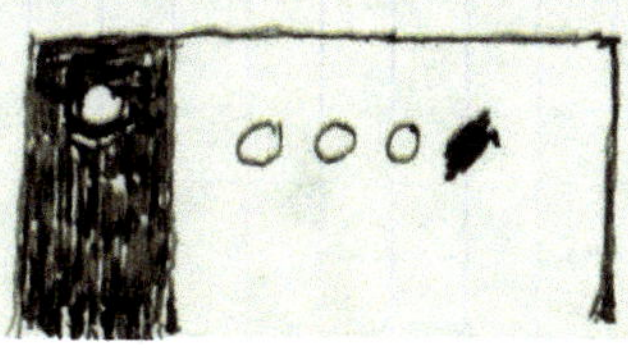

Steps = drumbeats
Each its pitch, descending
to Bam lowest

–

If fades too short start
beat before

–

Simplify text. Stimme [voice]
should not intervene in
"action".

Hauptproblem S. (Stimme).
Loudspeaker out. Perhaps
best Bam's face as in
action but modified
(entfernt). Different
light from PA (playing area),
different size. For PA
"the light of other days."[14]

–

PA lit throughout so as
to be present empty
when Bam – Bem go

–

No further need of shadow
surrounding PA. 3/4
of screen (PA) dimly lit.
Remainder in dark except
for S [Stimme] [*erasure*]
spot lit throughout

[Sketch]

S on
same level
as 3 or
higher[15]
?

1 – The colour differentiation, like the distinctive headdresses and the audible steps for entrances and exits cited below, was finally dropped in what became a ghostly, black-and-white film. Beckett referred to these embellishments in rehearsals as 'gimmicks' (see Asmus, 1986).

2 – Although only four characters are directly named in the play, a fifth is referred to: 'We are the last five.' With only four characters listed, the fifth may be the separate, remembering consciousness, the 'Voice of Bam', the voice, as it were, 'from beyond the grave', according to Beckett. Since Beckett also associated Rimbaud's sonnet 'Voyelles' with the play, the fifth character might be the already dispatched figure whose name might contain the missing fifth vowel. Bom does not appear, we may recall, but 'Reappears'; having already failed to elicit the required information from another (Bum?), he enters 'head bowed'.

In the *Stuttgart Nb* Beckett wrote that characters should be 'As alike as possible. Differentiated by colour.' Beckett then outlined the colour pattern following the one in Rimbaud's sonnet. The Paul Schmidt translation is as follows:

Vowels

Black A, white E, red I, green U, blue O – vowels
Some day I will open your silent pregnancies:
A, black belt, hairy with bursting flies,
Bumbling and buzzing over stinking cruelties,

Pits of night; E, candour of sand and pavilions,
High glacial spears, white kings, trembling Queen Anne's lace;
I, bloody spittle, laughter dribbling from a face
In wild denial or in anger, vermilions;

U, . . . divine movement of viridian seas,
Peace of pastures animal strewn, peace of calm lines
Drawn on foreheads worn with heavy alchemies;

O, supreme Trumpet, harsh with strange stridencies,
Silences traced in angels and astral designs:
O . . . OMEGA . . . the violet light of His Eyes.

(*Arthur Rimbaud: Complete Works*, translated by Paul Schmidt, Harper and Row, New York, 1975, p. 123).

3 – Beckett preferred this archaic form of the word 'high', which is related to the French 'haut' or 'haute' and which remains in English chiefly in the word 'haughty'.

4 – The pattern chosen finally was one of sequential exits with the potential torturer leading his victim away.

5 – The sounds of approaching and receding footsteps for the entrances and exits were dropped from production, but not before Beckett elaborated on the effect on the last page of the *Stuttgart Nb* where he contemplated using drumbeats for the steps with each character having his own pitch, 'descending to Bam lowest'.

6 – This page of the *Stuttgart Nb* contains essentially pre-production ideas. Subsequent notes were made during rehearsals and taping so that the final revised text of *What Where* was very much a direct product of production.

7 – This statement may stand as one of Beckett's most succinct summaries of his late aesthetics, but in some *What Where* productions Beckett felt that he had overcut his text. The play's mime (lines 34–54), the initial enactment of the play's pattern of appearance and disappearance (that is, another form of coming and going), was cut in the French text and performance, *QO* (PC), and initially in the English text, *WW*(SEG). Subsequently, Beckett felt that he overcut the French text and so restored the mime for the American première of the revised text. The revised text printed here follows Beckett's restoration of the mime, which he retained in his own Stuttgart production.

8 – The originally published set description, '*Playing area* (P) *rectangle 3m × 2m, dimly lit, surrounded by shadow, stage right as seen from house. Downstage left, dimly lit, surrounded by shadow,* V' was cut, and all references to P (i.e. playing area) were eliminated as well by Beckett – except for the final one (line 201 of the revised text), which he neglected to revise and which has been replaced with '{BAM}' by the editor. The excision above also eliminates the confusing stage direction of the original text, '*stage right as seen from the house*'. As the diagram for the original publication clearly indicates, the lit playing area was stage left (or audience right).

In place of the lit playing area, a stage within a stage which Beckett has called the 'field of memory', all three productions of the revised script used the '*Black ground unbroken*' (line 7) of the *Stuttgart Nb*, against which the '*Full face*[*s*] *throughout*' appear and disappear, silently. In the video productions, the TV screen itself becomes the 'field of memory'.

9 – 'V = *mirror reflection of* Bam's *face*', an enlarged and distorted death mask, replaced the suspended '*small megaphone at head level*' of the original

publication. As Beckett noted in the *Stuttgart Nb*, 'Loudspeaker out'. The image that now intrigued him was that of the hooded 'statue of John Donne in St Patrick's [*recte* Paul's] Cathedral in London', according to his cameraman, Jim Lewis (Fehsenfeld, 1986, p. 232). The new image, finally, represented 'The image of Bam in the beyond or beyond the grave or whatever you want to call it – the death mask thing that wasn't originally planned at all . . . That was the problem almost up to the end until I came up with this idea of enlarging the death mask . . .' (Fehsenfeld, 1986, p. 236). In the French production, however, the enlarged and distorted reflection of Bam's face was replaced by a ring of diffuse light. Pierre Chabert's production note is as follows: 'rond lumineux = source de Voix'. For the English stage première, Beckett suggested a return to a hologram of the distorted face of Bam.

The voice of Bam, moreover, notes Chabert, is not identical to Bam's voice: 'V ≠ voix Bam, i.e., 2 voix, souvenir & Bam.' In the Stuttgart television production and subsequent stage productions of the revised text the difference was achieved mechanically. 'There was a slightly higher frequency in [the voice] of the younger Bam, and a lower, deeper effect in the older Bam' (Fehsenfeld, 1986, p. 237). In both French and English stage productions, the difference in voice was similarly achieved by recording and altering v to produce, as Walter Asmus suggests, 'the ghost Bam, dead Bam, distorted image of a face in a grave, somewhere not in this world any longer, imagining that he comes back to life in the world, dreaming and seeing himself as a little face on the screen' (Fehsenfeld, 1986, p. 238). In the *Stuttgart Nb* Beckett wrote, 'S's [i.e. Stimme (voice)] prerecorded. Bam's but changed.' And shortly thereafter he added, 'Bam's voice in dialogue with some colour. S [Stimme] colourless.'

10 – Although Beckett revised the dialogue for *What Where* three times in three different languages for three separate productions, the only revision of the visual image is that in the *Stuttgart Nb*, which Beckett prepared *before* and modified during rehearsals for the German television adaptation of his stage play, which was aired by Süddeutscher Rundfunk on 13 April 1986, Samuel Beckett's eightieth birthday. Subsequently, Beckett prepared a revised French text for Pierre Chabert *QO* (PC) and a revised English text for S. E. Gontarski *WW* (SEG) (see Bibliography: Primary Sources for production details).

Beckett's original numbering of character positions is retained in the revised text but it now corresponds to the revised diagram.

11 – All three productions of the revised text, German, French and English, include some version of this new opening line.

12 – This is simply the cast list.

13 – Beckett associated yet another poem, or series of poems, with this play, the song-cycle Franz Schubert based on the poems of Wilhelm Müller and called *Die Winterreise* (*Winter Journey*). The seasons provide a formal, symmetrical structure and progression for the play, driving towards the final 'winter/Without journey' (lines 195–6), or death. It is difficult to single out one influential poem from the twenty-four that Schubert set to music since many of them, such as 'Gute Nacht' ('Good Night'), feature a disconsolate winter wanderer who has lost his love and whose 'winter journey' is towards death. The closing refrain of 'Der Wegweiser' ('The Signpost'), however, is particularly illustrative:

> And I see a single signpost
> Ever there before my gaze;
> There's one road that I must follow
> From which no one e'er returned.

14 – *What Where* is a memory play, and one poem Beckett associated with it is Thomas Moore's Scottish air 'Oft, in the Stilly Night', from the collection *National Airs*. In 1986 Beckett could still recite it from memory, emphasizing the shift from 'Fond memory brings the light/Of other days around me' in the first stanza to 'Sad memory brings the light/Of other days around me' of the second. Beckett in fact quoted the line in the *Stuttgart Nb*: 'For PA [playing area] "the light of other days".' The second stanza of the poem seems particularly apposite to the play:

> When I remember all
> The friends, so linked together,
> I've seen around me fall,
> Like leaves in wintry weather;
> I feel like one
> Who treads alone
> Some banquet hall deserted,
> Whose lights are fled,
> Whose garlands dead,
> And all but he departed!
> Thus, in the stilly night,
> Ere slumber's chain has bound me
> Sad memory brings the light
> Of other days around me.

(*Thomas Moore's Complete Poetical Works*, Collected by Himself, Thomas Y. Crowell & Co., New York, 1895, p. 224)

15 – In the final version of *Was Wo* worked out with cameraman Jim Lewis, 'v' was much larger, taking up almost one-third of the video screen, and so of necessity it was also higher than the other three heads.

CUTS AND CHANGES TO THE SÜDDEUTSCHER RUNDFUNK PRODUCTION TEXT (STUTTGART, 1985) AND TO THE THÉÂTRE DU ROND-POINT PRODUCTION TEXT (PARIS, 1986)

Stuttgart, 1985

Page references are to the text Beckett used to prepare for the Stuttgart television production of *Was Wo*, the Elmar and Jonas Tophoven translation published in *Theater Heute.* Reading University Library MS 3097.

Page 9

'Ich bin Bam' added as Bam's first words.

'ob wir noch wären' revised to 'wären wir noch'.

Twelve lines cut, beginning with first '*Das Spielfeld leuchtet auf*' through 'Ich mach' an'.

'So ist's besser' revised to 'Gut'.

Page 10

'So ist's gut' revised to 'Gut'.

'So ist's gut' revised to 'Gut'.

'BAM: Na?' cut.

'BOM: (*mit stets gesenktem Kopf*) Nichts' cut.

Page 11

First sixteen lines cut, from 'BAM: Er hat nichts gesagt?' to 'S: So ist's nicht gut, [/] Ich fang' nochmal an.'

'S: So ist's besser' cut.

Bam's 'Nein' given now to Bom.

'Du hast ihn gut bearbeitet' given to Bam.

'reagiert' revised to 'reagierte'.

'Pause' contemplated before 'So ist's gut' cancelled; line revised to 'Gut'.

Page 12

Seven lines cut, from 'BAM: Nimm ihn mit und bearbeite ihn, bis er gesteht' to 'S: Ich fang nochmal an.'

'S: So ist's besser' cut. 'BIM: Was? [/] BAM: Was' added in margin then deleted.
'Pause' contemplated before 'So ist's gut' cancelled; line revised to 'Gut'.
'Er hat es nicht gesagt' revised to 'Er hat nicht gesagt was?'
'es nicht gesagt?' revised to 'nicht gesagt was?'
Four lines cut, from 'S: So ist's nicht gut' to 'BIM: Nichts.'
Four lines cut, from 'S: So ist's besser' to 'BAM: Wo.'

Page 13

Contemplated cut of four lines, from 'BAM: Du hast ihn gut bearbeitet' to 'BIM: Nein', restored with 'Stet' in margin.
'reagiert' corrected to 'reagierte'.
'Pause' contemplated before 'So ist's gut' cancelled; line revised to 'Gut'.
Seven lines cut, from 'BAM: Ja' to 'BEM: Das ist alles?'
'S: So ist's besser' cut.

Page 14

'Pause' contemplated before 'S: So ist's gut' cancelled; line revised to 'Gut'.
'Pause' contemplated before 'S: So ist's gut' cancelled; line revised to 'Gut'.
'So ist's gut' revised to 'Gut'.
'ob ich noch wäre' revised to 'wäre ich noch'.
In Walter Asmus's text S's final 'Ich mach' aus' revised to 'Ich mache aus'.

Paris, 1986

Page references are to the two texts of *Quoi Où* that Beckett prepared for the French director Pierre Chabert (Les Editions de Minuit, 1983). As in the other revised texts stage directions were not revised. These French texts represent the most radical of revisions for *What Where*. In them Beckett eliminated not only Bam's 'interventions' (Beckett's word) into the text but the entire mime as well, 'First without words'. For the American production, however, Beckett restored the mime so that the English text essentially paralleled the German. Disparities between the two revised French texts are noted below.

Pages 8–11

Massive 56-line cut from V's first words, 'Nous ne sommes plus que cinq' to 'J'éteins. *L'aire s'éteint.*' The final stage direction, '*L'aire s'éteint*', is cut in only one text.

'Je recommence' cut and replaced by 'Ici Bam'.

After 'Nous ne sommes plus que cinq', 'Au présent, comme si nous y étions' was added in one of the texts.

'Cette fois parlant' cut twice, since, of course, the entire mime had been cut in this version.

Page 12

Eighteen lines cut from Bam's first 'Alors?' to V's 'Ce n'est pas bon. Je recommence.'

'V: C'est mieux' cut.

Page 13

First 'BAM' corrected to 'BOM' and after the 'Non' the following insertion:

BAM: Il n'a pas dit quoi?
BOM: Non.
BAM: Il n'a pas dit où.
BOM: Non.

Page 14

From 'BAM: Emmène-le et travaille-le jusqu'à ce qu'il avoue' to V's 'C'est n'est pas bon. Je recommence' cut.

Bam's 'Qu'il le lui a dit' revised to 'Qu'il lui a dit quoi'.

Bam's 'Et quoi' revised to 'Et où'. An alternative 'Ou où' is contemplated in one of the texts.

V's 'C'est mieux' cut.

Page 15

After Bam's 'Il ne l'a pas dit?' Beckett added:

BIM: Non.

BAM: Il n'a pas dit quoi?
BIM: Non.
BAM: Il n'a pas dit où?

The second text makes the addition after Bim's 'Non', but the results are the same in both revised texts.

Page 16

Fourteen lines cut, from V's 'Ce n'est pas bon' to Bim's second 'Non'.

Bam's 'Mais n'a pas dit où' revised to 'Mais ne l'a pas dit?'.

Page 17

Bam's 'Il t'a dit où' revised to 'Il te l'a dit'.

Bam's 'Avoue qu'il t'a dit où' revised to 'Avoue qu'il te l'a dit'.

Six lines cut, from Bam's 'Emmène-le et travaille-le jusqu'à ce qu'il avoue' to Bam's 'Oui'.

Page 18

V's 'Ce n'est pas bon. Je recommence' cut.

Bam's 'Qu'il lui a dit où' revised to 'Qu'il lui a dit quoi'.

V's 'C'est mieux' cut.

Page 19

Bam's 'Il n'a pas dit où' revised to 'Il ne l'a pas dit?' in one version and to 'Il ne te l'a pas dit' in another.

Bam's 'Il t'a dit où' revised to 'Il te l'a dit' in one version only.

Bam's 'Avoue qu'il t'a dit où' revised to 'Avoue qu'il te l'a dit' in one version only.

Bam's 'Il t'a dit où' revised to 'Il te l'a dit' in one version only.

Bam's 'Et où' revised to 'Ou où' in one text only and then only as a possibility.

APPENDIX

Not I

Samuel Beckett's Production Notes for *Not I* at the Royal Court Theatre, London, January 1973

FACSIMILE OF BECKETT'S PRODUCTION NOTES WITH TRANSCRIPTION

Note on the Manuscript

Beckett's notes for the Anthony Page production of *Not I* on 16 January 1973 are contained on a single sheet of stationery from the Hyde Park Hotel.

MS 1227/7/12/11

on reading university library
[illegible]

Reading University Library

Hyde Park Hotel
Knightsbridge London SW1 Telephone 01-235 2000 Telegrams Highcaste London SW1 Telex 262057

Pauses

p. l. 2 ✓ 1. after "godfor –" what Girl
" 15 ✓ 2. " "when –" what Seventy
" 22 ✓ 3. " "in the –" What (identity)
" 1 ✓ 4. " "SHE!" Long
" 12 ✓ 5. " "brain –" what (kneeling)
" 14 ✓ 6. " "brain –" what (lying)
" 45 ✓ 7. " "but –" what buzzing
3 " 22 ✓ 8. " "then listen" Long
" 24 ✓ 9. " "then listen again" Long
" 44 ✓ 10. " "she realiz – no part" what buzzing
" 47 ✓ 11. " "words were –" what (identity) Long
" 31 ✓ 12. " "all those –" "SHE" tongue
" 49 ✓ 13. " "all –" buzzing
" 4 ✓ 14. " "never –" tongue
" 44 ✓ 15. " "can't –" buzzing
6 " 8 ✓ 16. " "had to –" what (identity) Long
" 19 ✓ 17. " "had to –" buzzing
" " 28 ✓ 18. " "how she –" "SHE" had been / had to tell – — Long
" " 31 ✓ 19. " "something she –" Seventy
" " 38 ✓ 20. " "another few –" what (not that)
" " 45 ✓ 21 " "in the –" what (not that either)
" " 48 ✓ 22 " "nothing she –" what (identity) Long
" " 48 ✓ 23 " "SHE" buzzing
7 " 26 ✓ 24 " "Keep –" what (identity)
" " 29 ✓ 25 " "she was –" Long
m " 30 ✓ "SHE"

other breaks possible pp. 4 & 5 if needed

Hesitations to point

p. 2 l. 3 Before "lark)
p. 3 l. 8 " "torment"
" " 13 " "groan"
" " 14 " "agony"
p. 6 16 " "Fell"
p. 7 7 "Fell" (omitting "to")

p. 6 l. 8 reinsert something she

for
Reading
University
Library
—
Sam. Beckett

Hyde Park Hotel [logo]
Knightsbridge London SW1 Telephone 01–235–2000 Telegrams
Highcaste London SW1 Telex 262057

		Pauses			
P. 1[1]	l.	2 √	1.	after	"godfor–" {what} Girl
"	"	15 √	2	"	"when–" {what} seventy
"	"	22 √	3.	"	"in the –" what (identity)
2	"	1 √	4.	"	"SHE!" Long
"	"	12 √	5.	"	"brain –" what (kneeling)
"	"	14 √	6	"	"brain –" what (lying)
"	"	45 √	7.	"	"but –" what buzzing
3	"	22 √	8.	"	"then listen" Long
"	"	24 √	9.	"	"then listen again" Long
———		25 √			——— no part
"	"	44 √	10.	"	"she realiz–" W [what] buzzing
"	"	47 √	11.	"	"words were –" what (identity)
"	"	48 √			"SHE –" ——————— Long
4	"	31 √	12.	"	"all those –" tongue
"	"	49 √	13.	"	"all –" begging
5	"	4 √	14.	"	"never –" tongue
"	"	44 √	15.	"	"can't –" buzzing
6	"	8 √	16.	"	"had to –" what (identity) ——————— Long

Transcription continues on page 466.

<	”	10>√	17.	”	“had to –” buzzing
<	”	11>√			“She –” 1. [*illegible*] “had to tell” – Long
”	”	<22>√	18.	”	“how she –” had been
”	”	<31>√	19.	”	“something she –” seventy
”	”	38√	20.	”	“another few –” what (not that)
”	”	45√	21.	”	“in the –” . . what (not that either)
”	”	48√	22.	”	“nothing she –” what (identity)
”	”	48√	23.	”	“SHE” ——————— <u>Long</u>
7	”	24^2√	24.	”	“keep –” buzzing
”	”	29√	25.	”	“she was –” what (identity)
”	”	30√	–	”	“SHE” – Long

—

<Further> {Other} breaks
possible pp. 4–5
if needed

—

<u>Hesitations to point</u>

p. 2	l. 3	Before	“dark)	
p. 3	l 8	”	“torment”	p. 6 {l. 8} reinsert
” ”	13	”	“groan”	something she[3]
” ”	14	”	“agony”	
” 6	16	”	“tell”	
7	7	”	“tell” (omitting “to”)	

EDITORIAL NOTES ON THE HYDE PARK HOTEL MANUSCRIPT

1 – Beckett's page references below are not to the first publication of the play (*Not I*, Faber and Faber, London, 1973), which contains eleven unnumbered pages of text, but to the acting script retyped by the Royal Court Theatre whose pages are numbered 1.1–1.8. An unannotated, mimeographed copy is on deposit at the University of Reading Beckett Archive, MS 1227/7/12/9.
2 – Revised from 25.
3 – Beckett must have deleted this phrase only on his copy of the play since it appears in the unannotated copy on deposit at the University of Reading Samuel Beckett Archive, MS 1227/7/12/9.

BIBLIOGRAPHY

Manuscripts and Annotated Copies of Beckett Consulted

RUL = Reading University Library

Play

Primary Sources

Spiel in *Samuel Beckett Dramatische Dichtungen*, Band 2 (Englische Originalfassungen/Deutsche Übertragung von Erika und Elmar Tophoven/Französische Übertragung von Samuel Beckett), Suhrkamp Verlag, Frankfurt am Main, 1964, pp. 235–69. (The annotated copy Beckett prepared for the Schiller-Theater Werkstatt production 6 October 1978; cited throughout as *Spiel* (SB).)

Spiel in *Samuel Beckett Dramatische Dichtungen*, Band 2 (Englische Originalfassungen/Deutsche Übertragung von Erika und Elmar Tophoven/Französische Übertragung von Samuel Beckett), Suhrkamp Verlag, Frankfurt am Main, 1964, pp. 235–69. (A copy of annotated text above with additional production notes by Walter Asmus; cited throughout as *Spiel* (WA).)

Other Editions Consulted

Samuel Beckett Dramatische Dichtungen, Band 2 (Englische Originalfassungen/Deutsche Übertragung von Erika und Elmar Tophoven/Französische Übertragung von Samuel Beckett), Suhrkamp Verlag, Frankfurt am Main, 1964. (*Spiel*, pp. 235–69; '*Spiel wiederholen bis*' ('*Repeat play*'), pp. 268–9.)

'Play' and Two Short Pieces for Radio, Faber and Faber, London, 1964. ('Repeat play exactly', p. 22.)

'Play' and Two Short Pieces for Radio, Faber and Faber, London, 1969. ('Repeat play', p. 22, and 'Note on repeat', p. 24.)

'Cascando' and Other Short Dramatic Pieces, Grove Press, New York, 1968. ('Repeat play', p. 61, but no 'Note on Repeat'.)

Secondary Sources

Asmus, Walter D., 'Beckett inszeniert sein *Spiel*', in Klaus Völker (ed.), *Beckett in Berlin*, Edition Hentrich, Berlin, 1986, pp. 145–7. (An invaluable resource for Beckett's German productions.)

Gontarski, S. E., 'The Scoring of *Play*', *The Intent of Undoing in Samuel Beckett's Dramatic Texts*, Indiana University Press, Bloomington, 1985, pp. 90–100.

Kaiser, Joachim, 'Beckett's *Spiel* in Ulm – die Aufführung des Monats', *Theater-Heute*, no. 7 (July 1963), pp. 6–9.

'Dirigent für Beckett's Partitur: Ein Gespräch mit Derek Mendel dem Regisseur der Ulmer Aufführung', *Theater Heute*, no. 7 (July 1963), pp. 9–10.

Come and Go

Primary Source

'Kommen und Gehen', *Theater Heute*. (Director's copy used by Walter Asmus, with annotations and revisions in his hand; cited throughout as *KUG* (WA).)

Secondary Sources

Knowlson, James, 'Good Heavens', *Gambit: International Theatre Review*, vol. 7, no. 28 (1976): pp. 101–5.

Mitchell, Breon, 'Art in Microcosm: The Manuscript Stages of Beckett's *Come and Go*', *Modern Drama*, vol. 19, no. 3 (September 1976), pp. 245–54. (This text prints the opening four lines as in the French and German texts, which in English appear only in the first Grove Press edition, *'Cascando' and Other Short Dramatic Pieces*, Grove Press, New York, 1968, p. 67. The Grove Press edition of *The Collected Shorter Plays of Samuel Beckett* is a photo offset of the Faber and Faber edition, and so reverts to the corrupt versions by omitting the opening four lines.)

Eh Joe

Primary Source

Samuel Beckett/Film/He Joe (Englische Originalfassungen, Deutsche Übertragung von Erika und Elmar Tophoven, Französische Übertragung von Samuel Beckett), Suhrkamp Verlag, Frankfurt am Main, 1976, pp. 4–65. (The autograph presentation reads, 'for Rick [Cluchey]/ affectionately/from Sam/Stuttgart/January 1979'; cited throughout as *He Joe* (RC).)

Footfalls

Primary Sources

Footfalls, Faber and Faber, London, 1976. (The revised text Beckett prepared for the Royal Court Theatre production in 1976; cited throughout as *Footfalls* (SB), RUL MS 2828.)

Footfalls, Faber and Faber, London, 1976. (The revised text Beckett prepared for Calvin Israel and inscribed 'for Calvin & Joann/Sam. Beckett'; cited throughout as *Footfalls* (CI).)

Pas suivi de quatre esquisses, Les Éditions de Minuit, Paris, 1978.

Secondary Sources

Asmus, Walter, 'Rehearsal Notes for the German Première of Beckett's *That Time* and *Footfalls*', in S. E. Gontarski (ed.), *On Beckett: Essays and Criticism*, Grove Press, New York, 1986, pp. 335–49.

Gontarski, S. E., 'Texts and Pre-texts in Samuel Beckett's *Footfalls*', *Papers of the Bibliographical Society of America*, vol. 77, no. 2 (1983), pp. 191–5.

That Time

Primary Sources

Samuel Beckett: That Time/Damals (Englische und Deutsch. Deutsche Übertragung von Elmar Tophoven), Suhrkamp Verlag, Frankfurt am Main, 1976. (The revised text Beckett prepared for his 1976 Schiller-Theater Werkstatt production; cited throughout as *TT* (SB).)

That Time, Faber and Faber, London, 1976.

Secondary Source

Asmus, Walter, 'Rehearsal Notes for the German Première of Beckett's *That Time* and *Footfalls*', in S. E. Gontarski (ed.), *On Beckett: Essays and Criticism*, Grove Press, New York, 1986, pp. 335–49.

What Where

Primary Sources

Was Wo, Theater Heute. (The annotated Copy Samuel Beckett prepared before and during the filming of *What Where* in Stuttgart, 18–28 June 1985; cited throughout as *WW* (SB), RUL MS 3097.)

Quoi Où, Les Éditions de Minuit, Paris, 1983. (The revised French text Samuel Beckett prepared for Pierre Chabert's French stage première of the revised text, Théâtre de Rond-point, April 1986; cited throughout as *QO* (PC).)

What Where, Three Plays: Ohio Impromptu, Catastrophe, What Where, Grove Press, New York, 1984. (The revised English text Samuel Beckett prepared for S. E. Gontarski's English-language stage première of the revised text, Magic Theater, San Francisco, December 1986; cited throughout as *WW* (SEG).)

What Where, *Evergreen Review*, no. 98 (1984), pp. 47–51. (The first English publication of *What Where*; it includes drawing of playing area omitted from *Three Plays*.)

Secondary Sources

Asmus, Walter, 'All Gimmicks Gone', *Theater Heute* (April 1986), pp. 28–30.

Brater, Enoch, *Beyond Minimalism: Beckett's Late Style in the Theater*, Oxford University Press, London, 1987, pp. 159–64.

Fehsenfeld, Martha D., '"Everything Out But the Faces": Beckett's Reshaping of *What Where* for Television', *Modern Drama*, vol. xxix, no. 2 (June 1986), pp. 229–40.

Gontarski, S. E., 'Revision as Recreation: *What Where* II', *Review of Contemporary Fiction* vol. 7, no. 2 (summer 1987), pp. 120–23.

Not I

Not I, Faber and Faber, London, 1973.

SELECT LIST OF BOOKS ON BECKETT'S PLAYS

Admussen, Richard L., *The Samuel Beckett Manuscripts*, G. K. Hall and Co., Boston, 1979

Brater, Enoch, (ed.), *Beckett at 80/Beckett in Context*, Oxford University Press, New York and Oxford, 1986

Coe, Richard N., *Samuel Beckett*, Oliver and Boyd, Edinburgh and London, 1964; revised ed., Grove Press, New York, 1970

Cohn, Ruby, *Samuel Beckett: the Comic Gamut*, Rutgers University Press, New Brunswick, NJ, 1962

Cohn, Ruby (ed.), *Casebook on Waiting for Godot*, Grove Press, New York, 1967

Cohn, Ruby, *Back to Beckett*, Princeton University Press, Princeton, NJ, 1973

Cohn, Ruby (ed.), *Samuel Beckett, a Collection of Criticism*, McGraw Hill, New York, 1975

Doherty, Francis, *Samuel Beckett*, Hutchinson University Library, London, 1971

Duckworth, Colin (ed.), *Samuel Beckett, En attendant Godot*, Harraps, London, 1966

Esslin, Martin, *The Theatre of the Absurd*, Doubleday, New York, 1961, and Penguin Books, Harmondsworth, 1968

Esslin, Martin (ed.), *Samuel Beckett: a Collection of Critical Essays*, Prentice-Hall, Englewood Cliffs, NJ, 1965

Fletcher, Beryl, *et al.*, *A Student's Guide to the Plays of Samuel Beckett*, Faber and Faber, London, 1978

Fletcher, John, and John Spurling, *Beckett: a Study of his Plays*, Eyre Methuen, London, and Hill and Wang, New York, 1972

Gontarski, S. E., *Beckett's 'Happy Days': a Manuscript Study*, Ohio State University Libraries, Columbus, Ohio, 1977

Gontarski, S. E., *The Intent of Undoing in Samuel Beckett's Dramatic Texts*, Indiana University Press, Bloomington, 1985

Gontarski, S. E., *On Beckett, Essays and Criticism*, Grove Press, New York, 1986

Graver, Lawrence, and Raymond Federman, *Samuel Beckett: the Critical Heritage*, Routledge and Kegal Paul, London and Boston, 1979

Guicharnaud, Jacques, *Modern French Theatre from Giraudoux to Genet*, Yale University Press, New Haven, Conn., 1967

Hamilton, Kenneth and Alice, *Condemned to Life: the World of Samuel Beckett*, Eerdmans, Grand Rapids, Michigan, 1976

Hesla, David, *The Shape of Chaos. An Interpretation of the Art of Samuel Beckett*, University of Minnesota Press, Minneapolis, 1971

Janvier, Ludovic, *Pour Samuel Beckett*, Les Editions de Minuit, Paris, 1966

Kennedy, Andrew, *Six Dramatists in Search of a Language*, Cambridge University Press, London, 1975

Kenner, Hugh, *Samuel Beckett. A Critical Study*. New ed., University of California Press, Berkeley and Los Angeles, 1968

Kenner, Hugh, *A Reader's Guide to Samuel Beckett*, Thames and Hudson, London, 1973

Knowlson, James, and John Pilling, *Frescoes of the Skull, the Later Prose and Drama of Samuel Beckett*. John Calder, London, 1979, and Grove Press, New York, 1980

Mercier, Vivian, *Beckett/Beckett*, Oxford University Press, New York, 1978

Pilling, John, *Samuel Beckett*, Routledge and Kegan Paul, London and Boston, 1976

Reid, Alec, *All I Can Manage, More Than I Could*, Dolmen Press, Dublin, 1968, and Grove Press, New York, 1971 (revised ed.)